COMPUTER SCIENCE:
A MODERN INTRODUCTION

Prentice-Hall International
Series in Computer Science

C.A.R. Hoare, Series Editor

Published

BACKHOUSE, R. C., *Syntax of Programming Languages: Theory and Practice*
de BAKKER, J. W., *Mathematical Theory of Program Correctness*
DUNCAN, F., *Microprocessor Programming and Software Development*
HENDERSON, P., *Functional Programming: Application and Implementation*
JONES, C. B., *Software Development: A Rigorous Approach*
GOLDSCHLAGER, L. and LISTER, A., *Computer Science: A Modern Introduction*
REYNOLDS, J. C., *The Craft of Programming*
TENNENT, R. D., *Principles of Programming Languages*
WELSH, J. and ELDER, J., *Introduction to PASCAL,* 2nd Edition
WELSH, J. and McKEAG, M., *Structured System Programming*

COMPUTER SCIENCE:
A MODERN INTRODUCTION

by
L. GOLDSCHLAGER
University of Sydney

and
A. LISTER
University of Queensland

Prentice/Hall PHI International

ENGLEWOOD CLIFFS, NEW JERSEY   LONDON   NEW DELHI
SINGAPORE   SYDNEY   TOKYO   TORONTO   WELLINGTON

Library of Congress Cataloging in Publication Data

GOLDSCHLAGER, L.,   1951–
    Computer Science.

    Bibliography: p.
    Includes index
    1. Electronic data processing
    2. Electronic digital computers—Programming
I. Lister, A. (Andrew),   1945–
II. Title.
QA76.G589   001.64   81-21191
ISBN 0-13-165704-6 (pbk.)   AACR2

British Library Cataloging in Publication Data

GOLDSCHLAGER, L.
    Computer Science.

    1. Electronic digital computers
    I. Title
    II. Lister, A.
    001.64   QA76.5
    ISBN 0-13-165704-6

ISBN 0-13-165704-6

PRENTICE-HALL INTERNATIONAL, INC., *London*
PRENTICE-HALL OF AUSTRALIA PTY. LTD., *Sydney*
PRENTICE-HALL CANADA, INC., *Toronto*
PRENTICE-HALL OF INDIA PRIVATE LTD., *New Delhi*
PRENTICE-HALL OF JAPAN, INC., *Tokyo*
PRENTICE-HALL OF SOUTHEAST ASIA PTE., LTD., *Singapore*
PRENTICE-HALL, INC., *Englewood Cliffs, New Jersey*
WHITEHALL BOOKS LIMITED, *Wellington, New Zealand*

Printed and bound in Great Britain by SRP Ltd, Exeter

10 9 8 7

To Esther, Aaron and Danielle
and for Kate

CONTENTS

5   THE EXECUTION OF ALGORITHMS: SYSTEM SOFTWARE   171

6   ALGORITHMS IN ACTION: SOME COMPUTER APPLICATIONS   230

PREFACE

Computer science is a discipline with many facets, ranging from the impact of computers on society through to the technological details involved in computer design. An introduction to the discipline should give a broad overview of these many facets and their interrelationships, leaving a non-specialist with a fair perspective on computer science, and giving a student majoring in computer science a reasonable basis from which the choice of later year specialist subjects may be made. The "traditional" introductory course consisting only of computer programming does not fulfill these aims.

This book may be used in conjunction with a computer programming text to form a broad introductory course in computer science. The book is independent of any particular computer programming language and therefore, if used in conjunction with a programming text, the programming language can be of the instructor's choice. Alternatively, it may be used alone as a text in a computer appreciation course.

The unifying theme of this book is the notion of algorithm, which we believe to be the central concept of computer science. For example, many branches of computer science can be regarded in terms of the design, analysis, expression, execution and utilization of algorithms. To maintain independence of any particular programming language, we have chosen to express algorithms in stylized English, so that

    if you can understand this
      then continue reading
          enjoy the book
          attempt the exercises as you go
      else don't read on

is typical of the form in which algorithms are expressed. Rather than use

begin—end or some other statement bracketing convention found in programming languages, we have used indentation to define algorithm structure, as illustrated in the example above. All algorithms are built from the three fundamental concepts of sequence, selection and iteration, and these are explained together with algorithm design and elementary data structures in Chapter 2.

Chapter 3 discusses the theory of algorithms, indicating which tasks can be mechanically computed (computability), which tasks can be carried out using a feasible amount of resources (complexity), and the steps which can be taken to increase one's confidence in an algorithm's correctness. The design of computers forms the topic of Chapter 4. A flavor of the physical characteristics of the devices comprising computers is given, building up to gates and larger components, and culminating in the complete design of a simple microprogrammed computer. Chapter 5 deals with system software, describing the goals of language translators and operating systems, and the algorithms which are used to achieve these objectives. Applications in which computers are used are discussed in Chapter 6, with particular attention to data processing applications and to artificial intelligence. The final chapter is designed to widen a student's perspective of computer science and give some understanding of the impact of computers on the society in which we live.

The suggestions and constructive criticisms of many people are incorporated in this book. In particular, we would like to acknowledge the contributions of Paul Bailes, John Elder, Marshall Harris, Jan Hext, Henry Hirschberg, Tony Hoare, Maria Klawe, Brian Lings, Ian Parberry, Derek Partridge, Nick Pippenger, Paul Pritchard, Margaret Robinson, Ron Sacks-Davis, Dan Simpson, and John Staples. Thanks also to Alana Crangle and Tricia Howarth for a superb typing job. The greatest sacrifice was certainly made by our wives and children, who temporarily assumed the roles of widows and orphans during the writing of the book.

L.M.G
A.M.L

Brisbane, Queensland
July 1981

COMPUTER SCIENCE:
A MODERN INTRODUCTION

1 INTRODUCTION

1.1 COMPUTERS AND ALGORITHMS

We live in the age of the computer revolution. Like any revolution, it is widespread, all-pervasive, and will have a lasting impact. It is as fundamental to our economic and social order as was the industrial revolution. It will affect the thinking patterns and life style of every individual.

The industrial revolution was essentially the augmentation of man's *physical* powers; the amplification of man's muscle. The pressing of a button could cause a large machine to stamp a pattern in a metal sheet. The movement of a lever could result in a heavy scoop scraping out a mass of coal. Certain repetitive aspects of man's physical activities were replaced by machines.

By analogy, the computer revolution is the augmentation of man's *mental* powers; the amplification of man's brain. The pressing of a button can cause a machine to perform intricate calculations, to make complex decisions, or to store and retrieve vast quantities of information. Certain repetitive aspects of man's mental activities are being replaced by machines.

What is a computer, that it can have such a revolutionary impact? A first step toward an answer is to say that a computer is a machine which can carry out routine mental tasks by performing simple operations at high speed. The simplicity of the operations (typical examples are the addition or comparison of two numbers) is offset by the speed at which they are performed (about a million a second). The result is that large numbers of operations can be performed, and significant tasks can be accomplished.

Of course a computer can accomplish only those tasks which can be specified in terms of the simple operations it can execute. To get a computer to carry out a task one must tell it what operations to perform—in other

1

words, one must describe *how* the task is to be accomplished. Such a description is called an *algorithm*. An algorithm describes the method by which a task is to be accomplished. The algorithm consists of a sequence of steps which if faithfully performed will result in the task, or *process*, being carried out.

The notion of an algorithm is not peculiar to computer science—there are algorithms which describe all kinds of everyday processes. Some examples are given in Fig. 1.1. In these examples the processes are carried out by human beings. In general, the agent which carries out a process is called a *processor*. A processor may be a person, a computer, or some other electronic or mechanical device. A processor carries out a process by obeying, or *executing*, the algorithm which describes it. Execution of an algorithm involves execution of each of its constituent steps.

Process	*Algorithm*	*Typical steps in algorithm*
knitting a sweater	knitting pattern	knit one; purl one
building a model plane	assembly instructions	glue panel A to strut B
baking a cake	recipe	take 3 eggs; beat until smooth
making a dress	dress pattern	sew up side seam
playing a Beethoven sonata	musical score	♫

Figure 1.1   Algorithms for some everyday processes.

From the discussion above it is apparent that a computer is simply a particular kind of processor. Of course it is rather a special kind of processor; otherwise computers would not have had such a rapid and significant impact on so many areas of life. The features which make it special are described below.

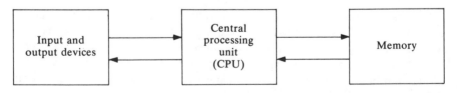

Figure 1.2   Components of a typical computer.

A present day computer has three major components, shown in Fig. 1.2. These are

(1)   the *central processing unit* (CPU), which performs the basic operations;

(2)   the *memory*, which holds

    (a)   the algorithm specifying the operations to be performed

    (b)   the information, or *data*, upon which the operations are to act;

(3)   the *input and output devices* (I/O devices), through which the algorithm and the data are fed into the memory, and through which the computer communicates the results of its activities.

These components comprise the computer *hardware*: that is, the physical units from which a computer is built. We shall describe the components in more detail in Chapter 4: for the moment our purpose is to highlight a few distinctive characteristics.

(1)   *Speed*

The CPU of a typical computer can perform between one million and ten million operations a second. Although these operations are very simple (we shall describe them in Chapter 4), the formidable speed with which they are performed means that even quite complex algorithms, requiring large numbers of operations, can be executed very quickly. By comparison the human brain is very slow, so it is not surprising that people have been replaced by computers in many activities where speed is a major requirement. Human beings do, however, currently retain significant advantages over computers. For example, it appears that the brain is capable of performing many operations at once whereas (with minor exceptions) a present-day computer can perform only one operation at a time. In Chapter 6 we shall look at other advantages retained by humans, and will examine the difficulties of inducing "artificial intelligence" in computers.

    The reader should also note that despite the high speed of computers there remain many processes which are simply too time consuming to be feasibly carried out. (An example is the formulation of a winning strategy for chess by studying all chess games which could possibly be played.) The distinction between feasible and infeasible processes will be discussed further in Chapter 3.

(2)   *Reliability*

Contrary to popular mythology computers seldom make mistakes, though they do occasionally break down. The mistakes which achieve prominence in the news media, such as an electricity bill for a million dollars or a false alert about nuclear attack, are almost invariably a result of a fault in the algorithm being executed or an error in the input data. On very rare occasions an electronic fault may cause a computer to execute an algorithm incorrectly, but the probability of this is minute, and in any case such malfunctions are usually detected immediately.

A computer is in a sense a totally willing and obedient slave: it will faithfully execute the algorithm it is given, and if necessary it will do so repeatedly without complaint. Such fidelity is of course both a strength and a weakness, since the computer will execute the algorithm quite blindly, whether or not it correctly describes the process intended.

(3) *Memory*

One of the prime characteristics of a computer is its ability to store vast quantities of information which it can access very quickly. Memory capacities and access speeds vary widely according to the storage medium used; some computers can store several thousand million items of information, and can access some of these items in as little as 100 nanoseconds (a nanosecond is 10^{-9} seconds, or one thousand millionth of a second). Impressive though these figures are, they are somewhat deceptive. As we shall see in Chapter 4, computer memory is organized in such a way that an item of information can be retrieved only if its location in the storage medium is precisely known. This means that a lot of effort must be put into keeping track of where information is located—effort which increases both the time to design an algorithm and the time to execute it.

By contrast, it is interesting to speculate on the working of human memory. Although no-one is sure of the mechanisms involved it seems that the key to the retrieval of information is not its location, but its association with other information. For example, we might remember the colors of the rainbow by using the mnemonic "*R*ichard *o*f *Y*ork *g*ave *b*attle *i*n *v*ain", and a snatch of melody might remind us of a teenage romance. The formation and use of such associations is little understood, so it is not surprising that algorithms for carrying out similar processes in computers have not yet been developed. We shall return to this topic in Chapter 6.

(4) *Cost*

Perhaps the feature of computers most responsible for their widespread impact is their low cost compared with the human labor needed to carry out the same tasks. The economic considerations vary widely according to the particular application. Some computers cost only a few dollars and can perform more calculations in a day than ten mathematicians in a lifetime. Other computers cost hundreds of thousands of dollars but can perform more operations than an army of clerks. Since the Second World War, when computers were first built, technological advances have been so spectacular that the cost of computers has steadily decreased, in contrast to most other commodities.

The significance of these characteristics is illustrated by the use of computers in airline reservation systems. A typical airline has many offices, geographically separated by large distances. Each office may employ a number of reservations clerks who answer queries from the public and book and cancel aircraft seats. The job of combining all the seat bookings and cancellations for each flight from a national or international network of offices, though routine, is enormous. Furthermore, the resulting information on seat availability must be disseminated back to all the offices to inform the reservations clerks of the status of all flights.

This routine collating task could be performed manually, but would require a massive number of employees and corresponding office space. A cheaper solution is to employ a computer for the task, and to provide each reservations clerk in every airline office with a computer *terminal*, or *visual display* (Fig. 1.3). These terminals are linked directly to the central compu-

Figure 1.3 A computer terminal.

ter. As soon as any booking or cancellation is made, a clerk enters the information into a terminal. Almost immediately, the information arrives at the central computer, which maintains in its memory an up-to-date record of the status of each flight. The computer can also send back to any terminal whichever piece of status information is requested by a reservations clerk. Thus the routine mental operation of collating information is performed by machine.

Significantly, these routine operations are performed much faster than any human could achieve. Humans might fall hours behind if they tried to collate the vast amount of booking information handled by a modern airline, but a computer can continuously maintain accurate status information for each flight, solely by virtue of its enormous speed. Thus a computer can provide some services faster than is manually possible.

Furthermore, a prospective passenger can have far more confidence in a computer-based reservation system than he could in a manual one. He can safely assume that if a reservation is made a seat will be available. The computer can perform the appropriate clerical tasks far more reliably than a human being, and (breakdowns apart) the accuracy of flight status information is assured.

Finally, the airline reservation example illustrates that computers can carry out certain routine processes more economically than is possible with human labor. The cost of purchasing and running a computer for the reservation system is far less than that of employing the large number of clerical workers that would be needed for even a modest manual system. In a wider context it is the economies made possible by advances in technology which are the major impetus behind the computer revolution.

1.2 PROGRAMS AND PROGRAMMING LANGUAGES

We saw in the last section that for a processor to carry out a process it must first be supplied with an appropriate algorithm. For example, the cook must be supplied with a recipe, the pianist with a score, and so on. In each case the algorithm must be expressed in such a way that the processor can understand and execute it. We say that the processor must be able to *interpret* the algorithm, meaning that it must be able to

(a)   understand what each step means, and

(b)   carry out the corresponding operation.

For example, to play a Beethoven sonata a pianist must firstly be able to read music (i.e. understand each piece of musical notation), and secondly be able to play the corresponding notes. Similarly, a person knitting a sweater must know what *purl one* means, and also be able to manipulate the needles and wool in the appropriate way. Summarizing, for an algorithm to be properly executed, each of its steps must be expressed in a form which the intended processor can both understand and carry out.

When the intended processor is a computer the algorithm must be expressed in a form called a *program*. A program is written in a *programming language*, and the activity of expressing an algorithm as a program is called *programming*. Each step in the algorithm is expressed by an *instruction*, or *statement*, in the program. Thus a program consists of a sequence of statements, each of which specifies certain operations the computer is to perform.

The nature of the statements in a program depends on the programming language being used. There is a large number of programming languages (the reasons for this diversity will be discussed in Chapter 2), and each language has its own repertoire of statements. The simplest languages, called *machine languages*, are designed so that each statement can be directly interpreted by the computer: that is, the CPU is capable of understanding each statement and performing the corresponding operations. (We shall see how this is done in Chapter 4.) However, since the statements are so simple (e.g. add two numbers), each one can express only a very small part of an algorithm. This means that a large number of statements is needed to express most algorithms, and programming in machine language is therefore very tedious.

To make programming easier, other types of languages have been developed. These *high level* languages are more convenient than machine languages, in that each statement can express a larger step of an algorithm. Of course each statement must still be interpreted by the computer, and it might appear that the capabilities of the CPU would have to be correspondingly enhanced in order to make this possible. Enhancement of the CPU is certainly one way to make interpretation of high level programs feasible, but in fact a cheaper and more flexible alternative is available. This is to *translate* high level programs into machine language before they are executed. The translation consists of transforming each statement in the high level program into an equivalent sequence of machine language statements. These machine language statements can then be interpreted by the CPU. The entire process is illustrated in Fig. 1.4.

The translation from high level language to machine language is a task which can itself be performed by the computer. A program for this task is called a *language translator*, which we shall describe in Chapter 5. Computer manufacturers supply language translators for most of the commonly used programming languages.

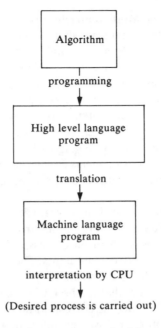

Figure 1.4   Stages in executing an algorithm on a computer.

Current programming languages fall in a spectrum from high level (examples are Pascal, PL/I, Algol and Cobol), through intermediate levels (Fortran and Basic), to the very low level of machine languages. High level languages can be viewed as making the task of programming easier, at the expense of making interpretation and translation more difficult. Since the former is performed by humans, and the latter by computers, there is no doubt where the balance of preference lies. (Low level languages do, however, have some advantages—we shall discuss the issues more fully in Chapter 5.)

1.3 THE SOFTWARE–HARDWARE HIERARCHY

We saw in the last section that a computer executes programs, which are simply the expression of algorithms for carrying out processes. Programs are often referred to by the generic term *software*, to distinguish them from the *hardware* (or physical equipment) from which the computer is built. Some software is written by the users of a computer system—to perform various tasks they wish to accomplish—but in fact most computer users do no programming at all. These people use computers as a tool, to perform tasks for which algorithms are well known and programs already written. For example, an accountant might use a computer to maintain ledgers; an engineer might use it in designing a bridge; a doctor might use it to monitor the condition of a patient; and a clerk might use it to prepare legal documents.

A set of programs for use in some particular application is called an *applications package*. There are applications packages for all the applications mentioned above, and for a multitude of others. The user of an applications package normally obtains it from a computer manufacturer, or from some other specialist vendor. The user's involvement in programming is limited to those occasions when the package may need modifying, possibly to meet some new circumstance or to satisfy some additional requirement.

There are, however, many occasions when a computer user wants to do something for which no applications package is available. On these occasions the user is forced to write his own programs, or to employ someone to write them for him. These programs might later be sold as a package to other users with similar requirements.

Applications packages and user written programs are generally categorized as *applications software*. For convenience, applications software is usually written in a high level programming language, and therefore relies on the existence of appropriate language translators. As we shall see in Chapter 5, language translators are not the only programs on which applications software relies. There are a number of other programs which provide vital services for the applications software; these programs, including the language translators, are collectively labelled *system software*. One notable element of system software is the *operating system*, whose services normally include management of the computer's input and output devices, the storage of information over long periods of time, and provision of access to the computer by several users simultaneously.

From the discussion above it is evident that a computer system can be viewed as a hierarchy of software and hardware components (Fig. 1.5). At the highest level is the applications software, which relies for its operation on the system software below it. The system software in turn relies on the computer's CPU, memory, and I/O devices. The hierarchy does not in fact stop here, since these hardware components are themselves constructed from simpler components in a way we shall describe in Chapter 4. The system software components of the hierarchy are described in Chaper 5, and various items at the applications level are described in Chapter 6.

We should point out that the distinction between the role of hardware and software is not as sharp as Fig. 1.5 might suggest. Each component of a computer system performs certain functions as outlined above. Some of

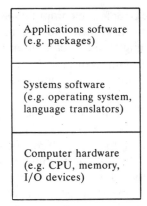

Figure 1.5   The software–hardware hierarchy

these functions (e.g. programming language translation) are traditionally performed by software; others (e.g. addition) are traditionally performed by hardware. Some functions, however, may sometimes be performed by software and sometimes by hardware. An example is multiplication, which is a function provided by all computer systems. One way of providing the multiplication function is to design a suitable algorithm, express the algorithm as a program (perhaps part of the system software), and then execute the program whenever multiplication is required. (The algorithm might perhaps be a version of the junior school algorithm which treats each digit separately and then adds the results.) Another way of providing the function is to embed the same algorithm in the hardware of the CPU—that is, design the CPU so that its internal components can execute the algorithm as a single operation. This hardware implementation has the advantage of speed—multiplication is much quicker than when implemented by software—but it has the disadvantage of additional complexity in the CPU and hence a higher cost for the computer.

In principle any function of a computer system can be provided either by software or by hardware. That is, an algorithm which describes how to perform the function can either be expressed as a program or be built into the physical components. (There is an analogy with maintaining a room at a constant temperature: an algorithm for performing this function can either be expressed as a "program" for manipulating various switches, or it can be built directly into the hardware of a thermostat.) In practice the choice between hardware and software depends on the speed–cost tradeoff involved. Complex functions, such as language translation and the design of bridges, are generally performed by software because the cost of building special hardware for these functions is prohibitive. Simple functions, or functions required very frequently, are generally performed by hardware so that greater speed can be attained. Summarizing, the boundary between hardware and software is a fluid one, and will probably change with advances in technology.

1.4 THE IMPORTANCE OF ALGORITHMS

We have seen that to carry out a process on a computer one must

(1) design an algorithm which describes how the process is to be performed;

(2) express the algorithm as a program in a suitable programming language;

(3) get the computer to execute the program.

The role of the algorithm is fundamental. Without an algorithm there can be no program, and without a program there is nothing to execute.

Algorithms are fundamental in another sense: they are independent of both the language in which they are expressed and the computer which executes them. For example, all airline reservation systems include an algorithm for booking a seat. In each system the algorithm may be expressed in a different programming language and executed on a different computer. However, in all cases the algorithm is fundamentally the same.

An analogy with everyday life may be helpful. A recipe for fruit cake can be expressed in English or in French. Whichever language is used the algorithm is the same. Moreover, if the recipe is followed faithfully, the same cake is produced irrespective of the cook using it (otherwise there would be little point in recipe books). All cooks are capable of the same basic operations (e.g. weighing ingredients, setting the oven temperature), and if the recipe is expressed understandably (e.g. in English or French as appropriate), then all cooks can produce the same cake. A novice cook may need the recipe to be spelt out in more detail, but this is a difference in expression and not in the recipe itself. Thus the recipe for fruit cake is independent of the language in which it is expressed and of the cook who uses it.

Moving back into the technical sphere, all computers (like all cooks) can perform roughly the same basic operations—there are differences of detail and of speed, but in a general sense the capabilities of all present-day computers are the same. Moreover, these capabilities are unchanged by technological innovation—such innovation does not affect *what* computers do, though it may affect the speed, cost, and reliability with which they do it. This means that algorithms can be devised and studied independently of the technology of the day—results will remain valid despite the advent of new computers and new programming languages.

To computer scientists, then, algorithms are more fundamental than either programming languages or computers (just as to those interested in food, recipes are more fundamental than languages or cooks). A programming language is simply a convenient medium for expressing an algorithm, and a computer is simply a processor for executing it. Both the programming language and the computer are means to an end—that of getting the algorithm executed and the corresponding process carried out.

We do not, however, wish to imply that computers and programming languages are unimportant. Developments in computer technology can lead to algorithms being executed more quickly, more cheaply, and more reliably. This in turn can open up areas of application which were previously infeasible. (For example, accurate weather forecasting relies on the solution of complex equations about the atmosphere. Algorithms for solving these equations have been known for some time, but until the recent advent of high-speed computers the time taken to execute them was so long that the weather would have passed before it had been predicted.) Programming languages, too, are important, since they govern the ease with which algorithms can be expressed, and hence affect the human effort expended on programming. Thus the development of new programming languages and new computers is a legitimate concern of computer science—but only as a means for the more effective expression and execution of algorithms.

Given that algorithms are fundamental to computer science, what aspects or properties of algorithms do computer scientists study? One extremely important aspect is the *design* of algorithms. Faced with a potential new application of computers, how does one design algorithms for carrying out the processes required? The design of an algorithm is a difficult intellectual activity—far more difficult than expressing the algorithm as a program. Computer scientists attempt to handle this difficulty by devising frameworks within which the design process can proceed. (One such framework is described in Chapter 2.) However, the design of most algorithms requires creativity and insight, and no general rules can be formulated. In other words, there is no algorithm for algorithm design.

This observation raises some interesting questions. Are there other processes for which no algorithm exists? Do such processes correspond to those we intuitively regard as creative? Given a process, how can one tell whether or not there is an algorithm which describes it? The last question is important, because if a process cannot be described by an algorithm there is no chance of it ever being executed by a computer—no matter how large, fast or expensive. These issues are collectively categorized under the heading *computability*—the study of what is computable and what is not. We shall look further at computability in Section 3.1.

Given that a process can be described by an algorithm, it is pertinent to ask how much computer resources are required to execute it. In particular, how long will it take to execute the algorithm, and how much memory will be needed? If there are several algorithms describing the same process, which of them is the "best", in the sense of consuming the least resources? What are the minimum resources required to carry out a given process—that is, what resources are used by the best possible algorithm? Can one discover what the best algorithm is? Are there processes for which the best algorithm requires so much resources that execution is infeasible, even on the biggest and fastest computers we can envisage? These issues—collectively referred to as the *complexity* of algorithms—will be discussed in Section 3.2.

Another topic of concern to computer scientists is the *correctness* of algorithms. Since the design of algorithms is so difficult, how can one be sure that the algorithms are correct? In other words, how can one be sure that a particular algorithm really does describe the process intended? Failure to be sure has led to some spectacular errors (e.g. the loss of a Venus space probe). As the application of computers widens, an increasing number of circumstances will arise in which an incorrect algorithm is potentially disastrous. We shall discuss these issues further in Section 3.3.

Summarizing, the notion of algorithm is fundamental to computer science. It is the unifying concept for all the activities which computer scientists engage in. The central role of algorithms is reflected in the rest of this book. In Chapter 2 we shall see how algorithms can be designed. In Chapter 3 we shall deal with the basic properties of algorithms, such as their complexity and correctness. Chapters 4 and 5 describe how computer systems which execute algorithms are built. In Chapter 6 we look at the algorithms used in some particular areas of computer application. Finally, in Chapter 7 we consider the social issues which are raised.

BIBLIOGRAPHY

Most introductory computer science books give an overview of the subject in their early chapters. The following three books are devoted largely to general issues.

M. A. Arbib, *Computers and the Cybernetic Society*, Academic Press, N.Y., 1977.
M. Bohl, *Information Processing* (2nd edn), Science Research Associates, Chicago, 1976.
R. Hunt and J. Shelley, *Computers and Common Sense*, Prentice-Hall International, London, 1975.

The following is a good refuge from jargon.

A. Chandor (ed.), *A Dictionary of Computers*, Penguin, Middlesex, 1970.

2 THE DESIGN OF ALGORITHMS

We argued in Chapter 1 that the notion of an algorithm is central to computer science. In this chapter we look more closely at algorithms, considering such issues as their structure, how they may be devised, and how they may be expressed in a form suitable for being executed.

2.1 ALGORITHMS, PROGRAMS AND PROGRAMMING LANGUAGES

We recall from Chapter 1 that an *algorithm* is a description of how to carry out a task, or *process*. There are algorithms for carrying out all kinds of useful processes—some examples were given in Fig. 1.1. In many cases a process interacts with its environment, accepting *input* and producing *output*. In fact production of the output is often the only reason for carrying out the process. In the first four examples of Fig. 1.1 the input includes wool, balsa wood, flour, and fabric, while the corresponding outputs are the sweater, plane, cake, and dress. The fifth example requires no specific input, and the output is the sound produced. Similarly, processes carried out by computers often require input in the form of information, and usually produce output in the form of more information. (For this reason some aspects of computer science are called "information processing".) As an example, the process of computing weekly wages requires as part of its input information about wage rates and hours worked; it produces among its output information about the wages payable and taxes deducted. Note that the input and output are part of the specification of the process, and hence part of any algorithm describing the process, but they are independent of the processor which carries it out. In this example the information on wage rates and so on would be required whether the processor were a computer or a

14

wages clerk, though as we shall see later it may be expressed in a different form in each case.

The processes in Fig. 1.1 all *terminate*: the sweater is completed, the plane built, the sonata played, and so on. However, there are many interesting processes which we regard as never terminating, such as

updating a library catalog
painting the Sydney harbour bridge
staying happy

Even processes carried out by computers may never terminate; examples are

controlling traffic signals
monitoring early warning radar systems
monitoring a patient in an intensive care unit

The termination or non-termination of a process is one of its prime characteristics. A major source of error in the design of an algorithm is that under certain circumstances the process described may not terminate whereas it is always supposed to do so. The algorithm devised by Prince Charming to find Cinderella was not a very good one in this respect. If Cinderella had emigrated or died the Prince would have spent the rest of his life touring the land trying to fit a glass slipper onto the foot of every girl he came across (unless he eventually cut his losses and found another bride). Only the fact that Cinderella was still around saved him from this ignoble fate. We shall say more about termination in Chapter 3.

As mentioned in Chapter 1, an algorithm can be executed only if it is expressed in a form the intended processor can understand. In all the examples of Fig. 1.1 the algorithms are expressed in a form suitable for understanding by people. It would be convenient if computers too could understand one of these forms of expression, particularly English. Unfortunately computers cannot at present do this, for the following reasons.

(1)   English has an enormous vocabulary and complex grammatical rules. For a computer to be capable of analyzing English sentences it would need to be supplied with appropriate algorithms to enable it to do so. Unfortunately the process of analysis is so complex and little understood that such algorithms have not yet been devised, except for simple restricted subsets of the language.

(2)   The interpretation of an English sentence depends not only on appropriate grammatical analysis, but also on the context in which the sentence appears. Many words have several meanings which can be resolved only by consideration of context; for example, the phrase *a funny situation* is ambiguous unless the meaning of the word *funny*

(peculiar or humorous) can be inferred from context. Even correct grammatical analysis is dependent on the meaning of words, as the sentence

Fruit flies like a banana

illustrates. The use of metaphor and other turns of speech also makes the interpretation of English difficult; for example, the sentence

Gather ye rosebuds while ye may

is not usually regarded as an invitation to pick flowers. The potential ambiguity of English is recognized in the means chosen to express the everyday algorithms of Fig. 1.1. In these algorithms the use of English, when it is used at all, is restricted to a very simple subset in which one hopes that instructions are unambiguous. Even so, many a small child has wondered precisely *which* piece of airplane is supposed to be glued on next.

Despite these difficulties, some advances have been made toward the understanding of natural language by computers. These advances (some of which are described in Chapter 6) have been achieved at the expense of severely limiting the vocabulary and style of expression used: they are currently inadequate to allow algorithms for computers to be expressed in English.

Since English text is too complex to be understood by computers, algorithms which are to be executed by computers must be expressed in a simpler form. We recall from Chapter 1 that an algorithm expressed in such a form is called a *program*, and that a program is written in a *programming language*. There are literally hundreds of programming languages: some of the better known ones are Fortran, Cobol, PL/I, Pascal, and Algol. The reason there are so many programming languages is threefold.

(1)   Computer programming is a comparatively recent activity, and ideas about how best to do it are still evolving. As new ideas emerge so do ideas about appropriate means of expression, and hence new programming languages are developed.

(2)   Computers are used for a wide variety of purposes. This implies that the algorithms used are of a diverse nature and cannot all be readily expressed in a single programming language. (Cf. musical notation, which evolved to express the algorithmic steps involved in playing an instrument, and the notation of knitting patterns, which was developed to perform a similar function in making sweaters.) Thus special purpose programming languages have been developed to express

algorithms arising in specific computer applications. For example, the algorithms used in business data processing are quite different from those used in controlling an industrial plant, and both are different from those used in simulating intelligence in robots. Consequently different programming languages (e.g. Cobol, Coral, and Lisp respectively) have been developed to express these different kinds of algorithm.

(3)   There is an inevitable tendency to reinvent the wheel. (This tendency stems partly from the "not invented here" syndrome—the belief that one's own wheels are better than anyone else's.)

By analogy with natural languages, each programming language has its own vocabulary and its own grammatical rules which dictate how the vocabulary may be used. In most cases the vocabulary consists of certain mathematical symbols and a few English words, and the grammatical rules are simple enough to allow computer interpretation of programs. Because of differences in vocabulary and grammar programming languages naturally differ in the forms of expression allowed; for example one of the steps in an accounting algorithm might be expressed in Cobol as

MULTIPLY *price* BY *quantity* GIVING *cost*

and in Pascal as

*cost := price * quantity*

Both forms of expression mean the same thing, namely an instruction to multiply a number called *price* by a number called *quantity* to give a number called *cost*. This is directly analogous to the two forms of expression

Donnez-le moi

and

Give it to me

which both mean the same thing.

The designers of programming languages attempt to meet several objectives, the most important of which are as follows.

(1)   The language must allow the easy and concise expression of algorithms in the application area for which it is designed.

(2)   The language must be readily comprehensible to a computer.

(3)   Programs written in the language should be readily understandable by humans, so that they can be easily modified and corrected where necessary.

(4)   The language should minimize the potential for error in the transformation of an algorithm into a program.

(5)   It should be easy to show, by inspection of a program, that its execution will indeed cause the desired process to be carried out.

It should be apparent that these objectives are not all mutually compatible. For example, conciseness of expression may militate against easy comprehension (cf. the use of acronyms in English), while a language designed for easy comprehension by humans may not be equally comprehensible to a computer (English is an extreme example).

In this book we shall need to express a large number of algorithms of various kinds. Fortunately we are operating under the considerable advantage that our algorithms do not need to be executed by computers, but "merely" understood by the reader. For this reason we shall not use a formal programming language to express our algorithms, but will rely on a stylized subset of English. The meaning of what we write will for the most part be intuitively obvious, though we shall of course explain our notation wherever necessary. The reader who wishes to learn a specific programming language is referred to the many programming texts available.

2.2   SYNTAX AND SEMANTICS

We recall from Chapter 1 that a processor must be able to *interpret* an algorithm if it is to carry out the process the algorithm describes. That is, the processor must be able to

(1)   understand the form in which the algorithm is expressed (e.g. a knitting pattern or a musical score);

(2)   carry out the corresponding operations.

In this section we shall look more closely at the first of these stages.

Understanding the expression of an algorithm itself falls into two stages. First the processor must be able to recognize and make sense of the symbols in which the algorithm is expressed, be they English words, abbreviations, mathematical symbols, or notes in a musical score. To do this the processor must have a knowledge of the vocabulary and grammar of the language in which the algorithm is expressed. It must know, to pursue earlier examples, that "sleeve" is an English noun, that "=" is a relation between two numbers, and that "#" is a symbol of musical pitch. The occurrence of any of these symbols outside its proper grammatical context, as in

sleeve the seams

or

$$a + = b$$

is a violation of the rules of the language concerned.

The set of grammatical rules which govern how the symbols in a language may be legitimately used is called the *syntax* of the language. Thus the syntax of English governs use of the word "sleeve", the syntax of mathematics governs use of the symbol "=", and the syntax of musical scores governs use of the symbol "#". A program which adheres to the syntax of the language in which it is expressed is said to be *syntactically correct*; that is, every symbol in the program is used legitimately. A deviation from the syntax of the language is called a *syntax error*. Syntactic correctness is usually a necessary prerequisite for interpreting a computer program; exceptions arise only when the processor is sophisticated enough to infer what form of expression was intended when it encounters a syntax error. As we shall see in Chapter 5, computers are not normally equipped with this degree of sophistication, so a program which is syntactically incorrect will not usually be executed.

The second stage in understanding the expression of an algorithm is to attach meaning to each step, in terms of the operations the processor is intended to carry out. For example, the meaning of

purl 1

is that the needles and wool are to be manipulated in a certain way; the meaning of

is that two particular notes are to be played; and the meaning of

cost := *price* * *quantity*

is that two numbers called *price* and *quantity* are to be multiplied together to give a third number called *cost*. The meaning of particular forms of expression in a language is called the *semantics* of the language. Programming languages are designed so that both their syntax and their semantics are relatively simple, and so that a program can be syntactically analyzed without reference to semantics. This is in sharp contrast to natural languages, in which, as we saw in the last section, syntax and semantics are very complex and often interrelated. In natural languages it is possible to write sentences which are syntactically correct but nevertheless meaningless. The sentence

Colorless green ideas sleep furiously

is a good example (due to Noam Chomsky), while

He went by the south and burned his mouth
By eating cold plum porridge

is a less extreme example which is often recited by small children. As another example,

The elephant ate the peanut

is a meaningful sentence, while

The peanut ate the elephant

is not, though both are syntactically correct. Similarly, a step in an algorithm can be syntactically correct but semantically meaningless. For example

write down the name of the 1st month of the year

and

write down the name of the 13th month of the year

are both syntactically correct algorithmic steps (expressed in English), but only the former has any meaning.

Detection of semantic inconsistencies relies on knowledge of the objects being referred to. In particular it relies on knowledge of the attributes of those objects, and of the relationships between them. Thus the absurdities above are recognized as such because the reader is aware of the relative attributes of elephants and peanuts, and so on. It follows that a processor can detect semantic inconsistencies while trying to understand the expression of an algorithm only if it knows enough about the objects the algorithm refers to; otherwise the inconsistencies will become apparent only when the algorithm is executed. Consider, for example, a processor faced with the command

write down the name of the 13th month of the year

If the processor knows that there are only 12 months in the year it can detect the semantic inconsistency in this command before trying to execute it. If, on the other hand, the processor is less knowledgeable, it will take the command at face value and attempt to execute it, possibly by looking up the name of the month in a calendar. It is only during execution, when the processor finds there is no such month, that the inconsistency becomes apparent.

Some semantic inconsistencies are more subtle, being a result of execution of an earlier part of the algorithm. For example, the algorithm

think of a number from 1 to 13
call this number N
write down the name of the Nth month of the year

contains a potential inconsistency which is realized only if execution of the first line results in the number 13. When an inconsistency is a result of executing an algorithm there is in general no chance of detecting it beforehand.

The discussion above can be summarized by saying that in order to interpret each step in an algorithm a processor must be able to

(1)   make sense of the symbols in which the step is expressed;
(2)   attach meaning to the step in terms of operations to be performed;
(3)   perform the appropriate operations.

Syntax errors can be detected in stage 1, and certain semantic errors can be detected in stage 2. Other semantic errors will not be detected until stage 3.

When the processor is a computer, stages 1 and 2 are performed by a *translator*, which transforms each step in the program into the appropriate operations the processor is to carry out. The translator is itself a program, whose design will be described in Chapter 5. A separate translator is required for each programming language used, and the translator for a particular programming language is equipped with full knowledge of the language's syntax. (This is quite feasible, since the syntax is by design a finite set of well-defined rules.) The translator can therefore detect any syntax errors in programs submitted for execution. However, we have seen that it is unreasonable to expect the translator to detect all (or even many) semantic errors, and those which remain undetected will become apparent only when the program is executed.

In addition to *syntactic* and *semantic* errors there is a third class of error which deserves mention. This is the *logical* error: a program may be syntactically correct and contain no semantic inconsistencies, but simply may not properly describe the desired process. For example, consider the following algorithm (expressed in English) for computing the circumference of a circle.

compute the circumference by multiplying the radius by π

This algorithm is syntactically and semantically correct (i.e. it is a correct and meaningful English command). However, it produces the wrong result—there is a logical error in the omission of a factor of 2.

A processor cannot detect logical errors, since it has no idea what process the algorithm is intended to describe. Logical errors can be detected only by comparing the desired process with the process actually carried out. Logical errors, and steps which may be taken to avoid them, will be discussed further in the next section.

2.3   STEPWISE REFINEMENT OF ALGORITHMS

We have seen that to get a processor to carry out a process one has to supply it with a suitable algorithm. The design of such an algorithm is usually surprisingly difficult, at least when the process to be carried out is non-trivial. The difficulties of designing an algorithm are compounded when the processor is a computer since, as we have seen, computers lack the intuition or common sense to realize that the algorithm may not describe precisely the process intended. A common fault among algorithms is that the process described is *almost* the intended one, but not quite.

An example in the human sphere is the friend who describes how to get to his house. The algorithm he gives, "Turn right at the shops, go straight ahead at the next crossroads, then take the third on the left, . . ." is quite likely to omit some small but crucial detail (e.g. precisely which shops to turn at) and send his visitor unwittingly to the wrong street or even the wrong suburb. At least in this case the processor is human, with probably sufficient sense to recognize the error and seek directions from a passer-by; computers, unfortunately, are not equipped with such resourcefulness.

Another common failing of algorithms is that execution *usually* results in the intended process being carried out, but in certain circumstances (unforeseen or overlooked by the designer) it does not. As an example, consider the following simple algorithm which describes how to calculate the flight time of an aircraft from an airline timetable.

> *look up departure time*
> *look up arrival time*
> *subtract departure time from arrival time*

The algorithm will usually give the correct result, but will fail to do so if the departure point and the destination are in different time zones. Even worse, if daylight saving is used at one end of the route but not the other the algorithm may give the correct result in winter but not in summer.

The moral of these examples is that the designer of an algorithm must take great care that the algorithm describes precisely the process he wants carried out, and that all possible circumstances have been allowed for. If the process to be carried out is at all complex, then the designer's task is a difficult one. Indeed the designer has very little chance of success unless he adopts a rigorously methodical approach. One such approach, known as *stepwise refinement* (or *top-down design*), is described in the following paragraphs.

Stepwise refinement is a latterday variation on the age-old theme of divide and conquer. The idea is to break the process to be carried out into a number of steps, each of which can be described by an algorithm which is smaller and simpler than that for the entire process. Because each such sub-algorithm is simpler than the whole thing, the designer usually has a clearer idea of how to construct it, and he can therefore sketch it in more detail than if he tried to handle the whole algorithm at one. The sub-algorithms can themselves be broken into smaller portions, which because of their greater simplicity can again be expressed with more detail and precision. Refinement of the algorithm continues in this way until each of its steps is sufficiently detailed and precise to allow execution by the processor concerned.

As an example, suppose that a robot which is to act as a domestic servant is being designed, and that it needs to be supplied with an algorithm describing how to make a cup of instant coffee. An initial version of the algorithm might be

(1)   *boil water*
(2)   *put coffee in cup*
(3)   *add water to cup*

The steps in this algorithm are probably not detailed enough for the robot to be able to interpret them. Each step must therefore be refined into a sequence of simpler steps, each specified in more detail than the original. Thus the step

(1)   *boil water*

might be refined into

(1.1) *fill kettle*
(1.2) *switch on kettle*
(1.3) *wait until boiling*
(1.4) *switch off kettle*

Similarly,

(2)   *put coffee in cup*

might be refined into

(2.1) *open coffee jar*
(2.2) *extract one spoonful of coffee*
(2.3) *tip spoonful into cup*
(2.4) *close coffee jar*

and

(3)   *add water to cup*

might be refined into

(3.1) *pour water from kettle into cup until cup is full.*

Note that the last refinement does not incease the number of steps in the algorithm, but simply re-expresses an existing step in more detail.

At this stage the original algorithm has been refined into three sub-algorithms, to be executed in sequence. If the robot can interpret all the steps in each sub-algorithm, then the process of refinement can stop and design of the algorithm is complete. However, some steps may still be too complex for the robot to interpret, and these must be refined further. Thus the step

(1.1) *fill kettle*

may need refinement into

(1.1.1) *put kettle under tap*
(1.1.2) *turn on tap*
(1.1.3) *wait until kettle is full*
(1.1.4) *turn off tap*

Other steps may need similar refinement, though there may be some, such as

(1.2) *switch on kettle*

which can already be interpreted by the robot and which need not be refined further.

Original algorithm	*First refinement*	*Second (final) refinement*
(1) *boil water*	(1.1) *fill kettle*	(1.1.1) *put kettle under tap*
		(1.1.2) *turn on tap*
		(1.1.3) *wait until kettle is full*
		(1.1.4) *turn off tap*
	(1.2) *switch on kettle*	
	(1.3) *wait until boiling*	(1.3.1) *wait until kettle whistles*
	(1.4) *switch off kettle*	
(2) *put coffee in cup*	(2.1) *open coffee jar*	(2.1.1) *take coffee jar from shelf*
		(2.1.2) *remove lid from jar*
	(2.2) *extract one spoonful of coffee*	
	(2.3) *tip spoonful into cup*	
	(2.4) *close coffee jar*	(2.4.1) *put lid on coffee jar*
		(2.4.2) *replace coffee jar on shelf*
(3) *add water to cup*	(3.1) *pour water from kettle into cup until cup is full*	

Figure 2.1 Refinement of a coffee-making algorithm.

Finally, after a number of refinements, every step in the algorithm will be interpretable by the robot. At this stage the algorithm is complete. The successive refinements are shown in Fig. 2.1. The final version of the algorithm (i.e. the program to be executed by the robot) is obtained by taking the last refinement of each step, as shown in Fig. 2.2.

{Algorithm for making a cup of coffee}
{first boil water}
(1.1.1)   *put kettle under tap*
(1.1.2)   *turn on tap*
(1.1.3)   *wait until kettle is full*
(1.1.4)   *turn off tap*
(1.2)   *switch on kettle*
(1.3.1)   *wait until kettle whistles*
(1.4)   *switch off kettle*
{put coffee in cup}
(2.1.1)   *take coffee jar from shelf*
(2.1.2)   *remove lid from jar*
(2.2)   *extract one spoonful coffee*
(2.3)   *tip spoonful into cup*
(2.4.1)   *put lid on coffee jar*
(2.4.2)   *replace coffee jar on shelf*
{add water to cup}
(3.1)   *pour water from kettle into cup*
          until cup is full

Figure 2.2   Final version of the coffee-making algorithm.

Those lines enclosed in curly brackets in Fig. 2.2 are simply *comments* to aid the human reader: they are not executable steps in the algorithm, and are to be ignored by the robot. Each comment describes the function of the part of the algorithm which follows it.

When using stepwise refinement the designer of an algorithm must of course know where to stop; that is, he must know when a particular step in the algorithm is sufficiently primitive to need no further refinement. This of course means that he must know what sort of step the processor can interpret. For example, the designer of the algorithm above must know that the robot can interpret

switch on kettle

which therefore needs no refinement, but that it cannot interpret

fill kettle

and refinement is therefore required.

Knowledge of a processor's capabilities is needed not only to terminate refinement but also to direct the way in which refinement proceeds. If an algorithm designer knows that the processor can interpet a particular kind of step, then he will organize the refinement to result in steps of that kind. To go back to the coffee-making example, the designer probably refined

boil water

into steps involving operations on a kettle because he realized that the robot knew all about kettles but nothing about saucepans or urns.

The foregoing discussion demonstrates that the stepwise refinement of an algorithm cannot proceed in a vacuum. The designer of the algorithm must be aware of the interpretive capabilities of the intended processor, so that he can push the refinement in particular directions and know when to terminate the refinement of each part. When the intended processor is a person the designer's task is complicated by the fact that people's interpretive powers vary widely: what is easily understood by one person may be quite unintelligible to another. The interpretive capabilities of a computer, on the other hand, are much more precisely defined: a computer can interpret anything which is properly expressed in a programming language. Thus the designer of a computer algorithm refines the algorithm in such a way that its steps can be expressed in an appropriate programming language, and terminates the refinement when every step is expressed in the language concerned.

2.4   SEQUENCE

The coffee-making algorithm of Fig. 2.2 is very straightforward, involving simple steps which are to be executed one after the other. We say that such an algorithm is a *sequence* of steps, meaning that

(1)   The steps are executed one at a time.
(2)   Each step is executed exactly once: none is repeated and none omitted.
(3)   The order in which the steps are executed is the same as that in which they are written.
(4)   Termination of the last step implies termination of the algorithm.

Throughout this book successive steps in a sequence will be written on successive lines.

An algorithm which is solely a sequence of steps is extremely inflexible, since its course of execution is fixed and cannot be modified by circumstances. What happens, for example, in the coffee-making algorithm if the coffee jar is empty? (The robot will probably either halt in confusion or serve up a cup of hot water.) Pursuing the same example, how can the robot handle a request for several cups of coffee (boil the water separately for each cup?), and how could the sequence of steps be extended to cater for optional milk and sugar?

As another example of the rigidity inherent in a sequence, consider the following algorithm which describes how to travel from central London to downtown New York.

> *catch Underground train to Heathrow airport, London*
> *fly by plane to Kennedy airport, New York*
> *take a cab from Kennedy to downtown New York*   (2.1)

Like the coffee-making example, this algorithm is very inflexible: it provides no alternative steps for the not unlikely circumstance of there being either an Underground strike in London or a cab drivers' strike in New York.

From these examples it is clear that a combination of steps in sequence is a very primitive structure for an algorithm. We shall examine less primitive structures in the next few sections.

2.5 SELECTION

We have just seen that when an algorithm is solely a sequence there is no possibility of its execution being modified by circumstance. Thus the domestic robot could not cope with an empty coffee jar, and an urban transport strike would disable the transatlantic traveller. In the case of the robot, what is required is the ability to execute a step such as

> *get new jar from cupboard*

if the current jar is empty, and to omit this step otherwise. This ability is called *selection*. The selection in the step above can be expressed by rewriting the refinement of step 2.1 as

> (2.1.1) *take coffee jar off shelf*
> (2.1.2) **if** *jar is empty*
>   **then** *get new jar from cupboard*
> (2.1.3) *remove lid from jar*

The crucial step is 2.1.2, which expresses both the step to be selected (*get new jar from cupboard*) and the condition (*jar is empty*) under which the selection is to be made.

Step 2.1.2 is a particular case of a step of the general form

> **if** *condition*
>   **then** *step*

where *condition* specifies the circumstance under which *step* is to be executed. If *condition* is true then *step* is executed; otherwise it is not. The processor must of course be able to interpret the conditions in an algorithm just as it must be able to interpret the steps. The conditions must therefore be refined until they are sufficiently detailed and precise to allow the processor to interpret them.

In the example above, selection is used to determine whether a particular step is to be executed or not. An extension of this form of selection is a form which determines which of two *alternative* steps is to be executed. For example, the transatlantic travel algorithm 2.1 can be greatly improved by rewriting its first step as

> **if** *Underground on strike*
> **then** *catch airport bus*
> **else** *catch Underground train*

This is a particular case of selection between alternative steps: the general form of such selection is

> **if** *condition*
> **then** *step* 1
> **else** *step* 2

where *condition* determines, in the obvious way, which of *step* 1 or *step* 2 is to be executed. Throughout this book we will use indentation (as above) to make the alternative steps stand out from the surrounding text.

It is apparent that the earlier **if** . . . **then** . . . form of selection is simply a special case of the **if** . . . **then** . . . **else** . . . form above, since

> **if** *condition*   **if** *condition*
> **then** *step*   and   **then** *step*
>   **else** *do nothing*

are equivalent. However, we shall continue to use the shorter **if** . . . **then** . . . form for conciseness whenever appropriate.

As a further example of the use of selection here is an algorithm for approaching a set of traffic signals:

> **if** *signal is red or signal is amber*
> **then** *stop*
> **else** *proceed*   (2.2)

A slightly better algorithm, which allows for the possibility of the signals being out of order, is

if *no signal*
   then *proceed with great caution*
   else if *signal is red or signal is amber*
      then *stop*
      else *proceed*   (2.3)

This algorithm contains two occurrences of selection, the second of which is *nested* inside the first and is executed only if the signal is working. Note how the use of indentation makes it quite clear to the human reader which steps in the algorithm are part of each selection. Without indentation the algorithm would be much more difficult to understand:

if *no signal*
then *proceed with great caution*
else if *signal is red or signal is amber*
then *stop*
else *proceed*   (2.4)

Another example of nested selection arises in the following algorithm, which describes how to determine the largest of three numbers given that the processor can compare only two of them at a time. If the numbers are called x, y and z, a first version of the algorithm is

if $x > y$
   then *choose between x and z*
   else *choose between y and z*

The choice between x and z can be refined into

if $x > z$
   then *choose x*
   else *choose z*

and the choice between y and z can be refined similarly. The final algorithm is therefore

if $x > y$
   then if $x > z$
      then *choose x*
      else *choose z*
   else if $y > z$
      then *choose y*
      else *choose z*   (2.5)

Note how indentation again makes clear which steps of the algorithm are part of each of the three selections. (The reader who still doubts the value of indentation might care to write the above algorithm without it, or attempt Exercise 2.2.)

The power of selection is that it allows a processor to follow different paths through an algorithm according to circumstance. Nested selections allow the number of paths to be arbitrary. Without selection it would be impossible to write algorithms of any significant practical use.

2.6 ITERATION

Consider the process of looking up a person's address, given his name, from a list of names and addresses. A possible algorithm is

> *consider the first name in the list*
> **if** *this name is the given name*
>   **then** *extract the corresponding address* $\left.\right\}$ S1
>   **else** *consider the next name in the list*
>   **if** *this name is the given name*
>   **then** *extract the corresponding address* $\left.\right\}$ S1
>   **else** *consider the next name in the list*
>   **if** *this name is the given name*
>   **then** . . .
>   . . .   (2.6)

The trouble with this algorithm (apart from a tendency to fall off the right-hand margin) is that its author doesn't know when to stop writing. More precisely, the author doesn't know how many times to write the step S1 to ensure that the given name is found. A similar problem arises in the following algorithm, which describes how to calculate the first prime number which is greater than a given "starting" number (which is assumed to be a positive integer).

> *obtain starting number*
> *add* 1
> *test number for primeness* $\left.\right\}$ S2
> **if** *number is prime*
>   **then** *write it down*
>   **else** *add* 1
>   *test number for primeness* $\left.\right\}$ S2
>   **if** *number is prime*
>   **then** *write it down*
>   **else** *add* 1
>   . . .   (2.7)

Again it is not clear how many times to write the sequence S2 to ensure that the processor produces a prime number. For example, S2 need be written only once if the starting number is 4, and four times if the starting number is 13, but how many times if the starting number is 7 394 485?

These examples show that sequence and selection are not by themselves sufficient to express algorithms whose length varies according to circumstance. What is required is a means of repeating certain steps in an algorithm an arbitrary number of times. To do this we shall introduce the words **repeat** and **until** into algorithms, so that algorithm 2.6, for example, may be rewritten as

> *consider the first name in the list*
> **repeat**
>   **if** *this name is the given name*
>   **then** *extract the corresponding address* $\left.\rule{0cm}{1cm}\right\}$ S1
>   **else** *consider the next name in the list*
> **until** *given name is found or list is exhausted*   (2.8)

Similarly, algorithm 2.7 may be rewritten as

> *obtain starting number*
> **repeat**
>   *add* 1
>   *test number for primeness*
> **until** *number is prime*
> *write down number*   (2.9)

These examples illustrate repetition, or *iteration*; the general form of such iteration is

> **repeat**
>   *portion of algorithm*
> **until** *condition*

which means that the portion of the algorithm between the words **repeat** and **until** is to be executed repeatedly until the condition specified after **until** is true. In algorithm 2.8 the portion which is repeated is the inspection of successive names in the list; repetition ceases when the sought for name is found or the list is exhausted. In algorithm 2.9 the repetition applies to the testing of successive numbers for primeness, and terminates when the first prime is encountered.

An occurrence of iteration is usually called a *loop*, and the part of the algorithm which is repeated (i.e. the part between **repeat** and **until**) is known as the loop *body*. The condition occurring after **until** is called the *terminating condition* of the loop. In this book we shall use indentation to make the body of a loop stand out from the surrounding text.

The power of iteration is that it allows a process of indeterminate duration to be described by an algorithm of finite length. This power carries with it a certain degree of responsibility: the responsibility to ensure that the iteration does indeed terminate when (and if) intended. In algorithm 2.9 the iteration terminates because there always exists a prime number greater than any given number. In algorithm 2.8 the iteration terminates because the terminating condition *given name is found or list is exhausted* eventually becomes true. Note, however, that omission of the second part of the terminating condition (*or list is exhausted*) is potentially disastrous, since if the name being sought is not present the processor will run off the end of the list. Failure to specify a terminating condition correctly is one of the most common errors in algorithm design.

Of course some processes, as suggested in Section 2.1, are not intended to terminate, and an algorithm describing such a process must contain a loop which is executed for ever. Such a loop can be written

repeat
   body of loop
forever

As a further example of iteration, consider again the prime-number algorithm 2.9. The loop in this algorithm contains the step

test number for primeness

It is unlikely that the intended processor will be able to tell directly whether or not a particular number is prime, so this step needs further refinement. By definition a prime number is one which has no factors (other than 1 and itself), so testing a number for primeness is the same as testing to see whether it has any non-trivial factors. This can be done by the following algorithm, in which the number being tested is called the *potential prime.*

divide potential prime by every number between 1 *and itself*
if *no division is exact*
   then *potential prime is prime*
   else *potential prime is not prime*

The first step clearly involves iteration, in which the potential prime is divided by successive possible factors starting with 2. The iteration can terminate either when one of the divisions is exact (in which case the potential prime has been shown not to be prime), or when the possible factor is equal to the potential prime (in which case the potential prime really is prime). In fact there is no need to prolong the iteration to the point at which the possible factor is equal to the potential prime: a little thought shows that it is sufficient to go only as far as the potential prime's square root. An algorithm for testing primeness is therefore

> *set possible factor to* 2
> **repeat**
>   *divide potential prime by possible factor*
>   *add* 1 *to possible factor*
> **until** *division is exact or possible factor* > $\sqrt{}$*(potential prime)*
> **if** *no division is exact*
>   **then** *potential prime is prime*
>   **else** *potential prime is not prime*   (2.10)

We recall that algorithm 2.10 is a refinement of the single step

> *test number for primeness*

in algorithm 2.9. Algorithm 2.9 can therefore be rewritten as

> *obtain starting number*
> *set potential prime to starting number*
> **repeat**
>   *add* 1 *to potential prime*
>   *set possible factor to* 2
>   **repeat**
>   *divide potential prime by possible factor*
>   *add* 1 *to possible factor*
>   **until** *division is exact or possible factor* > $\sqrt{}$*(potential prime)*
>   **if** *no division is exact*
>   **then** *potential prime is prime*
>   **else** *potential prime is not prime*
> **until** *potential prime is prime*
> *write down potential prime*   (2.11)

Note that this algorithm contains two loops, one nested inside the other. The outer loop is executed once for each potential prime, while the inner loop is executed once for each possible factor of a potential prime. Both loops are essential to the algorithm.

It is also worth noting how much processing time is saved by the use of square root in the terminating condition of the inner loop. This is an example of a common phenomenon: namely, that a little thought at the design stage can lead to considerable savings during execution. We shall return to this general point in Section 3.2.

The **repeat** . . . **until** . . . notation for iteration is fairly easy to understand, since it is only a slightly formalized version of English. However, there are important situations in which **repeat** loops are inappropriate for expressing the iteration required, for reasons we shall now discuss. A **repeat** loop has its terminating condition at the end, after the **until** which follows the loop body. This implies that the body is always executed at least once, even if the terminating condition is initially true, since the terminating condition is arrived at only after the body has been executed. The importance of this observation will become apparent through consideration of the following example.

Suppose we require an algorithm for determining the largest of a list of numbers. Such an algorithm can operate by scanning the list, comparing each number with the largest found so far, and updating the largest so far each time a larger one is found. Without too much effort we can therefore arrive at algorithm 2.12.

> *set largest so far to first number in list*
> **repeat**
>   *consider next number in list*
>   **if** *this number* > *largest so far*
>   **then** *set largest so far to this number*
> **until** *list is exhausted*
> *write down largest so far*   (2.12)

This algorithm seems to be correct, but it contains a serious error which becomes apparent if the list has only one number in it. In this case the processor will run off the end of the list as soon as it executes the body of the loop for the first time. Of course the terminating condition *list is exhausted* is intended to prevent this happening, but in this case it is ineffective since the processor does not test the terminating condition until it has executed the body at least once. What is required is a way of putting the terminating condition at the start of the loop rather than at the end, so that the processor can omit the loop body completely if it finds the terminating condition already true. An appropriate notation for this is

> *set largest so far to first number in list*
> **while** *list not exhausted* **do**
>   *consider next number in list*
>   **if** *this number* > *largest so far*
>   **then** *set largest so far to this number*
> *write down largest so far*   (2.13)

The loop body comprises everything which is indented below **while**, and the terminating condition appears before the loop body between **while** and **do**.

The general form of this type of loop is

while *condition* **do**
    body of loop

meaning that the body of the loop is to be executed repeatedly as long as *condition* is true. Because *condition* is tested before the body is executed this type of loop is called *pre-tested*; the **repeat** type of loop is called *post-tested*. Because of the different positions of the terminating condition the body of a post-tested loop is always executed at least once, whereas the body of a pre-tested loop may not be executed at all. A pre-tested loop may be regarded as a "look before you leap" loop, whereas a post-tested loop is a "fools rush in" loop. Despite this rather libellous characterization the post-tested loop is often useful in practice, and can be safely employed whenever it is known that the loop body is to be executed at least once. This was the case in all the Examples 2.8–2.11, where post-tested loops were used.

To consolidate the ideas about iteration which have been presented so far we shall look briefly at a very old algorithm: Euclid's algorithm, developed about 300 B.C., for determining the greatest common divisor (*GCD*) of two positive integers. (The *GCD* is also known as the highest common factor (*HCF*)). Euclid's algorithm is based on his discovery of the relation

$$GCD(x,y) = GCD(y, \text{remainder of } x/y) \qquad \text{if } y > 0$$

and

$$GCD(x,y) = x \qquad\qquad\qquad\qquad\qquad \text{if } y = 0$$

where x and y are any non-negative integers. The proof of this is quite straightforward (see Section 3.3). To illustrate the use of the relation, consider the problem of determining the *GCD* of 24 and 9:

$$GCD(24,9) = GCD(9,6) = GCD(6,3) = GCD(3,0) = 3$$

Generalizing, to determine the *GCD* of any non-negative integers x and y all we need to do is repeatedly divide x by y, then replace x by y and replace y by the remainder. The process continues as long as y is non-zero; when y is zero the answer is x. An appropriate algorithm is therefore

while $y \neq 0$ **do**
    calculate remainder of x/y
    replace x by y
    replace y by remainder
    write down the answer x   (2.14)

Note that the use of a post-tested loop in this case would be wrong, since the algorithm would fail (on division by zero) if y were initially zero.

Before finishing this section there is one more form of iteration we wish to discuss. This is a particularly simple form of iteration in which the number of repetitions is known before the loop is executed. For example, an algorithm for calculating the Nth power of a number x (i.e. for calculating x^N) will contain a loop in which x is multiplied by itself, and it is clear that this loop should be executed exactly N times. Such an algorithm can therefore be expressed as

> *obtain values of x and N*
> *set product to* 1
> **repeat** *N times*
>   *multiply product by x*
> *write down product*   (2.15)

This algorithm exemplifies a type of iteration of the general form

> **repeat** *N times*
>   *body of loop*   (2.16)

where N is an arbitrary positive integer, and the body of the loop is indented below **repeat**. Because the number of repetitions is defined in advance this type of iteration is known as *definite iteration*, as opposed to the earlier *indefinite iteration* in which the number of repetitions depends on what happens when the loop is executed. Definite iteration can of course be disguised as indefinite iteration:

> *set count of repetitions to* 0
> **while** *count of repetitions* $< N$ **do**
>   *body of loop*
>   *add* 1 *to count of repetitions*   (2.17)

but the form 2.16 is more concise and convenient. Everyday examples of definite and indefinite iteration, which may clarify the distinction between them, are

	Definite	*Indefinite*
(a)	*Play it again, Sam*	*Play it until you get it right*
(b)	*Keep walking for* 2 *miles*	*Keep right on to the end of the road*
(c)	*Wait here for* 5 *minutes*	*Wait here until I return*
(d)	*Bake for* 20 *minutes*	*Bake until brown*

The duration of definite iteration is determined on entry to the loop, and termination is therefore guaranteed. Indefinite iteration, on the other hand, depends on the terminating condition eventually becoming true. It is clear that definite iteration is the safer form, but of course it is by no means as powerful.

To illustrate a final piece of notation we introduce the two examples

repeat *for each wheel*
check tyre pressure

and

repeat *for each player*
deal a card

In each example the body of the loop is executed once for each instance of some object (wheel or player). The general form of the notation is

repeat *for each instance of an object*
body of loop

The notation implies definite iteration, since it is assumed that the number of instances is known before the loop is entered.

A more practical example of the notation arises in the following algorithm for calculating the product of the first N integers (i.e. the factorial of N).

obtain value of N
set product to 1
repeat *for each integer from* 1 *to N*
multiply product by integer
write down product   (2.18)

2.7 REVIEW OF SEQUENCE, SELECTION AND ITERATION

The last three sections have described three basic forms of algorithm construction: *sequence*, *selection* and *iteration*. Remarkably, these three forms are in fact sufficient for constructing any algorithm. More precisely, if it is possible to construct an algorithm for describing a particular process, then such an algorithm can be constructed from sequence, selection, and iteration alone. The sufficiency of the three basic constructs will be discussed further in Chapter 3. Our purpose in mentioning it here is to point out that the material we have covered so far in this chapter is sufficient to allow us to construct algorithms for any purpose. There are, however, other constructs which usefully supplement the three we have already discussed: we shall describe them in later sections.

In the meantime we shall reinforce the ideas already put forward by developing an algorithm for sorting a list of names into alphabetical order. The need to sort information occurs in many computer applications; indeed some computers spend more time in sorting than in anything else. Because sorting is such a common activity there are many algorithms for doing it: the one we shall develop here is a particularly simple one called the *bubble sort*. Although we shall develop the algorithm in the context of sorting names into alphabetical order it can also be used to sort any other kind of information into whatever order is required.

The basic idea is to pass through the list of names, comparing each name with its successor and interchanging them if they are out of order. If at the end of the pass all the names are in the correct order nothing further need be done; if not, another pass is made through the list and adjacent names are again interchanged where necessary. The passes must be repeated as long as any names are out of order. The process is illustrated in Fig. 2.3, which shows how particular names bubble upward or sink downward to their correct position in the list. An algorithm outlining the sorting process is

while *list not sorted* **do**
    make a pass through the list, exchanging adjacent names
        as necessary

Original list	*List after pass 1* (4 *exchanges done*)	*List after pass 2* (3 *exchanges done*)	*List after pass 3* (2 *exchanges done*)
John	John	Fred	Bill
Kate	Fred	Bill	Fred
Fred	Bill	John	Jill
Bill	Kate	Jill	John
Sam	Jill	Kate	Kate
Jill	Mary	Mary	Mary
Mary	Sam	Sam	Sam

Figure 2.3   Action of the bubble sort.

Note that a pre-tested loop is used in preference to a post-tested one, since the processor may be fortunate enough to find that the list is already in order and that there is nothing to do. (This decision will be reviewed when the algorithm has been refined further.) The second line of the algorithm can be refined into

    start at the top of the list
    repeat
        if *name alphabetically follows its successor*
            then *exchange name and successor*
        consider the next name in the list
    until *the end of the list is reached*

If the number of names is known (N, say) before the loop is entered, then the indefinite **repeat** loop can be replaced by a definite one, since there are exactly $N-1$ pairs of adjacent names to examine. Hence the complete algorithm can be written

> **while** *list not sorted* **do**
>   *start at the top of the list*
>   **repeat** $N-1$ *times*
>   **if** *name alphabetically follows its successor*
>   **then** *exchange name and successor*
>   *consider the next name in the list*   (2.19)

Algorithm 2.19 is adequate provided the processor is capable of telling (at line 1) whether or not the list is sorted. If the processor is incapable of this, perhaps because it cannot see the entire list at once, the terminating condition in line 1 needs further refinement. One way of telling whether the list is sorted is to remember whether any names needed exchanging during the last pass through it. If not, all the names must have been in the correct order, and the list is therefore sorted. Note that at least one pass through the list is required to see whether it is sorted to start with; thus the pre-tested loop of algorithm 2.19 is no longer appropriate, and should be replaced by a post-tested loop. With these refinements the algorithm becomes

> **repeat**
>   *start at the top of the list*
>   **repeat** $N-1$ *times*
>   **if** *name alphabetically follows its successor*
>   **then** *exchange name and successor*
>   *remember that an exchange has been performed*
>   *on this pass*
>   *consider the next name in the list*
> **until** *no exchange has been performed on this pass*   (2.20)

The change from the pre-tested loop of algorithm 2.19 to the post-tested loop of algorithm 2.20 is the reversal of an earlier decision. Such reversal is not uncommon in the stepwise refinement of algorithms. It is unduly optimistic to expect that refinement of each part of an algorithm can proceed entirely independently of other parts; as more details are filled in some early decisions which were taken without complete understanding of the algorithm may have to be reviewed. For this reason it is often a good idea to defer decisions as long as possible, so that they are taken with fuller knowledge and are less likely to need reconsideration. This cautious philosophy can be summarized in the rather cynical slogan *Always put off till tomorrow what is difficult to decide today.*

Algorithm 2.20 is a particularly simple sorting algorithm, but it is not always the fastest. There are other algorithms which in general involve the processor in the performance of fewer steps, and which are therefore quicker to execute. Algorithm 2.20 is at its best when the list is almost in order to start with, so that only a few passes through it are required. The algorithm is at its worst when the last name in the list happens to be alphabetically the first; in this case $N-1$ passes are needed to move this name up to first position. It can be shown that the average number of passes needed to sort the list is roughly proportional to N. Since each pass involves $N-1$ executions of the inner loop, the average number of steps executed is roughly proportional to N^2. The number of steps involved in the execution of an algorithm, and hence the time needed to execute it, are attributes of the algorithm which fall under the general term *complexity*. We shall discuss the complexity of algorithms further in Section 3.2.

We conclude this section by recalling that sequence, selection and iteration are adequate constructs for any algorithm. In the following sections we shall supplement these constructs by two others which are not strictly necessary but are nevertheless convenient.

2.8 MODULARITY

Earlier sections of this chapter have shown how algorithms can be developed through a process of stepwise refinement. At each step in the refinement the algorithm is divided into smaller components which can be specified in successively more precise detail. Refinement terminates when each component is expressed in such a way that the intended processor can interpret it.

The components arising during the refinement are often quite independent of the main algorithm in the sense that they can be designed without considering the context in which they are to be used. Such a component can be designed by someone other than the person developing the main algorithm, and can possibly be used as a component of a quite different algorithm. It can be regarded as a "plug-in" component, which once designed can be incorporated in any algorithm which needs it.

By way of illustration we shall consider the task of designing certain algorithms which are to be executed by a simple robot. The robot's function is to draw pictures: it is equipped with wheels which allow it to move around over a sheet of paper, and it has a pen which it can lower onto the paper when it wants to draw a line. The robot can interpret and execute commands of the form:

move(x)	*move forward x cm*
left(x)	*rotate x degrees to the left*
right(x)	*rotate x degrees to the right*
raise pen	*lift pen off paper*
lower pen	*put pen down to paper*

Suppose we want the robot to draw two concentric squares as shown in Fig. 2.4, given that it is initially at the center of the squares (point X) and facing up the page with the pen raised. An outline algorithm is

> *move to point A*
> *draw a square of side* 10 *cm*
> *move to point B*
> *draw a square of side* 20 *cm*   (2.21)

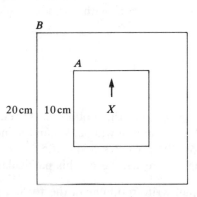

Figure 2.4   Concentric squares to be drawn by robot initially at point X.

The second and fourth steps of this algorithm involve drawing a square, which is a self-contained process quite independent of the rest of the algorithm. This implies that we can design a square-drawing algorithm without reference to the larger algorithm in which it is to be used. We can even, if we wish, get someone else to design a square-drawing algorithm without telling him what we are going to use it for. Once such an algorithm has been designed we can simply "plug it in" at the appropriate points of algorithm 2.21, and we can similarly plug it into any other algorithm in which a square needs to be drawn. An algorithm which can be plugged into another algorithm in this way is called a *module* (in some programming languages it is called a *procedure, routine, subroutine* or *function*). A module is a self-contained algorithm, and can be designed independently of the context in which it is to be used. An algorithm which uses a module is said to *call* the module. (For example, algorithm 2.21 calls the square-drawing module twice.)

For the square-drawing module to be generally useful it must be capable of drawing a square of *any* size. When the module is called, the *specific* size required must be indicated. Thus in algorithm 2.21 we might write

drawsquare(10) and *drawsquare*(20)

indicating that squares of side 10 cm and 20 cm are required. The square-drawing module itself can be written

module *drawsquare* (*size*)
{Draws a square of side *size* cm. The square is drawn anticlockwise, starting from the current position of the robot. The first edge is drawn according to the robot's current orientation. The robot returns to its initial position and orientation, with the pen raised.}
lower pen
repeat 4 *times*
  move(*size*)
  left(90)
raise pen   (2.22)

Size is called a *formal parameter* of the module: it is used in the body of the module to define how big the square will be. When the module is called, the *actual parameter* 10 (or 20) provides a specific value for *size*, and thus determines how big the square will be on this particular occasion.

In this book we shall write modules in the form

module *modulename*(*formal parameters*)
{specification of the process the module describes}
. . . *body of module* . . .

The comment in curly brackets is to help the human reader understand what the module does (recall Section 2.3); the body of the module expresses the details of how it does it. The body of a module is executed; the comment, of course, is not.

A call to a module will be written

modulename(*actual parameters*)

This is interpreted by the processor as a directive to execute the body of the module specified, with the module's formal parameters replaced by the actual parameters of the call. The formal parameters of a module can be regarded as representing the information the module needs when it is called.

The actual parameters are the pieces of information supplied for a particular call; these pieces of information take the place of the formal parameters when the module is executed. There must of course be the same number of formal and actual parameters.

An algorithm which is built from a number of modules is said to be *modular*. Each module is a self-contained component of the algorithm, and acts as a building block in the algorithm's construction. The interface between a module and its callers is twofold:

(1)   the interface explicitly expressed in the parameters (e.g. the size of the square to be drawn by *drawsquare*);
(2)   the interface implicit in the assumptions the module and its callers make about each other (e.g. that *drawsquare* finishes with the pen raised).

Both forms of interface should be described in the module specification; the second form, being implicit, should be particularly well described.

Using the *drawsquare* module as defined above we can refine algorithm 2.21 for drawing two concentric squares as follows:

> *left*(45)
> *move*($\sqrt{50}$)   {move to point *A*}
> *left*(135)
> *drawsquare*(10)   {draw inner square}
> *right*(135)
> *move*($\sqrt{50}$)   {move to point *B*}
> *left*(135)
> *drawsquare*(20)   {draw outer square}   (2.23)

Note that all the steps in this algorithm are calls to modules. We have not given the algorithms for the modules *move*, *left*, and *right*, since we have assumed that they are sufficiently simple for the robot to be able to interpret calls to them. If this is not the case, then each module needs to be defined in terms which the robot *can* interpret. Thus, for example, the *move* module might be defined as

> **module** *move*(x)
> {Moves robot forward *x* cm, leaving its orientation unchanged.
>   The pen is neither raised nor lowered}
> *set number of required wheel rotations to*
>   *x/(wheel circumference)*
> *call this number N*
> **repeat** *N times*
>   *rotate all wheels once*   (2.24)

This definition of *move* assumes that the robot can do division and knows how to rotate its wheels.

It is important to realize that the designer of algorithm 2.23 does not need to know how the module *drawsquare* works; all he needs to know is the effect of executing it. In other words, he does not need to understand the body of the module, but need only read the specification at its head. Thus he can make a clear separation of two design problems: the design of algorithm 2.23 and the design of *drawsquare*. This reduces the complexity of the design process, and hence leads to quicker and more reliable design. *Drawsquare* can be designed after algorithm 2.23 is finished, or it can be handed over to someone else to design in parallel. Alternatively, if the module already exists because it was previously needed in another algorithm it can simply be called without additional effort.

The power of using modules can be further illustrated by considering a different approach to the *drawsquare* module above. Since a square is simply a special case of a polygon it might be advantageous to design a module for drawing polygons and then call it with appropriate actual parameters whenever a square is required. A module for drawing polygons is

> **module** *drawpolygon(size, N)*
> {Draws an *N*-sided polygon with sides *size* cm long.
> The polygon is drawn anticlockwise, starting from the current position of the robot. The first edge is drawn according to the robot's current orientation. The robot returns to its initial position and orientation, with the pen raised.}
> *lower pen*
> **repeat** *N times*
>   *move(size)*
>   *left(360/N)*
> *raise pen*   (2.25)

The *drawsquare* module can now be rewritten very simply as

> **module** *drawsquare(size)*
> {Draws a square of side *size* cm. . . .}
> *drawpolygon(size,4)*

Similarly, a module for drawing a triangle can be written as

> **module** *drawtriangle(size)*
> {Draws an equilateral triangle of side *size* cm, . . .}
> *drawpolygon(size,3)*   (2.26)

Modules for drawing a pentagon, hexagon, and so on can be written with equal ease. Note that the new version of *drawsquare* does not require any alterations to algorithm 2.23, or to any other algorithm which calls it.

The advantages of using modules can be summarized as follows.

(1)   Modules fit naturally into stepwise refinement, giving a top-down design.

(2)   A module is a self-contained component of any larger algorithm which calls it. The design of the module and of the calling algorithm can be considered separately, thus simplifying the design process. Since algorithm design is usually quite difficult, any simplification is to be welcomed. The benefits of simplification are quicker design and lower probability of error.

(3)   To incorporate a module in an algorithm it is necessary to know only *what* the module does, and not *how* it does it. What a module does can be conveniently specified in a comment in its heading

(4)   Just as modules simplify the design of algorithms they also simplify the understanding of algorithms. For example, to understand algorithm 2.23 the reader need understand only the effect of the modules *move*, *drawsquare*, and so on, but need not understand how that effect is achieved. Ease of understanding is very important if, as often happens, an algorithm is to be modified (particularly by people other than its author). As we shall see in Chapter 3, it is also important for demonstrating that an algorithm is correct.

(5)   Once a module has been designed it can be incorporated in any algorithm which needs it. It is therefore possible to build up a "library" of modules, such as a sorting module, a module for solving simultaneous equations, a module for calculating income tax, and so on.

2.9 RECURSION

In Section 2.6 we presented an algorithm (2.18) for calculating the product of the first N integers (i.e. the factorial of N). That algorithm employed a loop, in which successive integers from 1 to N were multiplied together. An alternative approach is to utilize the fact that the factorial of N is simply the product of N and the factorial of $N-1$, i.e.

$$factorial(N) = N \times factorial(N-1)$$

This is true for any N which is greater than 1. Moreover, $factorial(1)=1$. Hence a possible algorithm for calculating the factorial of N is expressed by the following module.

module *factorial(N)*
{Computes factorial N for any integer $N>0$}
if $N=1$
    then *answer is* 1
    else *multiply N by factorial(N−1)*   (2.27)

The last line of the module implies that the module is to be executed again, but with actual parameter one less than before. Figure 2.5 illustrates execution of the module when N is 3. The figure shows how calculation of *factorial*(3) involves calculation of *factorial*(2), which in turn involves calculation of *factorial*(1). The boxes illustrate the three executions of the module which are required, and the numbers to the right of each box are the cumulative results after each such execution.

factorial (3):

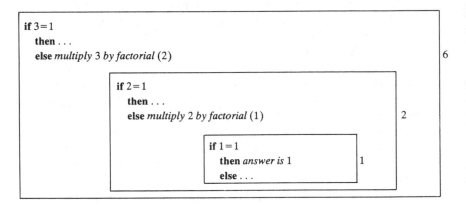

Figure 2.5   Calculation of factorial (3) by algorithm 2.27.

Algorithm 2.27, which is an algorithm for calculating the factorial of N, is expressed in terms of an algorithm for calculating the factorial of $N-1$. One can therefore regard the algorithm as being expressed in terms of itself, but with its input N being replaced by input $N-1$. The term used for this form of expression is *recursion*: a *recursive* algorithm is one which calls itself.

The apparent circularity of recursion is avoided by ensuring that the input to successive recursive calls becomes progressively "simpler" in some sense. There must then be a limiting case, in which the input is so "simple" that the process can be carried out without calling itself further. For example, the input N to algorithm 2.27 becomes progressively simpler by being reduced by 1 on successive calls. In the limit, when N is reduced to 1, the process can be carried out directly, with no further calls being needed. The limiting case may be regarded as an escape route which ensures that execution eventually terminates. Any recursive algorithm must provide such an escape route, and the input must be progressively simplified so that the escape route is eventually taken.

As another example of recursion, consider the process of reversing the order of the letters in an English word (e.g. turning *star* into *rats*). This can be done by removing the first letter of the word, reversing the rest of the word, and then appending the letter which was removed. The basis of a suitable algorithm is therefore

> *remove first letter*
> *reverse rest of word*
> *append removed letter*

The algorithm is clearly recursive, since it describes how to reverse a sequence of letters in terms of how to reverse a slightly shorter sequence of letters. On each recursive call a single letter is removed from the sequence to

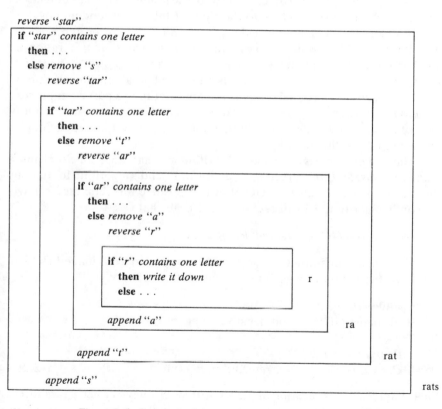

Figure 2.6   Reversal of the word "star" by algorithm 2.28.

be reversed, thus progressively simplifying the algorithm's input. In the limiting case, when the sequence has only one letter left, an escape from further recursive calls is provided by realizing that to reverse a single letter one need only write it down. Hence a complete algorithm for reversing a sequence of letters is

> **module** *reverse(sequence)*
> {Reverses the given sequence of letters}
> **if** *sequence contains only one letter*
> > **then** *write it down*
> > **else** *remove first letter from sequence*
> > > *reverse(rest of sequence)*
> > > *append removed letter*   (2.28)

Figure 2.6 illustrates execution of the module when the input is *star*. The boxes in Fig. 2.6 represent successive calls of the module, and the cumulative output from each call is shown to the right of the corresponding box.

Both of the recursive algorithms 2.27 and 2.28 can be replaced by iterative algorithms, which suggests that recursion is simply iteration in another guise. To some extent this is true; it can be shown that for any algorithm which uses recursion there is an equivalent algorithm which uses iteration. However, a recursive algorithm for describing a particular process is often far more concise than an iterative one, and in many cases it is much easier to derive and understand. In the following paragraphs we shall offer two examples in illustration.

The first example is a recursive algorithm which is more concise than its iterative equivalent. It is a recursive version of Euclid's algorithm for finding the greatest common divisor (GCD) of two positive integers: the iterative version is algorithm 2.14 of section 2.6. Recall that

$$GCD(x,y) = GCD(y, \text{ remainder of } x/y)$$

unless $y = 0$, in which case $GCD(x,y) = x$. This relation leads immediately to the following recursive algorithm for calculating $GCD(x,y)$.

> **module** *GCD(x,y)*
> {Calculates *GCD* of non-negative integers *x* and *y*}
> **if** $y = 0$
> > **then** *answer is x*
> > **else** *calculate GCD(y, remainder of x/y)*   (2.29)

Note that recursive execution of the algorithm terminates when *y* is reduced to zero, in which case the required result is *x*. Figure 2.7 illustrates execution of the algorithm to determine the *GCD* of 24 and 9.

calculate GCD (24,9)

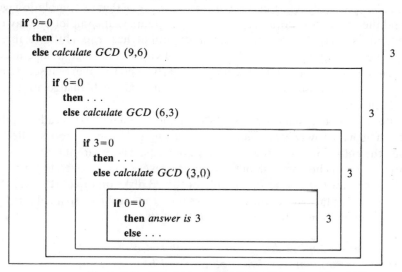

Figure 2.7   Calculation of GCD (24,9) by algorithm 2.29.

The second example is of a task for which it is easier to derive a recursive algorithm than an iterative one. The example is widely known as the *Towers of Hanoi*. According to legend an order of Buddhist monks in Hanoi has been engaged for many years in the following task. The monks have three vertical rods and a set of 64 circular disks of different sizes; each disk has a hole in the center which allows it to be slid onto any of the rods. Initially the disks were all placed on a single rod, one on top of the other in order of decreasing size, so that they formed a single tower as shown in Fig. 2.8. The task the monks have set themselves is to transfer this original tower to one of the other rods, moving only one disk at a time and ensuring that no disk ever

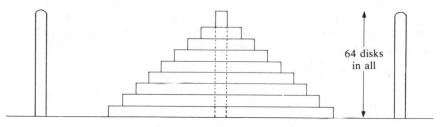

Figure 2.8   The Towers of Hanoi.

rests on top of a smaller one. The labor involved in carrying out this task is said to be spiritually uplifting, and the monks believe that its completion will herald the end of the world. (The reader who fears that completion may be imminent is advised to contain his anxiety until he has read a little further.) Since the strategy for moving disks is not obvious, and since a false move could undo many years work, the monks clearly need to adhere closely to an algorithm which describes how to achieve their goal. Such an algorithm can be developed as follows.

Let us suppose that the rod supporting the original tower is called a, the rod to which the tower is to be moved is called b, and the other rod is called c. Given the rules governing the movement of disks, it is apparent that the only way in which the bottom disk of the original tower can be moved to form the base of the new tower is to first of all get the 63 disks on top of it out of the way. The only place to put these 63 disks is on the third rod, so an algorithm for transferring the entire tower from rod a to rod b is

> *transfer the top* 63 *disks from rod a to rod c*
> *move the bottom disk from rod a to rod b*
> *transfer the* 63 *disks from rod c to rod b*

This algorithm describes the task of transferring 64 disks between two rods in terms of the task of transferring 63 disks between two rods. Similarly, the task of transferring 63 disks between two rods can be described in terms of transferring 62 disks between two rods, and so on. Generalizing, an algorithm for transferring N disks from a rod called *source* to a rod called *target* (given a third rod called *workspace*) is

> *transfer N−1 disks from source to workspace*
> *move 1 disk from source to target*
> *transfer N−1 disks from workspace to target*

This algorithm is clearly recursive, and the number of disks to be removed on each recursive call is successively reduced by 1. An escape route from successive calls is provided when only a single disk is to be transferred between rods: in this case all one needs to do is pick it up and move it. Hence a complete algorithm for transferring N disks from *source* to *target* is

> **module** *movetower(N,source,target,workspace)*
> {Moves a tower of N disks from *source* to *target*, using
> *workspace* where necessary}
> **if** $N = 1$
>   **then** *move disk from source to target*

else *movetower*($N-1$, *source, workspace, target*)
  move 1 *disk from source to target*
  movetower($N-1$, *workspace, target, source*)   (2.30)

Figure 2.9 illustrates execution of this module when the original tower contains only 3 disks and is to be transferred from rod *a* to rod *b*. Each box represents one call to the module, and the positions of the disks at each stage are shown at the right.

We can now reassure any reader who was anxious about the time it would take the monks to complete their task. Execution of the algorithm with $N = 64$ results in two executions with $N = 63$, each of which results in two executions with $N = 62$, and so on. Hence transfer of the complete tower requires $2^{64} - 1$ executions of the algorithm. Since one disk is moved during each execution, the total number of moves which have to be effected is $2^{64} - 1$. If the monks can move one disk every second, and never make a mistake, the time taken to transfer the whole tower will be about 600 000 000 000 years! (Furthermore, it can be proved there is no faster algorithm.)

As a final remark on the Towers of Hanoi it should be pointed out that algorithm 2.30 is a very concise and elegant solution to a decidedly non-trivial problem. Iterative algorithms do exist, but they are less concise and their derivation requires considerable insight (see Exercise 2.14).

It will be apparent by now that there is a helpful strategy for devising recursive algorithms. The first element of the strategy is the determination of how the process to be carried out can be expressed recursively; that is, how the process can be expressed in terms of similar processes which differ from the original only by having an input which is in some sense simpler (e.g. a smaller number, or a shorter sequence). The second element is to ensure that there is a limiting case in which the input is so simple that the process can be executed without recourse to further recursive calls. The limiting case then acts as an escape route from recursion. This strategy has been applied to the development of all the algorithms above, and we shall now illustrate it further by developing a recursive algorithm for sorting a list of names into alphabetical order. (Algorithm 2.20 was an iterative algorithm for the same process.)

The algorithm is based on the observation that a list can be sorted by breaking it into two halves (or roughly equal portions), sorting each half separately, and then merging the halves together. The outline of the algorithm is therefore

  sort first half of list
  sort second half of list
  merge the two halves together

It is easy to see that recursive calls can cease when the portion to be sorted is

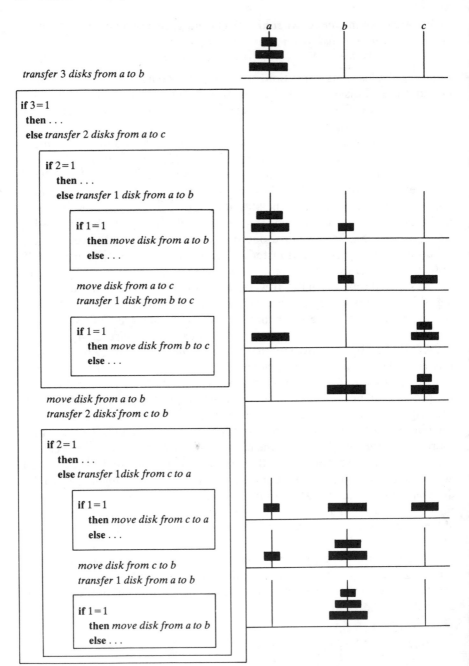

transfer 3 *disks from a to b*

if 3 = 1
then . . .
else *transfer* 2 *disks from a to c*

    if 2 = 1
      then . . .
      else *transfer* 1 *disk from a to b*

        if 1 = 1
          then *move disk from a to b*
          else . . .

      move disk from a to c
      transfer 1 *disk from b to c*

        if 1 = 1
          then *move disk from b to c*
          else . . .

  move disk from a to b
  transfer 2 *disks from c to b*

    if 2 = 1
      then . . .
      else *transfer* 1*disk from c to a*

        if 1 = 1
          then *move disk from c to a*
          else . . .

      move disk from c to b
      transfer 1 *disk from a to b*

        if 1 = 1
          then *move disk from a to b*
          else . . .

Figure 2.9   Execution of the Towers of Hanoi algorithm with 3 disks.

reduced to a single name, when there is nothing to do. Hence the algorithm for a list of N names is

    module *sort(list)*
    {Sorts given list of N names into alphabetical order}
    if $N>1$
       then *sort(first half of the list)*
           sort(second half of the list)
           merge the two halves together   (2.31)

The action of the algorithm on a list of seven names (the same list as was used to illustrate the iterative sorting algorithm 2.20) is shown in Fig. 2.10.

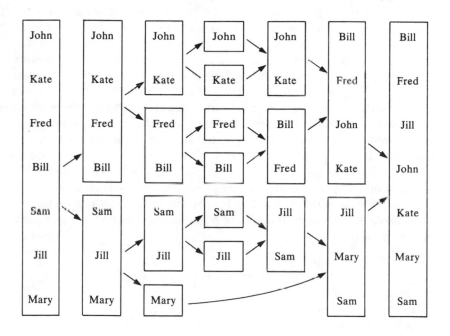

Figure 2.10   Action of recursive sorting algorithm 2.31

    The last line of algorithm 2.31 needs further refinement before most processors can execute it. We shall not give the refinement here, but refer the reader to Exercise 2.9 and to Section 6.1.2.

2.10 PARALLELISM

Each of the algorithms we have devised so far has been constructed on the assumption that only one processor is available to execute it. This assumption is justified for most current computers. However, recent advances in technology have made it possible to manufacture certain computer processors very cheaply, and it is therefore economically feasible to assign several processors to a single task. One of the potential advantages in doing so is that the task may be completed more quickly than if only a single processor is used.

The potential gain in speed can be realized only if the process to be carried out can be broken up into a number of subprocesses, each of which is carried out by one of the available processors. This implies that the algorithm describing the complete process must be broken into a number of components, each of which describes the subprocess to be carried out by an individual processor. The components of the algorithm are executed simultaneously by their respective processors, so that the time taken to execute the complete algorithm is no more than that taken to execute its longest component. This form of execution is called *parallelism*, or *concurrency*, and an algorithm whose components can be executed in this way is often referred to as a *parallel algorithm* (as opposed to a *sequential algorithm*, whose steps are executed one at a time). It is sequential algorithms which have occupied us so far in this chapter.

As a simple example of a parallel algorithm we shall consider the process of subtracting a list of purchase prices for various items from a list of sale prices for the same items. The results will be a list of the profits (or losses) made on each item. If there are N items concerned, a simple sequential algorithm is

> **module** *sequentialprofit*
> {Calculates a list of profits from lists of purchase
> and sale prices}
> *start at the top of each list*
> **repeat** *N times*
>   *subtract purchase price from sale price*
>   *place answer in profit list*
>   *consider the next item in each list*   (2.32)

Most of the time spent in executing this algorithm is spent in the body of the loop. Since the body is executed N times, the time taken to execute the complete algorithm is roughly proportional to N. Suppose, however, that N processors are available. In this case one processor can be allocated to calculating the profit on each item in the list, and since all the items are independent the processors can perform their calculations in parallel. If the processors are numbered from 1 to N an appropriate algorithm for the ith processor is

> **module** *parallelprofit(i)*
> {Algorithm for the ith processor to calculate the ith profit}
> *subtract purchase price of ith item from sale price of ith item*
> *place answer in ith position of profit list*   (2.33)

The time taken to execute this algorithm does not depend on the length N of the list. Since all the processors execute the algorithm in parallel their execution times all overlap, and hence the time taken to produce the complete profit list is also independent of N. Thus while the execution time of the sequential algorithm 2.32 increases in proportion to the length of the list, the execution time of the parallel algorithm is constant. The parallel algorithm can be regarded as giving an N-fold increase in speed at the expense of an N-fold increase in the number of processors. (For a more careful analysis of the speed-up see Exercise 2.17.)

As a slightly more complex example of parallelism, consider the process of adding up a row of N numbers. A sequential algorithm, designed for a processor which can perform only one addition at a time, is

> **module** *sequentialsum(N)*
> {Adds a row of N numbers}
> *set cumulative sum to 0*
> *start at the beginning of the row*
> **repeat** N *times*
>   *add number to cumulative sum*
>   *consider the next number in the row*   (2.34)

As with algorithm 2.32, most of the time taken to execute this algorithm is spent inside the loop. Thus the execution time is roughly proportional to N. The basis of a parallel algorithm can be seen in Fig. 2.11, which shows how the numbers in the row can be added in pairs. The first stage in the algorithm is to group the numbers into pairs and form the sum of each pair. The additions can be performed in parallel, provided the number of processors available is at least $N/2$ (more precisely, the integer part of $N/2$). The resulting sums can again be added in pairs, the number of processors required at this stage being only $N/4$. The parallel addition of pairs of numbers continues until a single sum results. Since the number of pairs to be added is halved at each stage, the number of stages which have to be gone through is approximately the logarithm of N using base 2, written $\log_2 N$. (More precisely, it is $\log_2 N$ rounded up to the nearest integer; in Fig. 2.11, for example, the number of stages is $\log_2 7$ rounded up, which is 3.) The

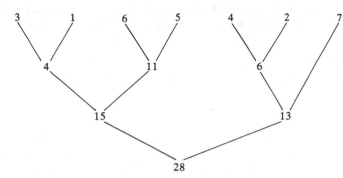

Figure 2.11   Pairwise addition of numbers.

number of processors required at each stage is also halved, so the maximum number required is that for the first stage, namely $N/2$.

If the processors are numbered from 1 to $N/2$, and the numbers in the row to be added are called num[1], num[2], num[3], ..., num[N], the algorithm executed by the ith processor is

module *parallelsum(i)*
{Summation algorithm executed by the ith processor}
repeat $log_2 N$ *times*
$\quad$ *set num[i] to num[2i−1] + num[2i]*   (2.35)

The parallel execution of this algorithm by all the processors is illustrated in Fig. 2.12. Note how the sums at successive stages (shown in heavy type) accumulate at the left of the row, the rest of the row being undisturbed.

original row	**3**	**1**	**6**	**5**	**4**	**2**	**7**
row after 1st addition	**4**	**11**	6	7	4	2	7
row after 2nd addition	**15**	**13**	6	7	4	2	7
row after 3rd addition	**28**	13	6	7	4	2	7

Figure 2.12   Execution of the parallel addition algorithm 2.35.

Since the output from each stage forms the input for its successor, no stage may start until the previous one has finished. This implies that all the processors must operate at the same speed, or at least wait for each other before starting successive executions of the bodies of their **repeat** loops. The general term for such a requirement is that the processors must *synchronize* with each other, or operate *synchronously.*

Since all the processors operate synchronously the time taken to add the complete row of numbers is the same as that taken by each processor to execute algorithm 2.35. This time is roughly proportional to $\log_2 N$. Hence the parallel algorithm is faster than the sequential algorithm by a factor proportional to $N/\log_2 N$. The practical implication is that 10- to 100-fold speed increases can be obtained for values of N between 100 and 1000.

As a final example of parallelism we shall develop a parallel sorting algorithm which makes use of the parallel addition algorithm above. Suppose, to use the same example as in Sections 2.7 and 2.9, we wish to sort a list of N names into alphabetical order. Recalling algorithm 2.20 we observe that the essence of sorting is the comparison (and possible exchange) of pairs of names. In that algorithm, which was designed for a single processor, the comparisons were necessarily performed one at a time. Given a large enough number of processors an obvious way to speed up the sorting process is to perform all the comparisons at once; that is, to compare simultaneously each name in the list with every other name in the list, thus determining for each name how many other names alphabetically precede it. Since there are N names to be compared with each other, the number of processors required is N^2.

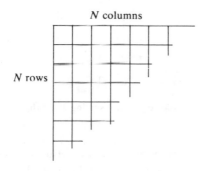

$N \times N$ grid to be filled with 0s and 1s

Figure 2.13

During the first phase of the sorting process the job of each processor is to compare two names, recording the result in one of the squares of an $N \times N$ grid (Fig. 2.13). The processor which compares the ith name in the list with the jth name in the list records its result in the square formed by the ith row and jth column of the grid. If the ith name alphabetically precedes the jth name, the processor puts a 0 into the square; otherwise it puts a 1 into the square. Thus the algorithm executed by the processor during this phase is

> **module** *parallelcompare(i,j)*
> {Each processor executes this with different values of i and j}
> **if** *name*[i] *alphabetically precedes name*[j]
>   **then** *put* 0 *into the ith row and jth column of the grid*
>   **else** *put* 1 *into the ith row and jth column of the grid*   (2.36)

All the processors execute this algorithm in parallel, each using different values of i and j. The resulting grid for the list

> John, Kate, Sam, Fred, Bill, Jill, Mary

is shown in Fig. 2.14. Note that the time taken to execute algorithm 2.36 is independent of N.

	John	Kate	Sam	Fred	Bill	Jill	Mary	Position in ordered list
John	1	0	0	1	1	1	0	4
Kate	1	1	0	1	1	1	0	5
Sam	1	1	1	1	1	1	1	7
Fred	0	0	0	1	1	0	0	2
Bill	0	0	0	0	1	0	0	1
Jill	0	0	0	1	1	1	0	3
Mary	1	1	0	1	1	1	1	6

Figure 2.14   Execution of the parallel sorting algorithm 2.36.

At the end of this phase the number of 1s in the ith row of the grid indicates how many names (including itself) alphabetically precede the ith name in the list. This in turn indicates whereabouts in the sorted list the ith name should be. For example, the grid in Fig. 2.14 has five 1s in the second row, indicating that five names (including itself) alphabetically precede the corresponding name in the original list (Kate), and hence that Kate should occupy fifth place in the sorted list. The number of 1s in each row, and hence the correct position in the sorted list for the corresponding name, is shown in the right-hand column of Fig. 2.14. (We are assuming for simplicity that all the names are different; if this is not the case the algorithm needs a slight modification to deal with the clash between two identical names.)

The second phase of the algorithm therefore consists of adding up the number of 1s in each row of the grid, thus determining the correct position of each name in the list. The addition of each row can be performed by means of the parallel algorithm developed earlier, each row requiring $N/2$ processors and taking time proportional to $\log_2 N$. The simultaneous addition of all the rows therefore requires $N^2/2$ processors (which is less than for the first phase of the algorithm), and can also be performed in time proportional to $\log_2 N$.

The sums resulting from the second phase of the algorithm are used to determine the position of each name in the sorted list. If the sum of the ith row is k, then the ith name in the original list should occupy the kth position in the sorted list. The final phase of the algorithm is therefore simply to move each name to its correct position in the sorted list. By using N processors all the names can be moved in parallel, so the time taken to perform this phase is no more than that required to move a single name, and is independent of N.

The only phase of the algorithm whose execution time does depend on N is the second, with an execution time proportional to $\log_2 N$. Hence the time taken to execute the entire algorithm is also roughly proportional to $\log_2 N$. This can be compared with the sequential algorithms given earlier: for example the execution times of algorithms 2.20 and 2.31 are proportional to N^2 and $N\log_2 N$ respectively. The dramatic difference in speed between the sequential and parallel algorithms can be seen in Fig. 2.15, which tabulates the values of $\log_2 N$, $N\log_2 N$, and N^2 for various values of N.

Size N of input data	$\log_2 N$ microseconds	$N \log_2 N$ microseconds	N^2 microseconds
10	0.000003 seconds	0.00003 seconds	0.0001 seconds
100	0.000007 seconds	0.0007 seconds	0.01 seconds
1000	0.00001 seconds	0.01 seconds	1 second
10000	0.000013 seconds	0.13 seconds	1.7 minutes
100000	0.000017 seconds	1.7 seconds	2.8 hours

Figure 2.15 Comparison of execution time of different algorithms.

Of course the increase in speed is not without cost. The sequential sorting algorithms use only a single processor, whereas the parallel algorithm sketched above requires $N^2/2$ processors. It is possible to achieve the same speed increase by using only $N\log_2 N$ processors, but no way of doing it with fewer processors is currently known. Thus the best known parallel algorithm can be regarded as giving an N-fold increase in speed at the cost of an $N\log_2 N$-fold increase in the number of processors.

2.11 DATA STRUCTURES

The majority of this chapter has concentrated on the *control structure* of algorithms; that is, on the constructs which can be used to control the order and circumstances in which the individual steps of an algorithm are executed. The choice of appropriate control constructs is an essential part of the development of an algorithm, but it cannot be performed without considering the information, or *data*, which the algorithm manipulates.

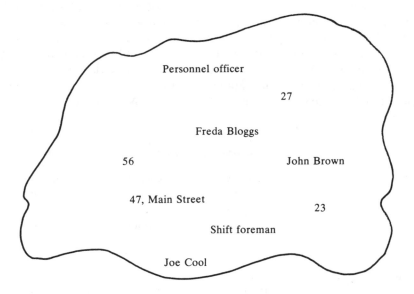

Figure 2.16   Example of unstructured data.

In general, the data manipulated by an algorithm are not merely an arbitrary collection of unrelated items, but rather consist of pieces of information which are in some way related to each other. As an example, consider an algorithm which is used in the maintenance of personnel information about a company's employees. The data manipulated by the algorithm consist of names, addresses, ages, positions held, and so on.

These pieces of data are not merely a random jumble of information, but possess logical relationships with each other. One obvious relationship between a particular name, address, age and position is that these items all describe the same person. The data can therefore be viewed not as a jumble of unrelated items (as shown in Fig. 2.16), but as a collection of *records*, each of which contains all the information about a particular employee (Fig. 2.17). These records may themselves have logical relationships between them reflecting the logical relationships between the people they describe. For example, particular employees (and hence the records describing them) may be related by working in the same section of the company, or one employee may be related to several others by virtue of being their immediate supervisor (Fig. 2.18). Data that are organized to reflect the logical relationships between their elements are said to be *structured*; the data elements and their interrelationships together form a *data structure*.

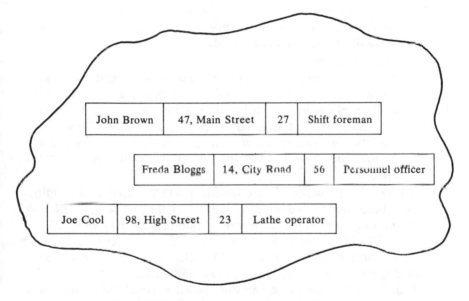

Figure 2.17 Example of data structured into records.

We have in fact been using data structures earlier in this chapter without explicitly mentioning them. For example the sorting algorithms we developed all operate on a list of names. Such a list is a simple data structure in which the individual names are related by their physical order: a name comes either before or after other names in the list. The sorting algorithms transform one list into another by altering the physical order of the names to coincide with their alphabetical order.

A list is an example of a particularly common type of data structure known as a *sequence*. A sequence is a set of items that is ordered such that every item except one (called the last) has a successor, and every item except one (called the first) has a predecessor. Examples of sequences are

(1)   An English word, which is a sequence of letters.

(2)   English text, which is a sequence of words separated by spaces and other punctuation symbols.

(3)   A number, which is represented in written form as a sequence of digits.

(4)   A railway train, which is a sequence of carriages (preceded by an engine).

(5)   A telephone directory, which is a sequence of records, each of which contains a name, an address, and a telephone number.

A sequence is a particularly useful structure for items which are to be processed one after another. An algorithm for describing such processing has the general form

> *start at the beginning of the sequence*
> **while** *end of sequence not reached* **do**
> *process next item*

If the sequence is known to contain at least one item the **while** loop can be replaced by a **repeat** loop; if the number of items is known, indefinite iteration can be replaced by definite iteration. Examples of algorithms acting on sequences according to this general scheme are 2.13 and 2.19.

Certain kinds of sequence occur so frequently that computer scientists have given them special names. For the sake of completeness we mention three of them here.

(1)   An *array* is a sequence of fixed length, in which each item is identified by its position. Thus we refer to the 1st item, the 2nd item, the ith item, and so on. An example is the row of numbers $num[1]$, $num [2]$, ..., $num [N]$ which were added by algorithm 2.35 of Section 2.10. Each number is identified by its position $[1], [2], . . . , [N]$ in the row, in a way analogous to the use of subscripts in mathematics.

(2)   A *queue* is a sequence of variable length in which items are always added at one end and removed at the other. It follows that the order in which items are removed is the same as that in which they are added. A queue is a particularly useful data structure for items which are to be operated upon on a first-come first-served basis.

(3)   A *stack* is a sequence of variable length in which items are added and removed at only one end. Thus the order in which items are removed is the reverse of that in which they are added. (The reader may find it helpful to think of waggons in a railway siding—the first waggon pushed into the siding is the last one out.)

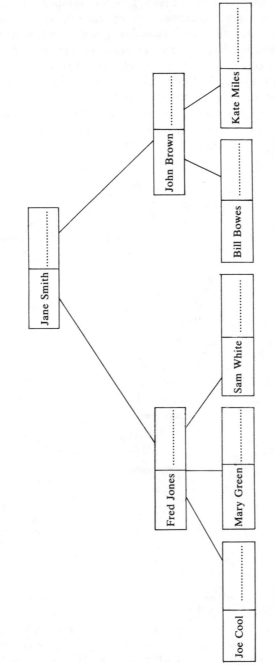

Figure 2.18 Logical relationships between records reflecting the organizational relationships between employees.

Another type of data structure is the *tree*, an example of which is shown in Fig. 2.18 (trees in computer science grow upside down!). The data in a tree is represented by its *nodes*, or branching points, and is hierarchically arranged. The *branches* of the tree represent logical relationships between an item of data at one level of the hierarchy and several items at the next level down. The node at the highest level of the hierarchy is perversely called the *root* of the tree; the nodes at the lowest extremities are called the *leaves*. A tree is clearly an appropriate data structure for expressing any hierarchical relationships, such as the company management structure of Fig. 2.18, the structure of an English sentence (Fig. 2.19), or the successive refinement of modules (Fig. 2.20).

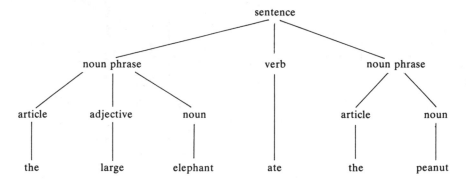

Figure 2.19   The tree structure of an English sentence.

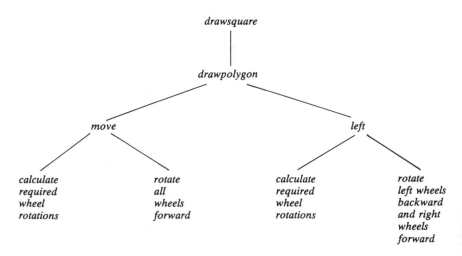

Figure 2.20   Tree showing the successive refinement of module *drawsquare* of Section 2.8.

Note that every node in a tree is itself the root of a smaller tree. Even the leaves can be regarded as the roots of trees—trees which are so small as to have no branches! In general, the smaller trees are called *subtrees* of the complete tree. Thus a tree is essentially a *recursive* data structure (recall Section 2.9), since any tree can be defined in terms of other trees as follows.

A tree is either

(1) empty, or
(2) a node plus a (possibly empty) set of branches,
     each leading to a tree

As we shall see shortly, the recursive structure of trees is particularly conducive to recursive algorithms.

In general, algorithms describe processes which transform one data structure (the input) into another data structure (the output). For example, the sorting algorithms mentioned earlier describe how to transform one sequence into another, while an algorithm for parsing English sentences describes how to transform a sequence of words into a tree such as shown in Fig. 2.19. Sometimes, as in the case of the bubble sort (algorithm 2.20), the transformation can be effected by simply manipulating the items within the framework of the original data structure. In many cases, however, some intermediate data structure(s) may be required, as illustrated in Fig. 2.21. The development of the algorithm in these cases is intimately linked to the choice of an appropriate data structure. (The grid in the parallel sorting algorithm of Section 2.10 is an example of an intermediate data structure between an input sequence of unsorted names and an output sequence of sorted names.)

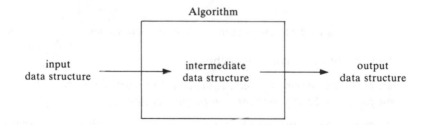

Figure 2.21   The use of an intermediate data structure in an algorithm.

By way of further illustration we shall develop yet another sorting algorithm, which uses a tree as an intermediate data structure in the transformation of the unsorted input sequence into the sorted output sequence.

The tree used is a special variety known as a *binary tree*, so called because each node has at most two branches coming from it. A binary tree is a particularly useful structure for sorting, since the two branches from each node can be used to represent "before" and "after" relationships. More precisely, a binary tree is sorted if the data at each node follows all the data in the node's left subtree (i.e. all the data that can be reached via the node's left branch) and precedes all the data in the node's right subtree (reached via the node's right branch). Figure 2.22 shows two alphabetically sorted binary trees; in Fig. 2.22(b), for example, John alphabetically follows every name in its left subtree and precedes every name in its right subtree. The same applies to every other node in the tree. Note that not every node need have its full complement of two branches; the number of branches depends on the alphabetic distribution of names in the tree, and on the way in which the tree is built up (which we shall discuss in a moment).

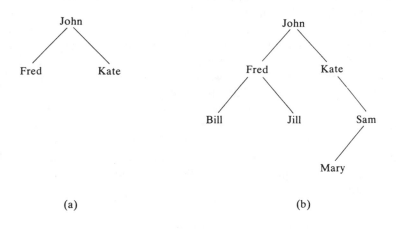

(a)   (b)

Figure 2.22   Two alphabetically sorted binary trees.

The basis of the sorting algorithm is

transform the unsorted input sequence into a sorted binary tree
transform the binary tree into an output sequence

Since the two steps are independent, we can write each of them as a separate module. The two modules needed are *buildtree* which constructs the tree from the input, and *outputtree* which produces the output list from the tree. We develop each of these modules in turn, using the input list

John, Kate, Sam, Fred, Bill, Jill, Mary

as illustration.

The tree is built by starting with nothing and adding each name from the input list in turn. A first approximation to the *buildtree* module is therefore

module *buildtree(L,T)*
{Builds a sorted binary tree *T* from an input list *L* of names}
start at the beginning of L
while *L not exhausted* **do**
    add next name to T   (2.37)

The process of adding a name to the tree (the last line of algorithm 2.37) can be described by a recursive module. If the tree does not yet exist (i.e. it is empty) a new tree is created with the name as its root and only node. If the tree does exist the name to be added is compared with the name at the root. If it alphabetically precedes the name at the root then it must be added to the left subtree, otherwise it must be added to the right subtree. The module for adding a name is therefore

module *addname(name, T)*
{Adds *name* to sorted binary tree *T*}
if *T is empty*
    then *create a new subtree with name as its root*
    else if *name precedes name at root of T*
        then *addname(name, left subtree of T)*
        else *addname(name, right subtree of T)*   (2.38)

Note that the recursion eventually ceases, since the tree which is the actual parameter of the module gets smaller with each successive call. When it gets so small as to be empty the new name is added as the root (and only node) of a new subtree, and the recursion terminates. Figure 2.23 illustrates the addition of the name Jill to a partially built tree. On successive recursive calls of *addname* Jill is added to the left subtree of John and the right subtree of Fred. Since this latter subtree is empty a new subtree is created with Jill as its only node.

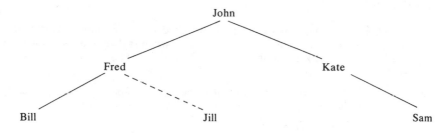

Figure 2.23   Addition of "Jill" to a partially built binary tree.

The complete *buildtree* module is

module *buildtree(L,T)*
{Builds a sorted binary tree *T* from an input list *L* of names}
start at the beginning of L
while *L not exhausted* **do**
    addname(next name, T)   (2.39)

where the module *addname* is defined above (algorithm 2.38).

The module *outputtree* which produces a sorted list from the binary tree can also be written recursively. The output of a complete tree in the correct order is accomplished by outputting the root's left subtree, then the root, and finally the root's right subtree. Recursion ceases when the tree to be output is reduced to being non-existent, when there is nothing to do. The module is

module *outputtree(T)*
{Outputs all the nodes of binary tree *T* in left to right order}
if *T is not empty*
    then *outputtree(left subtree of T)*
        write down name at root of T
        outputtree(right subtree of T)   (2.40)

The complete sorting algorithm can now be written

module *sort(L)*
{Sorts list *L* into alphabetical order}
start with an empty tree called T
buildtree(L,T)
outputtree(T)   (2.41)

EXERCISES

1   Devise an algorithm which describes how to find a book in a library. Ensure that the algorithm describes some sensible process when (a) the book is not held by the library, and (b) the book is held by the library but is not currently on the shelves.

2   The following two algorithms both describe how to behave when approaching traffic signals.

    if *signal is working*
        then if *signal is red or signal is amber*
            then *stop*
            else *proceed*

if *signal is working*
then if *signal is red or signal is amber*
    then *stop*
else *proceed*

In what circumstances do the algorithms describe different behavior? Which algorithm do you consider the more satisfactory?

3 How is iteration expressed in (a) musical scores, and (b) recipes?

4 The following algorithm purports to describe how to find a perfect marriage partner.

repeat
    send ten dollars to Compute-a-Date
    go out with selected person
until *the perfect partner is found*

Under what conditions does this algorithm fail? Amend the algorithm appropriately.

5 Suggest improvements to algorithm 2.11 for finding the first prime number greater than a given number.

6 Using algorithm 2.11 as a base, design an algorithm for finding the first N prime numbers, where N is an arbitrary positive integer.

7 The following algorithm (called a *binary search*) describes one method of finding an arbitrary name in an alphabetically ordered list containing N names.

set FIRST to 1
set LAST to N
while *FIRST* $\leqslant$ *LAST and name not found* **do**
    set I to the integer part of $(FIRST + LAST)/2$
    if *the Ith name is not the wanted name*
    then if *the Ith name precedes the wanted name*
        then *set FIRST to* $I+1$
        else *set LAST to* $I-1$

Trace the execution of this algorithm in searching for the name Jones in any convenient length list in which (a) Jones appears, and (b) Jones does not appear.

How many names are looked at in each case? How many names would be looked at if algorithm 2.8 were used instead?

In the general case, when the length of the list is N, how many names must be looked at before it is clear that a particular name is not present? How many names must be looked at if algorithm 2.8 is used?

8 Write down how sequence, selection and iteration are expressed in any programming language you know.

9 Devise an algorithm which describes how to merge two ordered lists of names into a single ordered list of names (i.e. a refinement of the last line of algorithm 2.31).

10 Devise yet another algorithm for sorting a list of names into alphabetical order. (*Hint*: try moving the alphabetically first name to the head of the list, then the alphabetically first name of the remainder to second position in the list, and so on.)

11 Devise an algorithm to find all the prime numbers less than an arbitrary positive integer N. (*Note*: this is quite different from finding the first N prime numbers as in Exercise 2.6.)

12 Devise an algorithm for determining the day of the week on which your birthday will fall in any year, given the day of the week and the date on which you were born.

13 Devise an algorithm for determining the letter which occurs most often in a given piece of English text.

14 Devise an iterative (rather than recursive) algorithm for solving the Towers of Hanoi problem. (*Hint*: Consider the three rods to be arranged in a triangle, and show that odd-numbered disks always move in a clockwise direction whereas even-numbered disks always move in an anticlockwise direction.)

15 Show how the following tasks can be split up into processes which can be executed in parallel:
(a)   making a cup of coffee;
(b)   multiplying two matrices;
(c)   searching an unsorted binary tree for a particular element.

16 Modify the parallel sorting algorithm of Section 2.10 to cater for multiple occurrences of the same name.

17 A careful study of the design of parallel computers shows that algorithm 2.33 really has an execution time proportional to $\log_2 N$ (rather than constant as claimed) because it takes time proportional to $\log_2 N$ for N processors to communicate and coordinate with each other. Show that it is still possible to achieve a speed increase proportional to the increase in the number of processors. (*Hint*: use only $N/\log_2 N$ processors, each one processing a group of $\log_2 N$ items sequentially.)

18 Repeat Exercise 2.17 for algorithm 2.35.

BIBLIOGRAPHY

The following books are concerned with algorithm design and expression.

O. J. Dahl, E. W. Dijkstra and C. A. R. Hoare, *Structured Programming*, Academic Press, London, 1972.

E. W. Dijkstra, *A Discipline of Programming*, Prentice-Hall, N.J., 1976.

G. Dromey, *How To Solve It By Computer*, Prentice-Hall International, London, 1982.

M. J. Jackson, *Principles of Program Design*, Academic Press, London, 1975.

N. Wirth, *Algorithms + Data Structures = Programs*, Prentice-Hall, N.J., 1975.

E. Yourdon, *Techniques of Program Structure and Design*, Prentice-Hall, N.J., 1975.

The following books are an introduction to data structures.

D. Coleman, *A Structured Approach to Data*, Macmillan, London, 1978.

M. Elson, *Data Structures*, Science Research Associates, Chicago, 1975.

E. S. Page and L. B. Wilson, *Information Representation and Manipulation in a Computer* (2nd edn), Cambridge University Press, 1978.

M. J. R. Shave, *Data Structures*, McGraw-Hill, London, 1975.

The following are devoted to the use of recursion.

D. W. Barron, *Recursive Techniques in Programming*, Macdonald-Elsevier, London and New York, 1968.

P. J. Hayes, A note on the Towers of Hanoi problem, *Computer Journal*, **20**(3), 282–285, 1977.

Finally, a book covering the development of programming languages.

J. Sammet, *Programming Languages: History and Fundamentals*, Prentice-Hall, N.J., 1969.

3 THE THEORY OF ALGORITHMS

We have seen that algorithms are a fundamental concept of computer science, and we have developed some insight into how to construct them. In this chapter we will step back a pace to see if there are any interesting properties we can discover about algorithms in general. We will investigate the sort of problems for which algorithms exist, and the sort of algorithms which are feasible in terms of their usage of physical resources. Finally we will study methods of increasing one's confidence in an algorithm's correctness.

This chapter is essentially a survey of the theory of algorithms. Some of the results presented are deep and perhaps counter-intuitive. Such results require careful mathematical proofs which can be found in the technical literature, but which are omitted or only sketched briefly here. Thus the reader is not expected to see why all the results are true, and such understanding is not required in order to follow the thrust of the chapter.

3.1 COMPUTABILITY

Many examples of algorithms have been presented in Chapter 2. We know there exist algorithms for knitting a sweater, building a model plane, baking a cake, making a dress, and playing a Beethoven sonata. We know that computers can control traffic signals, production lines and chemical plants. They can book airline flights, control robots and produce payrolls. There are algorithms for making a cup of coffee, finding the largest of a set of numbers, discovering whether or not a number is prime, and printing the greatest common divisor of two numbers. From our schooldays we remember that there exist algorithms for adding, subtracting, multiplying and dividing numbers, and for computing square roots. No doubt there are algorithms for computing logarithms, finding the frequency of words in a given piece of text, and controlling a nuclear submarine. Is there any job which a computer *cannot* do—any job for which no algorithm exists?

The surprising answer is Yes! There are many things a computer cannot do. In fact, the number of things which can be computed is infinitesimal compared with the number of things one might like to compute. Computers cannot do most things!

3.1.1 History of Computability

The idea of having an algorithm, or recipe for performing some task, has existed for thousands of years. For many years, people also held the following belief: if any problem could be precisely stated, then with enough effort a solution could eventually be found (or else a proof that no solution exists could eventually be provided). In other words, it was believed that there was no problem which was so intrinsically difficult that, in principle, it could never be solved.

One of the great supporters of this belief was the famous mathematician David Hilbert (1862–1943). He once said

"Every definite mathematical problem must necessarily be susceptible of an exact settlement either in the form of an actual answer to the question asked, or by the proof of the impossibility of its solution and therewith the necessary failure of all attempts . . . one of the things that attracts us most when we apply ourselves to a mathematical problem is precisely that within us we always hear the call: here is the problem, search for the solution; you can find it by pure thought, for in mathematics there is nothing which cannot be known."

Hilbert's aim was to devise a formal mathematical system in which all problems can be precisely formulated in terms of statements which are either true or false. His idea was to find an algorithm which, given any statement in the formal system, would determine whether or not that statement was true. If Hilbert had achieved this objective, then any problem which was well-defined could have been solved simply by executing the algorithm. Deciding the truth of a given statement in the formal system was called the *Entscheidungsproblem* by Hilbert, who considered it to be a fundamental open problem in mathematics.

Unfortunately for Hilbert's objective, the 1930s brought a wave of research which showed that the Entscheidungsproblem is not computable. That is, no algorithm of the type for which Hilbert longed, exists. A cynic might say that mathematicians could heave a sigh of relief, for if such an algorithm did exist, they would all be out of a job just as soon as the algorithm was found! In fact, however, mathematicians were stunned by this remarkable discovery.

The first news of the discovery came in 1931 when Kurt Gödel published his now famous *incompleteness theorem*. Among other things, this showed that there is no algorithm whose input can be any statement about the integers and whose output tells whether or not the statement is true. Closely following on Gödel's heels, further mathematicians such as Alonso Church, Stephen Kleene, Emil Post, Alan Turing and many others, found more problems which had no algorithmic solution. Perhaps the most remarkable feature of those early results on problems which cannot be solved by computers is that they were obtained in the 1930s, before the earliest computers had been built!

3.1.2   The Church–Turing Thesis

There is one major obstacle in proving that no algorithm for a particular task exists. We must first know exactly what we mean by an algorithm. Each of the mathematicians mentioned in the previous section had to overcome this obstacle, and each overcame it by defining "algorithm" in a different way! Gödel defined an algorithm as a sequence of rules for forming complicated mathematical functions out of simpler mathematical functions. Church used a formalism called the lambda calculus, whilst Turing used a hypothetical machine we call a Turing machine. Turing defined an algorithm as any set of instructions for his simple machine. In Chapter 2 we defined an algorithm as consisting of basic operations on integers and other data structures, controlled by sequence, selection and iteration.

Now why should any one pay any attention to results about algorithms defined in such various and obscure ways? The answer is that all the seemingly different and independently contrived definitions turn out to be equivalent. That is, if something can be computed by an algorithm defined in one way, then it can also be computed by an algorithm defined in any of the other ways. As this equivalence was increasingly realized by researchers in the 1930s, the following two statements became widely believed:

(1)   All reasonable definitions of "algorithm" which are known so far are equivalent.

(2)   Any reasonable definition of "algorithm" which anyone will ever make will turn out to be equivalent to the definitions we know.

These beliefs have come to be known as the *Church–Turing thesis* (or sometimes Church's thesis) after two of the earliest workers who realized the fundamental nature of the concept they had defined. To this day, no evidence has arisen to the contrary, and the Church–Turing thesis is widely believed.

The Church–Turing thesis merely states that we think we have a good definition for what an algorithm is. Everyone has an intuitive feeling for what it means to perform some task in a routine or mechanical manner. People have an intuitive grasp of the concept of devising a set of instructions or steps to perform some task, and then giving the instructions to a person or machine for purely routine execution. Such a set of instructions is what we think of as an algorithm, and the Church–Turing thesis reassures us that the precise definitions of "algorithm" used in computer science do indeed match these informal ideas that people have. In short, we believe that whenever we write down some set of steps which we feel could be executed in a purely routine manner, then there is a formal algorithm, in the computer science sense of the word, for the same task.

In a modern setting, we can define "algorithm" as anything which can be executed on a computer. Fortunately, the particular computer chosen is irrelevant to the definition, since any algorithm which can be implemented on one computer can also be implemented on any other computer. This is true because all computers can *simulate* each other: that is, given any two computers, we can write a program for one computer which can understand and execute any program written for the other. Such a program is called an *interpreter* (or *simulator*, or *universal program*).

The equivalence between all modern computers, and their equivalence to Turing machines and to the numerous other means of defining "algorithm", is further evidence for the Church–Turing thesis.

The existence of interpreters, as discussed above, is in itself an interesting and remarkable property of algorithms. Although it is not self-evident, it is nevertheless true that for any programming language there exists an interpreter which, given the description of any program in the language, can simulate that program. Therefore, the interpreter (or universal program) can perform any task which any other program can perform. This remarkable property of algorithms is called *universality*.

Loosely speaking, universality means that any computer is equivalent to all other computers in the sense that they can all perform the same tasks. Why then, do people choose one computer over another? The reason is that some computers run faster than others, some are easier to program, some already have programs written for them and it may be uneconomical to re-write the program for another computer, and some have more memory so that larger programs can execute faster on them. Thus although all computers can perform the same tasks, they do not necessarily consume the same amount of resources while performing a given task. We shall return to this point in Section 3.2.

3.1.3 The Halting Problem

At the beginning of this chapter we mentioned that there are many problems which are non-computable. That is, no algorithm exists for solving such a problem. This is a very strong statement. We are saying something much deeper than that we *don't know* an algorithm for solving the problem. We are saying that we will *never know* such an algorithm—that we never *can* know such an algorithm, because no such algorithm exists.

In this section we will show how to convince oneself that particular problems are non-computable. The reader may like to pause at this point to try to visualize any method for proving that no algorithm can possibly exist for solving a particular problem. Certainly, it is not obvious.

We have already mentioned one problem which is not computable. That was Hilbert and Gödel's problem concerning facts about numbers. Are there problems of more direct interest to computer science which are not computable? The following paragraphs describe an apparently simple computer science problem and prove that no algorithm can solve it.

A common problem among computer installations the world over is that when writing programs people often make mistakes which prevent their programs from terminating. In popular jargon, programmers say "My program went into an infinite loop!" It would clearly be beneficial if programmers could detect the existence of infinite loops in their programs before wasting computer resources in executing them. Hence the problem one would like to solve is that of determining whether an arbitrary program contains an infinite loop. Putting this another way, the problem is to determine whether an arbitrary program halts or not. This is called the *halting problem*. Its solution is an algorithm which, given an arbitrary program P and its input data D, can tell us whether or not P would eventually halt when executed with input data D.

Now the "solution" to the halting problem used by most computer installations is to time each program whilst it is being executed, and to forcibly abort the program if it uses more time than was allocated to it. However, this is an undesirable solution for two reasons. Firstly, non-terminating programs will waste the entire time allocated to them. Secondly, it may happen with certain programs that the programmer cannot calculate the time required, and therefore a program may be aborted a short time before it would otherwise successfully halt.

Thus one might expect that computer installations around the world are investing considerable effort in attempts to devise an algorithm which solves the halting problem. If they are, they are wasting their time, because no such algorithm exists. The halting problem is non-computable. This can be proved as follows.

Let us assume for the moment that there *is* an algorithm for solving the halting problem. Call this algorithm *halttester*. As mentioned above, the algorithm has two inputs *P* and *D*, so that *halttester(P,D)* prints the answer *"OK"* if program *P* would terminate when executed with input data *D*, and it prints *"BAD"* otherwise. The action of *halttester* is illustrated in Fig. 3.1(a).

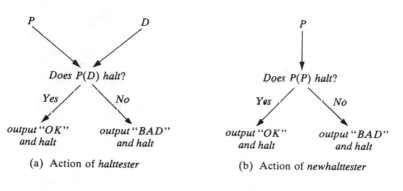

(a) Action of *halttester*   (b) Action of *newhalttester*

Figure 3.1

Since *halttester* tests the termination of a program *P* for any data *D* we can use it to construct a more limited algorithm which tests the termination of *P* when the data is *P* itself. The reader may find it strange that a program can be used as data in this way, but the situation is not unusual. A program is a representation of an algorithm and simply consists of a sequence of characters (such as letters and digits). Any sequence of characters can be input to a computer program. Whether the program does anything sensible with the input is a separate issue. Actually there are many programs of practical interest whose input is a sequence of characters representing another program: examples are compilers and editors (see Chapter 5).

Let us give the name *newhalttester* to this limited version of *halttester*. *Newhalttester* can be written

module *newhalttester(P)*
{Checks whether program *P* halts if executed with data *P*}
halttester(P,P)   (3.1)

The action of *newhalttester* is illustrated in Fig. 3.1(b).

If we assume that an algorithm *halttester* exists, and that therefore *newhalttester* exists, we may construct the following algorithm, called *funny*, which has just one input *P*.

module *funny(P)*
{In order to write this module we are assuming
that *halttester* exists}
if *newhalttester(P) outputs* "*BAD*"
  then *halt*
  else *loop for ever*   (3.2)

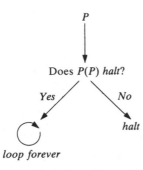

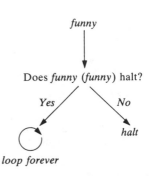

(a) Action of *funny (P)*   (b) Action of *funny (funny)*

Figure 3.2

The action of algorithm *funny* is illustrated in Fig. 3.2(a).

Finally, we consider what happens during execution of *funny(funny)*—that is, during execution of *funny* with its own program text as the input *P*. (This is quite legitimate, since *P* can be *any* sequence of characters.) The execution of *funny(funny)* is illustrated in Fig. 3.2(b), which is the same as Fig. 3.2(a) but with *funny* substituted for the input *P*. Figure 3.2(b) clearly demonstrates a contradiction, since it shows on the one hand that if *funny(funny)* halts then it loops for ever, but on the other hand that if *funny(funny)* loops for ever then it halts! In other words the execution of *funny(funny)* can neither halt nor loop for ever.

The contradition can be resolved only by admitting that the algorithm *funny* cannot exist. However, the only assumption made in deriving *funny* was that *halttester* exists. Hence if *funny* cannot exist then neither can *halttester*. We have therefore shown that no algorithm *halttester* for solving the halting problem can exist, and hence that the halting problem is non-computable.

The proof above can be summarized as follows:

(1)   Assume we can write a program *halttester*.
(2)   Use it to construct another program *funny* (via an intermediate program *newhalttester*).

(3)   Show that *funny* has some impossible property (it can neither halt nor loop for ever).

(4)   Conclude that the assumption in step 1 must be wrong.

We have shown that there is no algorithm which can solve the halting problem. What does this mean? Surely there are some programs which are so simple that it is obvious whether or not they halt. Of course there are—but there are lots of others where it is by no means so obvious. Consider, for example, an algorithm for testing the truth of Fermat's last theorem. This theorem states that there are no positive integers a, b, and c such that $a^n + b^n = c^n$ when $n > 2$. At present no proof or disproof of this theorem is known, though Fermat did claim to have a proof. A plausible algorithm for testing the theorem is

module *Fermat(n)*
{Tests Fermat's last theorem on input n}
repeat *for a* = 1,2,3, . . .   {for ever}
  repeat *for b* = 1,2,3, . . .,*a*
    repeat *for c* = 2,3,4, . . . ,*a* + *b*
    if $a^n + b^n = c^n$
      then *output a,b,c, and n, and halt*   (3.3)

The algorithm exhaustively tests all positive integers a, b, and c, and halts only if it finds a, b, and c such that $a^n + b^n = c^n$. If the algorithm halts for some particular input $n > 2$ then Fermat's last theorem will be disproved.

It is easy to see that the algorithm will halt when the input n is 1, since when $a = 1$, $b = 1$, and $c = 2$ we know that $a^1 + b^1 = c^1$. Similarly, when the input n is 2 it is easy to work out that the algorithm will halt, since $a^2 + b^2 = c^2$ when $a = 3, b = 4$, and $c = 5$. When the input n is 3 it is not easy to see whether or not the algorithm will halt. However, with ingenuity one can prove that the algorithm will never halt. What happens when $n = 37$? Again, a great deal of human ingenuity can show that the algorithm will never halt. What if n is very large? At present nobody knows.

The example illustrates that in some cases the halting problem is easy to solve. In other cases it is very difficult, and a great amount of *creativity* is required. In further cases, such as a very large input to the algorithm above, the halting problem has yet to be solved. The important point is that there is no purely *mechanical* method (i.e. no algorithm) which is guaranteed to solve the halting problem in every case.

Of course, it is possible to design an algorithm which will solve the halting problem in certain cases, but the algorithm is bound to fail on some other inputs. In fact it is not hard to show that any proposed algorithm for the halting problem must fail on infinitely many inputs (Exercise 3.5). Even more interesting is the fact that there exists an *algorithm* which, given any proposed algorithm for the halting problem, can produce an input on which the proposed algorithm must fail (Exercise 3.6). In other words, not only must every proposed *halttester* algorithm fail, but it is not too hard to determine *where* it will fail!

In this discussion we have touched on the difference between a *routine algorithm* and the application of *human creativity* in the solution of a problem. We shall return to this point in Chapters 6 and 7.

3.1.4   More Non-computable Problems

We have just seen a problem which has no algorithmic solution. The halting problem cannot be solved by any program written in any language for any computer. The natural question, to which we now turn, is which other problems are non-computable.

The proof method of the previous section (which, incidentally, is called "diagonalization" and is related to Cantor's proof that there are more real numbers than integers), is tedious and perhaps difficult to follow. Therefore rather than repeat a similar proof for each non-computable problem, we will merely show that if the problem at hand were computable, then so would be the halting problem. Of course we know that the halting problem is not computable and so neither could be the problem at hand.

Recall that the halting problem is to determine whether or not an arbitrary program P will halt when executed with arbitrary input data D. A related question is whether or not an arbitrary program P will halt on *all* inputs. This is called the *totality problem*. We say that P is *total* if $P(D)$ halts for all input data D.

Not surprisingly, the totality problem is non-computable. Otherwise, given any P and D, we could simply construct a special program for that P and D which ignores its input and simulates $P(D)$. This special program could be called *funnypd* and written

> **module** *funnypd*(I)
> {I is the input, but the module doesn't use it}
> *simulate program P on input data D*   (3.4)

Now asking whether *funnypd* is total is the same as asking whether $P(D)$ halts. So an algorithm for the totality problem would also give us the following algorithm for the halting problem.

> **module** *halttester*(P,D)
> {In order to write this module we are assuming
>   that an algorithm for the totality problem exists}
> *construct the text of the program funnypd*
> **if** *funnypd is total*
>   **then** *output "OK" and halt*
>   **else** *output "BAD" and halt*   (3.5)

However, we know that no algorithm for the halting problem exists. Hence the assumption that there exists an algorithm which solves the totality problem is false. We have therefore proved that the totality problem is not computable.

Another non-computable problem arises in the context of a company which is installing a new computer. Suppose the company has a large number of programs which have been running error-free for years on its old computer. The programmers have just written a suite of new programs for the same tasks to run on the new computer. How can the company be sure that the new programs will be as reliable as the old ones?

Clearly the company needs an algorithm which takes any two programs, an old and a new, and compares them to see if they perform the same job (i.e. for the same input they produce the same output). This is called the *equivalence problem*. Unfortunately, the equivalence problem is not computable. Otherwise, given any P, we could simply construct for that P a special program which simulates P, and outputs "13" if P eventually halts. (Of course if P doesn't halt, the simulating program just keeps on simulating P for ever.) This special program could be called *funnyp* and written

> **module** *funnyp(D)*
> {Outputs "13" if $P(D)$ ever halts}
> *simulate program P on input data D*
> {the previous step may loop for ever, but if it doesn't then ...}
> *output* "13"   (3.6)

Now consider a simple-minded program which always outputs "13".

> **module** *simple(D)*
> {D is the input, but the module ignores it and
>   outputs "13" regardless}
> *output* "13"   (3.7)

Now asking whether *funnyp* is equivalent to *simple* is the same as asking whether P is total. The reason is that if P halts on every input, then *funnyp* will output "13" on every input, whereas if there is some input on which P does not halt, then *funnyp* will not halt and will not output "13" on that input. So an algorithm for the equivalence problem would also give us an algorithm for the totality problem as follows:

> **module** *total(P)*
> {In order to write this module we are assuming
>   that an algorithm for the equivalence problem exists}
> *construct the text of the program funnyp*
> *construct the text of the program simple*
> **if** *funnyp and simple are equivalent*
>   **then** *output "P is total"*
>   **else** *output "P is not total"*   (3.8)

However, we proved earlier in this section that there is no algorithm for the totality problem. Hence the assumption that there exists an algorithm for the equivalence problem is false. We have therefore proved that there is no algorithm for solving the equivalence problem.

Perhaps the reader is getting the feeling that almost any interesting question we ask about algorithms is not computable. A remarkable theorem, called *Rice's theorem*, which is not obvious and involves a detailed proof, confirms this feeling to some extent. Think of any task which some algorithms perform and others don't (such as outputting "28", or computing the square root of the input). Rice's theorem says there is no algorithm to tell whether or not an arbitrary program performs the task!

Most of the non-computable problems we have encountered have concerned questions about algorithms. We complete this section by mentioning some other non-computable problems which have a different flavor.

Many programming languages have a fairly simple grammatical structure which can be expressed by something called a *Backus–Naur form* (or *BNF*, or *context-free*) grammar—see Chapter 5. Even though these grammars are simple, many questions concerning them are not computable. For example, given two arbitrary BNF grammars, the question of whether or not they represent the same programming language is non-computable. In fact, there is no algorithm to tell whether or not there exists *any* sequence of characters which is grammatically correct in both languages. One might at least hope that, given an arbitrary BNF grammar, it is possible to tell whether there exists any ungrammatical sequence of characters. But even this is non-computable.

Fortunately, certain important properties of BNF grammars *are* computable. For example, given a BNF grammar and a sequence of characters, there is an algorithm to check whether or not the sequence is grammatically correct. The determination of grammatical correctness is called the *parsing problem*, and is further discussed in Chapter 5.

Finally, here is a non-computable problem with a mathematical flavor. Given an arbitrary equation (such as $(a + 1)^2 + (b + 1)^3 = (c + 1)^4$), one would like to determine whether or not the equation is satisfied by any integers. This is called the *Diophantine equation* problem, and it is known that no algorithm exists for solving arbitrary Diophantine equations.

3.1.5 Partial Computability

There are a large number of problems which are not computable, and some have been presented above. However, some non-computable problems are less computable than others. For the sake of definiteness we shall restrict our attention to problems which require only a "YES" or "NO" answer.

Consider once again the halting problem. For an arbitrary program P and data D, we would like to know whether or not $P(D)$ halts. Now if $P(D)$ does halt, there is no difficulty because we can simply execute the program until it halts and then we certainly know that it halts. The difficulty only arises if $P(D)$ does not halt. Then there is no general (i.e. algorithmic) method which can discover that $P(D)$ does not halt. No matter how long we execute the program, if it has not yet halted, we cannot say that it will never halt.

The halting problem is called *partially computable* because there is an algorithm which outputs "YES" if $P(D)$ halts, though it loops for ever if $P(D)$ doesn't halt. The difference between computable and partially computable is illustrated in Fig. 3.3.

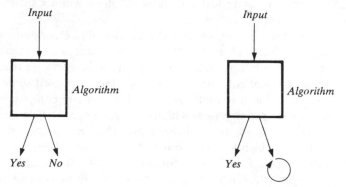

(a) A computable problem   (b) A partially computable problem

Figure 3.3

In contrast to the halting problem, the totality and the equivalence problems are not partially computable. Thus there is no algorithm which, when given P, is able to output "YES" if P halts on all inputs, even if the algorithm is permitted to loop when the answer is "NO".

The distinction between not computable and not even partially computable is more important than appears at first sight. The distinction relates to our concept of being able to prove something. Mathematicians talk about *proof systems* which are general frameworks, or methodologies, for proving things. Usually we think of a proof system as a set of axioms (or basic assumptions) and some rules of inference. Then a proof is just a sequence of lines, the early ones being axioms and the remainder following from previous ones by using the rules of inference. The last line of the proof is the item (or "theorem") which we set out to prove.

It is possible to show that problems are partially computable if and only if they have a proof system. The halting problem is an apt example. Although it is not computable, it is partially computable and therefore has a proof system. This means that if a program does halt on some input data, it is possible to write down a convincing proof of this fact. Indeed, the proof can just be a step by step trace of the execution of the program. It is then easy to check through the trace and convince oneself that the program really does halt on the given input data (see also Exercise 3.8).

However, the situation is quite different for the totality and equivalence problems. Neither are partially computable. Therefore, even if two programs are equivalent, there is no uniform framework for proving this fact. Thus we conclude that proofs of program equivalence will in general require a great deal of creativity, and routine hack-work alone will not suffice. We shall return to this idea in Section 3.3.

At the start of this chapter, we mentioned Gödel's celebrated incompleteness theorem. It follows from this theorem that there is no algorithm to decide whether or not arbitrary statements·about the integers are true. We say that "arithmetic is not computable". In fact, Gödel proved something stronger. He showed that arithmetic is not even partially computable. It · follows that there is no proof system which can prove every true statement about the integers. Thus, in any arithmetic proof system, there are statements about integers which are true, but cannot be proved!

In summary, problems can be computable, partially computable, or not even partially computable. If a problem is computable, there is an algorithm which can correctly answer "YES" or "NO" for every input. If the problem is only partially computable, there is no such algorithm, but at least there is an algorithm for answering "YES" if that answer is correct (though it may loop for ever if the answer is "NO"). Finally, if the problem is not even partially computable, there is no algorithm which can always correctly answer either "YES" or "NO". In terms of proof systems, for any problem which is computable or partially computable there is a method of proving that the answer is "YES" whenever it is. However, if the problem is not even partially computable, there is no general method of proving the correctness of a proposed answer.

3.1.6   The Recursion Theorem

In our investigation of some properties of algorithms, we have considered algorithms which operate upon (or "talk about") other algorithms. From this property there followed many interesting facts. Let us now consider algorithms which talk about themselves.

One of the fascinating facts which has been discovered about algorithms which talk about themselves is called the *recursion theorem*. This is a deep theorem about algorithms and it has both amusing and important implications. In this section we will investigate some of these implications, indicating how they follow from the recursion theorem. However, we shall not give a proof of the recursion theorem itself.

The recursion theorem states, essentially, that algorithms can compute, and operate upon, a copy of themselves. More precisely, for any algorithm which operates in some way upon some arbitrary sequence of characters D, there exists an algorithm which operates in the same way upon the sequence of characters which is its own text. The algorithms obtained in this manner are self-referential. In a sense they can talk about themselves and compute properties of themselves.

The simplest fact which follows from the recursion theorem is that in every programming language there exists a program which prints itself! (For simplicity in this section, we will assume that the set of characters used to write programs is the same as the set of characters used for input and output. It is possible to relax this assumption, but only at the cost of a more cumbersome discussion.) It is almost trivial to see how the existence of a self-printing program follows from the recursion theorem. Certainly for any arbitrary sequence of characters D, there is a program which can print D. Such a program can be written as follows.

module *print*
{Outputs the sequence of characters D}
output D   (3.9)

Therefore the recursion theorem states that there is a program which can operate in the same way upon its own text. Namely, the program can print a copy of its own text.

let x be ' ; *let y be x with every* " *changed to* '''' ; *output* (" *let x be* '''''' *y* '''''''' *x*) ; ' ;

let y be x with every ' *changed to* " ;

output (' *let x be* ''' *y* '''' *x*) ;

Figure 3.4   A program which prints itself.

The existence of a self-printing program is mainly of recreational interest. One such program is sketched in Fig. 3.4, and the reader is challenged to write a self-printing program in some real programming language (Exercise 3.11). Figure 3.5 provides a clue to the workings of the program in Fig. 3.4.

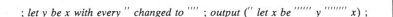

x is | ; *let y be x with every* ' *changed to* " ; *output* ('*let x be* ''' y '''' x) ;

y is | ; *let y be x with every* " *changed to* '''' ; *output* ('' *let x be* '''''' y '''''''' x) ;

Figure 3.5   The values of x and y after the first two
statements in Fig. 3.4 are executed.

The program uses certain conventions concerning sequences of characters. A sequence of characters is represented by enclosing it between two single quotes. Two adjacent quotes inside a sequence of characters represents one single quote (a quite usual convention in many programming languages). Two adjacent sequences of characters are simply joined together to form one longer sequence. The reader can now verify that the program of Fig. 3.4 does indeed print itself.

A further recreational fact which follows from the recursion theorem is that there are two algorithms which print each other (see Exercise 3.12).

Another implication of the recursion theorem is that there always exist alphabetically adjacent programs which perform the same task. In any programming language, a program can be represented by a sequence of characters. It is easy to place the sequences in alphabetical order. For example, if the set of characters for a particular programming language consists of only A and B, the sequences can be ordered A, B, AA, AB, BA, BB, AAA, AAB, ABA, and so on. Now consider the following program which operates upon an arbitrary sequence of characters D.

> **module** *copycat(I)*
> {Finds the alphabetically next syntactically correct
> program after D, and simulates it on input I}
> *set P equal to D*
> **repeat**
>   *set P equal to the alphabetically next sequence*
>   *of characters after P*
> **until** *P represents a syntactically correct program in*
>   *the language*
> *simulate the program P on input I*   (3.10)

It follows from the recursion theorem that there is a program which operates in the same way as *copycat* when D is a copy of the program's own text. A little thought shows that this program and the program following it in alphabetical order perform the same task. Thus an implication of the recursion theorem is that for any programming language, if one lists the syntactically correct programs in alphabetical order, then there are two adjacent programs which perform the same task!

There are also some serious and useful applications of the recursion theorem. It has long been the dream of some programmers to find an algorithm which generates an adequate set of test data for an arbitrary program. The hope is that if a program is tested successfully on the test data, then it will execute successfully for all input data. However, the recursion theorem shatters this dream. Assume that there does exist an algorithm to generate an adequate set of test data for an arbitrary program. Now consider the following program which operates upon an arbitrary sequence of characters D.

module *shatter*(I)
{The specification of this module is that its output
 is the square of its input.
 In order to write the module, we are assuming the existence of
 an algorithm to generate an adequate set of test data
 for an arbitrary program}
generate an adequate set of test data for program D
if I *is in the set*
   then *output I multiplied by I*
   else *output* 17   (3.11)

The recursion theorem shows that there is a program which operates in the same way as *shatter* when D is a copy of the program's own text. This program uses the assumed algorithm to generate an arbitrary set of test data for itself, and outputs the square of any item of that test data with which we present it. Thus the program operates correctly on all the test data, but we can see that it operates incorrectly on every other input. The test data is therefore not adequate, and so no algorithm exists for generating an adequate set of test data for an arbitrary program. We learn that automatic testing is not a generally workable method of verifying an algorithm's correctness. Other methods form the topic of Section 3.3.

3.2 COMPLEXITY

The study of computability described in Section 3.1 leads to an understanding of which problems admit algorithmic solution, and which do not. Of those problems for which there do exist algorithms, it is also of interest to know how much computer resources are required for their execution. Only those algorithms which use a feasible amount of resources are useful in

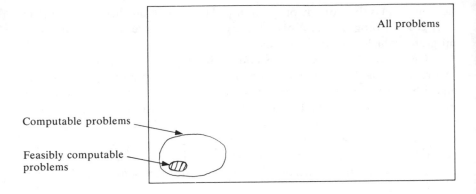

Figure 3.6   The universe of problems.

practice. It is the computer science field called *complexity theory* which asks, and attempts to answer, questions about the use of computational resources.

Figure 3.6 presents a pictorial representation of the universe of problems. Those which can be computed algorithmically form an infinitesimally small subset. Those which are *feasibly computable*, taking into account their resource requirements, comprise a minute portion of that already infinitesimally small subset. Nevertheless, the class of feasibly computable problems is so large that computer science has become an interesting, practical, and flourishing science.

3.2.1   Computer Resources

The major computer resources of interest are time, memory, and hardware. *Time* is simply the elapsed period from start to finish of the execution of an algorithm. *Memory* is the amount of storage required by the algorithm. The need for memory arises when partial results, calculated at some time during the execution of an algorithm, are required again at a later stage. *Hardware* is the amount of physical mechanism required for the execution of an algorithm. In a parallel machine, for example, hardware is closely related to the number of parallel processors needed by an algorithm (recall Section 2.10).

Algorithms usually accept input data and perform some processing on it. Therefore the amount of any resource used by an algorithm may vary with the size of the input data. Consider an algorithm which multiplies two numbers. Figure 3.7 gives an example of the standard "junior school" algorithm. If the algorithm is presented with two n-digit numbers, it will need to add together n rows, each containing n (or $n + 1$) digits. Each row can be

$$\begin{array}{r} 1984 \\ \times \quad 6713 \\ \hline 5952 \\ 1984 \\ 13888 \\ 11904 \\ \hline 13318592 \end{array}$$

Figure 3.7   The junior school multiplication algorithm.

computed in about n steps, or n units of time, and there are n separate rows. Adding the rows takes $n \times n$ (or n^2) units of time. Hence the execution time of the whole algorithm is proportional to n^2.

There are faster algorithms for multiplication of numbers. The algorithm shown in Fig. 3.8 takes time proportional to $n^{1.59}$, for reasons which will be explained later. The fastest known algorithm for a sequential machine has execution time proportional to $n \log n \log \log n$. (We shall use the notation $\log n$ to mean the logarithm of n using the base 2. Of course, when only proportionality is being considered the base of the logarithm is irrelevant.) On a parallel computer, numbers can be multiplied in time proportional to $\log n$.

$$\begin{array}{rrr} AC = & 19 \times 67 & = & 1273 \\ (A + B)\,(C + D) - AC - BD = (103 \times 80) - 1273 - 1092 = & & 5875 \\ BD = & 84 \times 13 & = & 1092 \\ & & & \overline{13318592} \end{array}$$

Figure 3.8   An $n^{1.59}$ multiplication algorithm

The multiplication algorithms discussed above illustrate two important points. The first is that a problem can be solved by quite different algorithms which perhaps use different amounts of resources. In many cases, it is interesting to find the best algorithm, namely that which uses the least resources. Sometimes, as one attempts to reduce some resource, such as time, some other resource, such as memory or hardware, must necessarily be increased. In these cases, the programmer must choose that *trade-off*, or balance, between resources which best matches the application at hand.

The second point illustrated by the multiplication algorithms is that the amount of resource used depends on the *size* of the input data. The more digits there are in the numbers to be multiplied, the longer it will take to perform the multiplication. In general, if there are n characters of input data, we can express the amount of resource used as a function of n, such as n, $3n^2 + 5n$, or $2n\log n + n + 17$.

Note that as n grows larger, some term in the function which expresses the amount of resource used may begin to dominate the other terms. For example, if the execution time is $3n^2 + 5n$, then as n grows larger, $3n^2$ grows very much larger than $5n$, and therefore $5n$ becomes increasingly less significant. The dominating term ($3n^2$) is called the *asymptotic* behavior of the algorithm. Although ideally it would be nice to fully understand the behavior of any algorithm and to be able to write down the exact function of n which represents the amount of resource used, in practice this task is often very difficult. One must sometimes be content to know only the asymptotic behavior of the algorithm.

Size n of input data	$\log_2 n$ microseconds	n microseconds	n^2 microseconds	2^n microseconds
10	0.000003 seconds	0.00001 seconds	0.0001 seconds	0.001 seconds
100	0.000007 seconds	0.0001 seconds	0.01 seconds	10^{14} centuries
1000	0.00001 seconds	0.001 seconds	1 second	astronomical
10000	0.000013 seconds	0.01 seconds	1.7 minutes	astronomical
100000	0.000017 seconds	0.1 seconds	2.8 hours	astronomical

Figure 3.9   Execution time of four algorithms.

In any case, it is the asymptotic behavior which ultimately governs whether or not a particular algorithm is feasible. Figure 3.9 illustrates the behavior of four algorithms which use $\log n$, n, n^2 and 2^n microseconds (i.e. millionths of a second) to solve some problem. Notice that the 2^n algorithm is infeasible even for relatively small sizes of input data. The n^2 algorithm is much better, but will also use too much computer time for large input data.

The algorithm whose execution time is n is eminently satisfactory. Its execution time is proportional to the number of characters of input data. Therefore, if twice as much input data is presented to the algorithm it will take twice as long to execute. This is quite a reasonable performance. On a sequential computer, the time taken by an algorithm must at least be proportional to the size of the input data, since, in all but the most trivial problems, the algorithm must at least look through the input data. Algorithms which run as fast as $\log n$ occur only on parallel computers which can consider many parts of the input data simultaneously (see Section 3.2.6).

Algorithms whose asymptotic behavior is 2^n, or more generally c^n for some constant c, are called *exponential* algorithms. Exponential algorithms are infeasible for all but the smallest input data sizes. Algorithms whose asymptotic behavior is n, n^2, or more generally n^c for some constant c, are called *polynomial* algorithms. Many polynomial algorithms are feasible for practical input data sizes, although, unfortunately, many are not. This point will be further discussed in Section 3.2.3.

Complexity theory studies various computer resources. The amount of resource used by an algorithm is expressed as a function of the input size. However, for a given input size, there are many different inputs, and it is not unusual that an algorithm uses different amounts of resource on different input data, even when the different inputs have the same size. This can occur because algorithms can *test* their data and perform different steps depending on the outcome of the test. (This does not occur, however, in the multiplication algorithms mentioned above, which execute the same steps whatever the data.)

When algorithms may use different amounts of resource for different inputs of the same size, a number of interesting resource questions may be posed. For example, it may be important to know the largest possible amount of resource used by an algorithm on any input of a given size. For example, if a computer is controlling a nuclear reactor, or landing a rocket on Mars, it is vital to know the longest time required by the computer to respond to some emergency. This is called the *worst-case* complexity of the algorithm.

Alternatively, the average amount of resource used over all the inputs of a given size may be the most useful knowlege. This is called the *average-case* complexity. Sometimes, it is interesting to know the chance of the algorithm remaining close to its average behavior on a given input. In such cases, the *standard deviation* of the resource usage should be calculated.

So far, we have been discussing the complexity of *algorithms* with respect to some resource. It is also meaningful to talk about the complexity of *problems* with respect to a resource. The complexity of a problem is just the complexity of the best algorithm which solves that problem.

Unfortunately, at present we do not know the exact complexity of many naturally occurring problems. In many cases all we know is the complexity of the best algorithm found so far for the problem. This is referred to as an *upper bound* on the complexity of the problem. Conversely, it is sometimes possible to prove that no algorithm can solve the problem without using *at least* a certain amount of resource. This amount of resource is called a *lower bound* on the complexity of the problem.

For example, the best known sequential algorithm for integer multiplication uses time proportional to $n \log n \log \log n$. On the other hand, it is easy to prove that no sequential algorithm can do better than using time proportional to n, because that is the size of the input and each digit in the input must be considered at least once. Thus the upper bound $(n \log n \log \log n)$ is larger than the lower bound (n), leaving unanswered questions concerning the exact complexity of integer multiplication. Can a faster algorithm be found? Alternatively, can one prove that no faster algorithm exists? These are currently open questions.

The example of integer multiplication is typical of the current state of affairs in complexity theory. For given problems, the upper and lower bounds rarely match, and computer scientists attempt to burn the candle at both ends, raising the lower bounds, and finding better algorithms in order to lower the upper bounds.

3.2.2   Divide and Conquer

A very common and elegant method of devising an efficient algorithm for a problem is to divide the problem into smaller pieces, thus leaving only smaller problems to be solved. An example of this approach was presented in Chapter 2, namely sorting n names with algorithm 2.31:

> **module** *sort(list)*
> {Sorts given list of n names into alphabetical order}
> **if** $n > 1$
> > **then** *sort(first half of the list)*
> > *sort(second half of the list)*
> > *merge the two halves together*   (3.12)

What is the time complexity of this algorithm? In other words, how long does this algorithm take to sort n names? Let $T(n)$ represent the time taken by the algorithm to sort n names. Now the algorithm begins by sorting the first half of the names. This will take time $T(n/2)$. Sorting the second half also takes time $T(n/2)$. Finally, the reader can check that merging the two halves can be carried out in time proportional to n (say cn for some constant c). Thus the total time taken is

$$T(n) = 2T(n/2) + cn$$

Also $T(1) = k$ for some constant k, since when $n = 1$ only the test $(n > 1)$ need be carried out.

Equations of the form above are called *recurrence relations*, and it is typical to find them resulting from a divide and conquer approach. Some recurrence relations are fairly difficult to solve. Indeed, whole books have been written on the subject. However, the recurrence relation above has the solution (see Exercise 3.17)

$$T(n) = cn \log n + kn$$

In other words, the asymptotic execution time of the merge-sorting algorithm is proportional to $n \log n$.

As a further example, consider the integer multiplication algorithm of Fig. 3.8. This algorithm uses a divide and conquer approach, since in order to multiply two numbers it splits each into halves (A,B and C,D), and then performs three multiplications of numbers only half the original length: AC, BD and $(A + B)(C + D)$. If $T(n)$ is the time taken by the algorithm to multiply two n digit numbers, then

$$T(n) = 3T(n/2) + cn$$

because the time needed to add and subtract the pieces is only cn, for some constant c. Also $T(1) = k$ for some constant k, since one digit numbers are very easy to multiply. The solution to this recurrence relation (Exercise 3.17) is

$$T(n) = (2c + k)n^{\log 3} - 2cn$$

Thus the asymptotic behavior is proportional to $n^{\log 3}$, which is about $n^{1.59}$.

Another application of divide and conquer is in obtaining fast algorithms for matrix multiplication. Figure 3.10 shows the standard algorithm for multiplying two $n \times n$ matrices A and B to give the answer D. Each element of D is obtained by combining one row of A with one column of B, using n multiplications and $n-1$ additions. As there are n^2 elements of D, the standard algorithm takes time proportional to n^3.

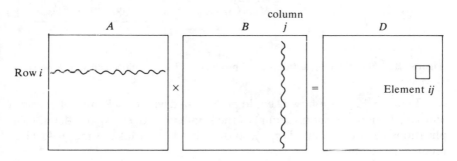

Figure 3.10   The standard matrix multiplication algorithm.

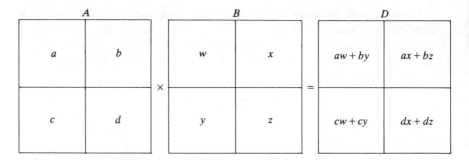

Figure 3.11   Multiplying $n \times n$ matrices by 8 products of $(n/2) \times (n/2)$ matrices.

Figure 3.11 illustrates how the divide and conquer approach begins by dividing each matrix into four quarters. Now D can be obtained by eight multiplications and four additions of smaller matrices, each of size $(n/2) \times (n/2)$. Each of these multiplications takes time $T(n/2)$, and each addition takes time $n/4$. The resulting recurrence relation is

$$T(n) = 8T(n/2) + cn$$

which has a solution whose dominating term is proportional to n^3. This is no faster than the standard algorithm. In fact, Fig. 3.11 is the standard algorithm in disguise.

8 additions and subtractions	7 multiplications	7 additions and subtractions
$S_1 = c + d$	$M_1 = S_2 S_6$	$t_1 = m_1 + m_2$
$S_2 = S_1 - a$	$M_2 = a\,w$	$t_2 = t_1 + m_2$
$S_3 = a - c$	$M_3 = b\,y$	The answer D is:
$S_4 = b - S_2$	$M_4 = S_3 S_7$	
$S_5 = x - w$	$M_5 = S_1 S_5$	
$S_6 = z - S_5$	$M_6 = S_4 z$	
$S_7 = z - w$	$M_7 = d\,S_8$	
$S_8 = S_6 - y$		

$m_2 + m_3$	$t_1 + m_5 + m_6$
$t_2 - m_7$	$t_2 + m_5$

Figure 3.12   Matrix multiplication with 7 products and 15 additions and subtractions.

Figure 3.12 shows how D could be obtained with only 7 multiplications and 15 additions (or subtractions) of the smaller matrices. Again, the multiplications each take time $T(n/2)$, and each addition takes time $n/4$. The recurrence relation now is

$$T(n) = 7T(n/2) + cn$$

whose solution has its dominating term proportional to $n^{\log 7}$, which is about $n^{2.81}$. Therefore the asymptotic behavior of this algorithm is superior to that of the standard algorithm. The complete solution of the recurrence relation (see Section 3.3.5) shows, however, that the faster execution time becomes noticeable only for very large values of n, whilst for values of practical interest the standard algorithm is faster. Although it is important to know the asymptotic behavior of an algorithm, this example illustrates that the asymptotic behavior by itself is not the full story.

This section has shown how divide and conquer can sometimes be used to derive interesting, elegant and efficient algorithms. Recurrence relations express the resource usage of such algorithms, and the solution of the recurrence relations gives the resource usage in a clearer form. The algorithms themselves are best expressed using the recursion feature of a modern programming language (recall Section 2.9).

3.2.3   The Sequential Computation Thesis

In Section 3.2.1, the difference between algorithms which use a polynomial (n^c) and an exponential (c^n) amount of some resource was described. Polynomial algorithms *tend* to be feasible for reasonable sizes of input data. Of course, many polynomial algorithms are infeasible, such as one which takes $5n^{1000}$ hours to solve a problem. Conversely, exponential algorithms tend to exceed the available resources even for small amounts of input data. Again there are exceptions. An algorithm which uses $2^{0.0001n}$ seconds may be quite reasonable for values of n up to about $10\,000$.

With our present poor understanding of the behavior of algorithms, the best *first approximation* we can make to distinguish between feasible and infeasible algorithms is to say that algorithms executing in a polynomial amount of time are feasible, and all others are infeasible. One of the primary aims of complexity theory is to improve this classification of algorithms, and thereby improve our understanding of the difference between feasible and infeasible problems.

The first approximation mentioned above is attractive for a number of reasons. One expects certain properties to hold for feasible algorithms, and these do indeed hold for algorithms running in polynomial time. For example, if an algorithm is constructed by taking two feasible algorithms and placing them sequentially one after the other, the constructed algorithm ought to be feasible. Similarly, if some step of a feasible algorithm is replaced by a call to a module representing a second feasible algorithm, the new combined algorithm should also be feasible. These *closure* properties do indeed hold for polynomial time algorithms.

There is another reason for associating "feasible" with "polynomial time". In order to measure *exactly* the amount of time used by an algorithm, it is essential to know all the details of the computer on which the algorithm will be executed. There are many different computers, and some can execute certain operations faster than others. When defining the concept of "feasible algorithm", which computer should be chosen? Actually, it would be most unfortunate if the definition of feasible algorithm depended on the details of just one computer, for then the whole theory would depend on the whims of one computer manufacturer, or on some passing technological fad. When that computer became outdated, the entire theory of feasible algorithms would be useless!

Fortunately, all reasonable sequential computers have related execution times. Not only can they all simulate each other (recall Section 3.1.2), but the time losses associated with the simulations are not excessive. In fact, any algorithm which executes in polynomial time on one computer can be run in polynomial time on any other computer. Thus it makes sense to talk about polynomial time algorithms *independently* of any particular computer. A theory of feasible algorithms based on polynomial time is machine independent.

The belief that all reasonable sequential computers which will ever be dreamed of have polynomially related execution times is called the *sequential computation thesis*. This thesis may be compared to the Church–Turing thesis of Section 3.1.2. It is a stronger form of that thesis, because it claims not only that the computable problems are the same for all computers, but also that the feasibly computable problems are the same for all computers. The major evidence for the sequential computation thesis is that it holds for all current computers and for all known reasonable definitions of sequential computation.

To summarize, our intention is to classify and understand feasibly computable problems. The best (although far from perfect) definition to date is that the feasibly computable problems are those which have polynomial time (sequential) algorithms. This definition matches practical experience quite well, and seems to be machine independent.

3.2.4 Infeasible Problems

Following the discussion above, it is of great interest to know which problems are computable in polynomial time. Many interesting and practical problems are in this category, a few examples being the problems in Section 3.2.2

Some problems have been proved not to be polynomial time computable. Such proofs are usually very difficult, as it is necessary to show that *no algorithm* which runs in polynomial time can solve the problem. An example of a problem which has been proved to require exponential time is a generalization of the game of chess to an $n \times n$ board. Given an arbitrary position of the black and white pieces on an $n \times n$ chess board, the problem is to determine which of the two players has a winning strategy. The infeasibility of the problem may explain why people still find chess interesting. On the other hand, for an 8×8 board, there may be a simple winning strategy which no-one has yet discovered. If such a strategy is ever discovered, the 8×8 chess game will become very boring. However, we can be sure that the simple strategy will not generalize to a $n \times n$ board, and thus a larger version of the game could still prove challenging.

There is a large number of problems for which the existence of a fast (i.e. polynomial time) algorithm remains an open question. No fast algorithms have been discovered for such problems, but neither has anyone yet been able to prove that no such algorithm exists. Many of these problems have practical application, as well as presenting an interesting challenge to computer scientists.

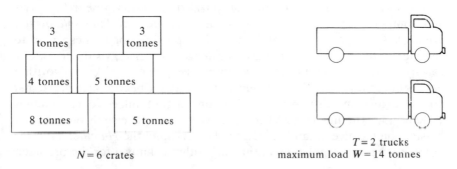

$N = 6$ crates

$T = 2$ trucks
maximum load $W = 14$ tonnes

Figure. 3.13   A simple case of the bin-packing problem.

An example of such a problem arises in connection with trucking companies. Suppose a trucking company has a number N of crates of different weights. The problem is to determine if T trucks, each of which can carry a load W, are sufficient to transport the crates. This is called the *bin-packing* problem (Fig. 3.13). Clearly, there are also many other applications in which the bin-packing problem arises. Unfortunately, every known algorithm for this problem uses exponential time. (Can the reader find a polynomial time algorithm? One might at first think of repeatedly loading the largest crate which still fits onto a truck until no more crates fit, and then proceeding to the next truck. However, Fig. 3.14 illustrates that this algorithm is not guaranteed to work.)

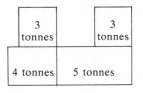

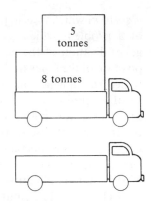

maximum load $W = 14$ tonnes

Figure 3.14   After loading one truck with the "largest crate first" algorithm, the remaining crates need not fit onto the other truck.

Another open problem which has puzzled operations research experts and computer scientists for years is the so-called *travelling salesperson problem*. Given a roadmap of N cities, is it possible for a salesperson to complete a round trip within a given mileage allowance, visiting each city exactly once? Despite numerous attempts, no polynomial time algorithm has ever been found for this problem, nor has anyone been able to prove that no such algorithm exists. A related (and one might think easier) problem is to determine whether a round trip which visits each city exactly once is even possible on the given map (Fig. 3.15). This is called the *Hamiltonian cycle* problem. Again, no polynomial time algorithm is known for the problem.

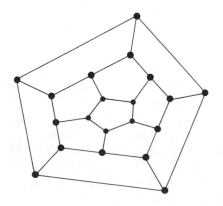

Dots represent cities
Lines represent roads

Figure 3.15   A simple case of the Hamiltonian cycle problem.

The *time-tabling* problem is also a problem of great practical interest for which no polynomial time algorithm is currently known. In this problem, one is given a list of subjects and the students enrolled in them, as well as the number of time slots available. The problem is to time-table the subjects so that no student has a clash.

Whether or not there exist polynomial time algorithms for any of the above problems is an interesting question which we shall further address in the next section. In the meantime, what should computer scientists do when a computer solution to any of these problems is required? The answer is that it is necessary to lower our sights in one of the following ways.

Firstly, rather than seek an algorithm which provides an exact solution, it will sometimes be adequate to provide an *approximate* solution only. For example, in the time-tabling problem, a solution with only a few clashes is better than no solution at all, and may be acceptable in the application at hand. A similar comment applies to the travelling salesperson problem. Rather than using an infeasible amount of computer time to calculate the absolutely minimum mileage round trip, a fast algorithm (if one can be found) which produces a reasonably short round trip may be of greater utility.

A second method of lowering one's sights when faced with a possibly infeasible problem is to try to produce an algorithm which executes quickly on the *average* input data, but which nevertheless exhibits an exponential behavior in the worst case. The hope is that the algorithm will terminate reasonably quickly on most of the data which it encounters in practice. Of course, this approach can be dangerous in a time-critical application (such as the nuclear reactor or Martian rocket of Section 3.2.1), where a short response time must be guaranteed.

A third, and seemingly bizarre, method of lowering one's sights is to relax the condition that the algorithm must be correct. Although no fast, correct algorithm may be known for the problem, it may be useful in certain circumstances to try to produce a fast algorithm which is known to contain an error!

A cute example of a useful algorithm with an error arises in the *primality* problem, for which no polynomial time algorithm is presently known. Given an n digit number as input, the problem is to determine whether or not the number is prime (i.e. contains no divisors other than itself and 1). The most obvious algorithm (see algorithm 2.10) is to divide the input number by every smaller number and check if the remainder is ever zero. This is an exponential algorithm, and becomes quite infeasible, even for moderate values of n (the number of digits) such as 20 or 30. A slightly faster algorithm results from dividing only by prime numbers, and then only up to the square root of the input number. However, this algorithm is still infeasible.

Consider the following mathematical fact concerning any odd number x. If x is prime, then every number y between 1 and $x-1$ satisfies the following condition:

$$GCD(x,y) = 1 \quad \text{and} \quad y^{(x-1)/2} \bmod x = J(y,x)$$

GCD is the greatest common divisor (Section 2.6) and J is called the Jacobi function. We need not worry about the details here, except to say that both can be computed quickly. It turns out that if x is not prime, then at least half the possible values of y will fail to satisfy the condition. Thus the following algorithm can be used to check if x is prime.

module *prime(x)*
{Tests any odd integer x for primality. If x is prime then
"PRIME" is output. If x is not prime then *"NOT PRIME"*
will probably be output, but there is a very small chance of
the algorithm outputting *"PRIME"* erroneously}
repeat *e times*
    randomly pick a number y between 1 *and* $x-1$
    if $GCD(x,y) \neq 1$
        then *output "NOT PRIME" and halt*
    if $y^{(x-1)/2} \bmod x \neq J(y,x)$
        then *output "NOT PRIME" and halt*
output "PRIME"   (3.13)

In this algorithm, e is a constant such as 20 or 30. The algorithm is fast, because it is easy to compute the conditions inside the loop.

If x is prime then, assuming the mathematical fact given above, it is easy to see that the algorithm outputs *"PRIME"*. Furthermore, if x is not prime, then each time around the loop there is at least a one in two chance that the randomly chosen y satisfies either $GCD(x,y) \neq 1$ or $y^{(x-1)/2} \bmod x \neq J(y,x)$. Therefore, after e times around the loop, the chance of not finding an appropriate y is less than one in 2^e. If e is 20, the chance is less than one in a million. If e is 30, the chance is less than one in a billion. Therefore, if x is not prime then the algorithm will probably output *"NOT PRIME"*, the chance of making an error being less than 1 in 2^e.

This type of algorithm—which may make an error, but very infrequently—is called a *probabilistic* algorithm. It can be argued that such algorithms are quite practical, because the constant e can be adjusted to make the probability of error as small as desired. If e is around 40, then the algorithm is probably more reliable than the computer on which it is being executed.

3.2.5 NP-completeness

Consider again some of the open problems described in the previous section, such as the bin-packing problem, the travelling salesperson problem, the Hamiltonian cycle problem and the time-tabling problem. No polynomial time algorithms are currently known for these problems.

Given arbitrary values of the inputs, or an arbitrary *instance* of the problem, there seems to be no fast method of *finding* the solution. However, these problems have a very interesting property in common. Once a solution is found for a particular instance of the problem (e.g. a particular time-table which works is discovered), it is easy to *verify* that the solution is correct. More precisely, for each of these problems there exists an algorithm which, given a particular instance of the problem and a proposed solution, can verify in polynomial time whether or not the solution is correct. Figure 3.16 illustrates a solution to the bin-packing example of Fig. 3.13, and Fig. 3.17 gives a solution to the Hamiltonian cycle example of Fig. 3.15. In each case it is easy to verify that the solution is correct, although it may have been much harder to find the solution in the first place. Is this not a common occurrence in real life? A solution to a puzzle seems difficult to obtain, but once found, the solution appears obvious and is easy to communicate to friends. The set of problems which have a fast verification algorithm as described above is

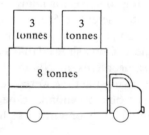

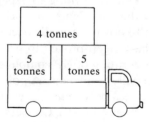

Figure 3.16   A solution to the bin-packing example of Fig. 3.13.

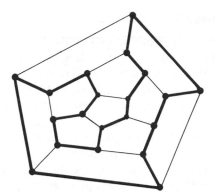

Figure 3.17   A solution to the Hamiltonian cycle example of Fig. 3.15.

called NP. (The name NP derives from a more precise mathematical definition of the set.)

Notice that all feasible problems are certainly in NP, since for feasible
problems it is not only possible to *verify* in polynomial time that a solution is
correct, but it is possible in polynomial time to *find* the solution in the first
place. What makes the set NP interesting is that, as well as containing all the
feasible problems, it contains many of the open problems which different
disciplines have been trying to solve for many years.

In 1971 the computer scientist Stephen Cook discovered a most
remarkable fact concerning many open problems in NP. Although we shall
not reproduce his proof here, Cook showed that a number of open problems
were among the *hardest* problems in NP in the following sense. If an
algorithm which runs in polynomial time were ever found for any one of the
problems, then there would be a polynomial time algorithm for *every* problem in NP. Any problem which is one of these hardest problems in NP is
called *NP-complete*.

Following Cook, Richard Karp and other computer scientists have
proved that the bin-packing, travelling salesperson, Hamiltonian cycle,
time-tabling and many other problems are each NP-complete. There are
literally thousands of well-known, naturally occurring and practically interesting problems which have been proved to be NP-complete.

It follows from the definition of NP-complete that all the NP-complete
problems are computationally equivalent. A polynomial time algorithm for
any one of them would give a polynomial time algorithm for all the others
(and indeed for all the problems in NP). Conversely, if there is any problem
in NP which is ever proved infeasible, it will be an NP-complete problem. Of
course, it will then follow that all the NP-complete problems are infeasible.

It is widely believed that the NP-complete problems are infeasible. Although this has not yet been proved, it does seem believable for the following reasons. Many different "experts" have attempted to find polynomial algorithms for NP-complete problems in their area of specialization. All have failed. However, this may be a poor argument, since many experts have attempted to prove NP-complete problems infeasible, and they have failed too!

Another reason for believing that NP-complete problems are infeasible is that we experience the same dichotomy in real life between problems which are easy to solve and those which are hard to solve but whose solution appears obvious once it is found. For example, many people who were lost without water would have great difficulty seeing how to get water even if green leaves and a plastic sheet were at hand. However, if they were shown the old scouting solution of Fig. 3.18 they would have no difficulty in

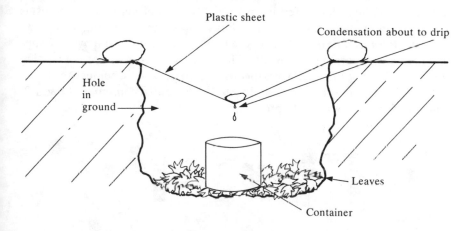

Figure 3.18   Old scouting trick for collecting water by condensation.

recognizing its utility. If there were an easy method of finding solutions to problems in NP, then the method would be most useful for human survival, which has depended mainly on our brains and our problem-solving ability. We might wonder why, if such a method existed, evolution had not built it into our brains.

One practical benefit of NP-completeness is that if one is having difficulty finding a polynomial time algorithm for a problem, then one can alternatively check if the problem is NP-complete. If so, one can reason "great experts could not solve my problem, so I probably can't either". Then one must seek a method of lowering one's sights.

Unfortunately, there are problems for which no fast algorithm is known, but neither does the problem appear so difficult that it has been proved NP-complete. An example is the primality problem, referred to in the previous section. No fast algorithm is available, nor is any ready excuse for not finding such an algorithm!

Summarizing, feasible problems have a fast algorithm for finding their solutions. Problems in NP may or may not have such an algorithm, but at least proposed solutions are easy to verify. NP-complete problems are the hardest problems in NP, and it is widely believed that they do not have fast algorithms.

3.2.6 Parallel Computers

Traditionally, complexity theory has concentrated upon sequential time and memory as the two resources of greatest importance. Now, with increasing awareness of the technical feasibility of highly parallel computers, interest is focussing on "parallel time" and number of processors as resources worthy of study. *Parallel time* is the time taken to execute an algorithm by a number of processors operating in unison. There are various ways of connecting processors so that they can work together. Two possible schemes are shown in Fig. 3.19. This may be contrasted with the sequential computer of Fig. 1.2, which includes only a single processor.

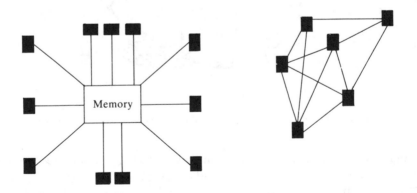

Figure 3.19   Two possible schemes for connecting many processors together (shaded boxes represent processors)

The parallel computers considered here have two distinguishing features. Firstly, they contain a vast number of processors, in the same way that modern computers contain a vast amount of memory. A parallel computer may contain one hundred thousand or one million processors, all simultaneously computing some portion of the problem at hand. Such machines are currently uneconomical to build, but it is believed that within a decade or two advances in technology will make them economically viable.

If the concept of one million parallel processors seems staggering, consider the memories of current computers. These have a comparable number of elements, and are manufactured from basic components which in different configurations could perform simple calculations rather than just passively storing information. The human brain, too, appears to have billions of active processing elements, all computing in parallel.

The second distinguishing feature of the parallel computers considered here is that they operate *synchronously*. In other words, the parallel processors are all synchronized with each other, performing their computations step by step in unison. Although machines can be built to operate asynchronously, synchronous machines are easier to design and build. They are also considerably easier to program, since the programmer need not worry about critical timing problems, or the complex task of communicating between machines at a point in time when the relationship between their computations is not known.

There are many different designs of parallel computers, in the same way as there are many different designs of sequential computers. Fortunately, there is a *parallel computation thesis*, analogous to the sequential time thesis and the Church–Turing thesis, which states that all parallel computer designs are closely related in their computational abilities. Thus in choosing a particular parallel computer design the main considerations are economic, or are related to ease of programming. More precisely, the parallel computation thesis states that, given the same number of processors, an algorithm running on one parallel computer can be simulated in about the same amount of time on any other parallel computer. Thus parallel computation can meaningfully be studied more or less independently of any particular parallel machine.

Another part of the parallel computation thesis relates parallel time to a resource which has long been studied on sequential computers: namely, the amount of memory used by an algorithm. Surprisingly, parallel time is roughly equivalent to amount of memory. Therefore, any problem which can be solved on a sequential machine using a small amount of memory can also be solved on a parallel machine in a small amount of time.

Of course, the speed-ups which are possible by using a parallel computer are not free. The price is investment in a more expensive machine comprising many processors. Parallel time and number of processors can often be traded for one another to achieve the desired balance of computational speed and available finance.

Some parallel algorithms which illustrate these points were presented in Section 2.10. A sequential machine requires time proportional to n to add together n numbers, whereas a parallel machine can perform the task in time proportional to $\log n$, but at a cost of n processors. Also presented was an algorithm for sorting n numbers with n^2 parallel processors running for time proportional to $\log n$. A slightly more complicated algorithm can achieve the same time using only $n \log n$ processors. The fastest sequential algorithms require time proportional to $n \log n$.

The problems of addition and multiplication of n digit numbers also have significant speed-ups on parallel machines, at the cost of using more hardware. Both problems can be computed in time proportional to $\log n$ on a parallel machine, but the best known sequential algorithms take time proportional to n and $n \log n \log \log n$ for the two problems respectively.

Another problem which has an impressive speed-up on a parallel machine is the *connectivity problem*. Given a road map showing n cities and the freeways which connect some of them, the problem is to determine whether or not every city can be reached from every other one without leaving a freeway. This problem can be solved in time proportional to n on a sequential computer. A parallel computer can solve the problem in time proportional to $(\log n)^2$, using n processors.

All the problems mentioned above can be computed extremely quickly on a parallel machine (in time proportional to $(\log n)^k$ for some constant k), while still using a feasible number of processors (n^c for some constant c). An interesting open question in the theory of parallel computers is whether or not every problem with a feasible sequential algorithm can be similarly speeded up. It is generally believed that there are *inherently sequential* problems which do not admit any significant speed-up on a parallel machine, but, so far, no problem has been *proved* inherently sequential (unless artificial restrictions are placed on parallel machines).

3.3 CORRECTNESS

In this section we turn to a major problem confronting all algorithm designers: the correctness of the algorithm. Important issues include the meaning of correctness, different types of correctness, and methods of increasing one's confidence that an algorithm is correct.

3.3.1 Bugs

It is an unfortunate fact that most computer programs in current use contain errors, or *bugs*. Even programs which have executed successfully for a number of years may contain bugs which would cause them to fail in certain circumstances. Indeed, a significant amount of programmer effort is deployed in fixing errors in such programs. The process of finding and correcting errors is referred to as *debugging*.

It is not surprising that computer programs are so error-prone. Algorithms can be complex objects. They require creativity to design, and they are often not easy to understand. It is essentially a human's lack of complete understanding of an algorithm that leads to major bugs in a computer program.

Methods of producing programs without bugs, or with fewer bugs, can be grouped into two categories: *testing* and *proving*. Testing a program consists of executing it on a particular set of data, called *test data*. The execution may be carried out on a computer, or by manually tracing through the program step by step in order to discover what results the program would output on the test data. The important feature of testing is that the effect of the program is discovered only for the particular chosen set of test data. (Recall Section 3.1.6 which showed that there is no algorithm to generate an adequate set of test data for an arbitrary program.) In contrast, proving a program correct means certifying its correctness on *all* permissible input data. Thus proving correctness involves saying something about a program's overall behavior, rather than about its behavior on a limited set of inputs.

Program testing has been the debugging technique most emphasized in the past, because testing can be carried out with less thought than proving. The lack of correctness proofs partly explains the proliferation of bugs in commercially available programs. The correct execution of a program on some input data is no guarantee of its correct execution on all permissible input data.

Even proving the correctness of a program does not leave one fully confident that no bugs are present, since it is possible to make a mistake in the proof! However, experience has shown that even short, informal proofs, such as those appearing in the remainder of this chapter, contribute significantly to one's confidence in a program's correctness.

It is possible to increase this confidence by making an informal proof increasingly more detailed and formal. Of course, the proof becomes correspondingly more tedious, longer and less palatable, but slowly one approaches a hundred percent confidence. Such a level of confidence may be important in particularly critical applications involving human life or health (e.g. monitoring patients in an intensive care unit), or perhaps involving the well-being of very costly machinery. Producing an extremely formal proof is an expensive exercise, and in practice some balance must be found between the level of detail of the proof, and the desired level of confidence in a program's correctness. For most applications, it appears that informal proofs provide an acceptable level of confidence without requiring an infeasible amount of programmer time.

An informal proof of correctness is nothing more than a representation of good understanding of the program at hand. It is therefore quite straightforward to produce the proof at the same time as designing the algorithm. Indeed, writing down the proof can in turn aid the design process by crystallizing some important point in the algorithm. Understanding is essential when designing an algorithm. A proof of correctness is just a representation of that understanding. Thus an algorithm design and a correctness proof can and should proceed hand in hand. Each provides feedback for the other, until eventually the design process yields a correct algorithm, and a correctness proof is written down as a by-product.

Much has been said over the years about *documentation*. Documentation means leaving a written record of what a program achieves, and how the program works. In a sense, good documentation is the same as writing down an informal proof of correctness. Another related concept is that of *desk-checking*. This term refers to reading carefully through one's program and understanding it, in order to check its correctness. This is yet another manifestation of an informal proof of correctness.

The key to producing a correct algorithm is for the algorithm designer to be able to "see" how the algorithm works. Desk-checking is the process of checking the algorithm by understanding how it works. A proof of correctness is a written version of this understanding. Documentation is the recording of the proof of correctness for future use, both for the algorithm designer and for others who might want to understand the program at a later date.

It is in fact meaningless to talk of an algorithm in isolation as being correct or incorrect. Correctness is meaningful only in relation to a set of beliefs regarding the purpose of the algorithm. Such beliefs are commonly called the *specifications* of the algorithm. An algorithm is correct with respect to its specifications if the algorithm produces the results specified for those input values defined by the specifications.

Discovering whether or not a program is correct with respect to its specifications is not a computable problem. The task is similar to the equivalence problem mentioned in Sections 3.1.4 and 3.1.5. It is for this reason that confidence in a program's correctness relies on the creative process of understanding the particular algorithm under consideration, rather than on any general mechanical method of churning out a demonstration of correctness.

There are a number of facets to a program's correctness, all of which are important to the final product. Firstly, it would be reassuring to know that whenever an algorithm terminates (or performs an output operation), the result produced is the one expected. This property is called *partial correctness*. Note that if an algorithm is partially correct, it may not terminate or produce a result in every circumstance. The only guarantee is that if ever a result is produced, that result is correct. Some examples of proofs of partial correctness can be found in Section 3.3.3.

The second important facet of a program's correctness is *termination*. Methods of proving that an algorithm terminates are discussed in Section 3.3.4. A program which always terminates, and which is partially correct, is called *totally correct*.

A third important property of programs is *feasibility*. Using the techniques of complexity theory described in Section 3.2, one may prove bounds on the amount of various resources consumed by an algorithm. Resource bounds are often an important facet of a program's correctness and may appear as part of its specifications (see Section 3.3.5).

3.3.2 Induction

Consider the following algorithm:

> **module** *exponentiate*(x)
> {Outputs 2^x assuming x is a non-negative integer}
> *set SUM equal to* 1
> **repeat** x *times*
>   *set SUM equal to SUM + SUM*
>   ***
> *output SUM*   (3.14)

Suppose the specifications for this algorithm are that it must output 2^x, where x is any non-negative integer. In order to prove the algorithm correct, it is essential to read it through until it is understood. In this simple case, it is sufficient to realize that when the position marked *** is reached for the nth time, SUM will equal 2^n. It is then straightforward to see that, provided the output statement is reached, 2^x will be output.

The previous paragraph is an adequate informal proof of the algorithm's correctness (actually we proved partial correctness, but it is trivial to see that the algorithm also terminates). In practice, one can use the yardstick that an informal proof is adequate if it would convince one's colleagues. Documentation should be added to help readers of the algorithm as follows.

> **module** *exponentiate*(x)
> {Outputs 2^x assuming x is a non-negative integer}
> *set SUM equal to* 1
> **repeat** x *times*
>   *set SUM equal to SUM + SUM*
>   {The nth time this point is reached, SUM will equal 2^n}
> *output SUM*   (3.15)

If even greater confidence in the correctness of the algorithm is desired, the proof can be made slightly more formal as follows.

(1)   The first time ∗∗∗ is reached, $SUM = 2$ (which equals 2^1)

(2)   Assume that the nth time ∗∗∗ is reached, $SUM = 2^n$. Then the $(n + 1)$th time, $SUM = 2^n + 2^n = 2^{n+1}$

(3)   Therefore for *every* n, the nth time ∗∗∗ is reached, $SUM = 2^n$

(4)   If the output statement is ever reached, there are two possibilities. Either the loop was never executed, in which case $x = 0$ and so the initial value of SUM was never changed. Therefore $SUM = 1$ (which equals 2^0). Or the loop was executed, in which case ∗∗∗ was reached x times. So $SUM = 2^x$.

(5)   In either case, if the output statement is reached, 2^x will be output.

This proof illustrates a technique which is used time and again in proofs of correctness: *induction*. Induction is useful when it is desired to prove that some statement is true in every case under consideration. The idea is to prove the statement for a small case, and then show that whenever the statement is true for a particular case, it is also true for the next larger case. It follows that the statement is true in every case.

For example, consider steps (1)–(3) of the proof above. The intention is to prove statement (3), namely that for every n, when ∗∗∗ is reached for the nth time, SUM will equal 2^n. Step (1) shows that the statement is true when $n = 1$. Step (2) shows that if the statement is true for any particular value of n, then it is also true for $n + 1$. Combining (1) and (2), it follows that the statement is true for $n = 2$, and then $n = 3$, and then $n = 4$, and so on. Thus we have proved that statement (3) is true for every value of $n \geqslant 1$.

In a proof by induction, the statement to be proved (step (3) in the example above) is called the *inductive hypothesis*. Step (1) is called the *basis*, because it proves the starting, or base, case. Step (2) is called the *inductive step*. It is the inductive step which allows one to step forward from the basis to progressively larger cases.

A neat method of setting out a proof by induction is the following.

Inductive hypothesis: The nth time ∗∗∗ is reached, $SUM = 2^n$

Basis: When $n = 1$, SUM is set to $1 + 1$ which equals 2^1

Inductive Step: Assume the inductive hypothesis is true for a particular value of n. The $(n + 1)$th time ∗∗∗ is reached, SUM is set equal to the previous value of SUM added to itself. By the inductive hypothesis, the previous value of SUM is 2^n. Therefore the new value is $2^n + 2^n = 2^{n+1}$. So the inductive hypothesis also holds for $n + 1$.

Conclusion: From the basis and the inductive step it follows that the inductive hypothesis holds for every value of $n \geqslant 1$.

Consider Euclid's greatest common divisor (GCD) algorithm (algorithm 2.14), reproduced below.

module $Euclid(x,y)$
{Outputs the greatest common divisor of the non-negative integers
x and y}
while $y \neq 0$ **do**
  calculate remainder of x/y
  set x equal to y
  set y equal to remainder
  ***
output x   (3.16)

The specifications are: when the inputs x and y are non-negative integers, the algorithm outputs their greatest common divisor, $GCD(x,y)$. In order to prove that the algorithm is correct (with respect to the specifications), one must first understand the algorithm.

The Euclidean algorithm is a reminder that understanding an algorithm is by no means always a trivial task. However, the algorithm must be understood in order to have reasonable confidence that it is correct. No amount of testing can replace this fundamental prerequisite. But once the algorithm is understood, then an informal proof of correctness is immediately available.

A key fact that Euclid needed to reveal in order for his algorithm to be understood is that at the place marked ***, the greatest common divisor of x and y is always equal to g, the GCD of the original x and y which were input. This fact can be proved by induction as follows.

Inductive hypothesis: Whenever *** is reached, $GCD(x,y) = g$
Basis: Originally, $x = gx'$ and $y = gy'$ for two numbers x' and y' which have no common factors. Now suppose $x = my + r$, so that r is the remainder when x is divided by y. Then $gx' = mgy' + r$, so $r = g(x' - my')$ and thus r must have g as a factor. The equation $gx' = mgy' + r$ also implies that r/g cannot have any factor in common with y', or else x' would have the same factor, which would contradict the fact that x' and y' have no common factors. Thus y and r have g as their greatest common factor. Therefore, $GCD(x,y)$ the first time *** is reached equals $GCD(y$, remainder of $x/y) = GCD(y,r) = g$.
Inductive step: The paragraph above also shows that the $(n + 1)$th time *** is reached, $GCD(x,y)$ will equal the GCD of the values of x and y at the nth time *** is reached. That number is g if one assumes that the inductive hypothesis holds for n. Therefore the $(n + 1)$the time *** is reached

$GCD(x,y)$ is also equal to g. Therefore the inductive hypothesis also holds for $n + 1$.

Conclusion: The inductive hypothesis holds for every value of $n \geqslant 1$, i.e. whenever *** is reached.

The proof by induction helps us understand the effect of the algorithm every time *** is reached. It is not immediately clear that the output statement will ever be reached, but if so, we know that $GCD(x,y) = g$ at that point, and that $y = 0$. Therefore $x = g$ and the program will output g as required.

The proof above demonstrates the partial correctness of the Euclidean algorithm. If the output statement is reached, the algorithm will produce the correct result. The termination and therefore total correctness of the algorithm will be proved in Section 3.3.4.

We have stressed the importance of understanding an algorithm in order to be able to certify it correct. It might be concluded that algorithms which are difficult to understand might be difficult to prove correct, and therefore that correctness proofs are not practical. A more appropriate conclusion, however, is that the correctness proof should be carried out by the algorithm designer during the design process. At that time the algorithm designer ought to have an excellent understanding of the algorithm. This is the time to certify correctness, and to document the proof by way of comments in the program. The documentation will then aid future readers to understand the program.

The documented Euclidean algorithm would appear as

module *Euclid*(x,y)
{Outputs the greatest common divisor of the non-negative integers
x and y}
while $y \neq 0$ **do**
  calculate remainder of x/y
  set x equal to y
  set y equal to remainder
  {at this point $GCD(x,y)$ is equal to
  the GCD of the original inputs, because . . .}
output x (3.17)

Proof by induction can also be used to prove the correctness of recursive algorithms. Consider the following easy example (algorithm 2.40, reproduced below) which outputs all the nodes in a binary tree in left to right order. Recall that a binary tree may have a root, a left subtree and a right subtree. The left and right subtrees are themselves trees, and they may be empty (i.e. contain no nodes).

module *outputtree(T)*
{Outputs all the nodes of binary tree T in left to right order}
if T *is not empty*
  then *outputtree(left subtree of T)*
    output root of T
    outputtree(right subtree of T)   (3.18)

Inductive hypothesis: The algorithm outputs all the nodes in the tree T in left to right order.

Basis: If T contains zero nodes, then it is empty and the algorithm does nothing. It is true to say that all the nodes in the tree are output in the correct order, since there aren't any!

Inductive step: Suppose T has n nodes and that the inductive hypothesis holds for all trees with fewer than n nodes. The left subtree is a tree with fewer than n nodes (since it does not contain the root), and so by the inductive hypothesis all its nodes are output in left to right order. The algorithm then outputs the root. Finally, applying the inductive hypothesis again, all the nodes of the right subtree are output in left to right order. Thus all the nodes in the tree T are output in the correct order, proving that the inductive hypothesis also holds for trees with n nodes.

Conclusion: The inductive hypothesis holds for any binary tree.

    This proof of correctness is so simple that in practice one would not write it down. In this case, an adequate informal proof of correctness just consists of reading through the algorithm and understanding it.

    A more complicated example of induction occurs with McCarthy's so called 91 algorithm:

module $f(x)$
{If $x > 100$ the result is $x - 10$, otherwise it is 91}
if $x > 100$
  then result is $x - 10$
  else result is $f(f(x + 11))$ (3.19)

Inductive hypothesis: If $x > 100$ the result is $x - 10$, otherwise it is 91.

Basis: If $x > 100$, clearly the answer is $x - 10$. If $x = 100$, the answer is $f(f(111)) = f(101) = 91$.

Inductive step: Suppose $x < 100$ and assume the inductive hypothesis holds for all numbers greater than x. There are two cases:

(a) if $x + 11 > 100$ then $f(x) = f(f(x + 11)) = f(x + 1)$ which equals 91 by the inductive hypothesis. (Recall that we are assuming the inductive hypothesis holds for all numbers greater than x, and $x + 1 > x$.)

(b)   if $x + 11 \leq 100$ then $f(x) = f(f(x + 11)) = f(91)$ by the inductive hypothesis (which applies because $x + 11 > x$). Since $91 > x$, we can apply the inductive hypothesis again, giving $f(91) = 91$.

Therefore the inductive hypothesis holds for x as well.

Conclusion: The inductive hypothesis holds for any value of x.

This proof by induction has shown that whenever $x \leq 100$, McCarthy's algorithm outputs 91. Note that the induction proceeded in reverse. The basis was at $x = 100$, while the induction step proved correctness for progressively smaller values of the input.

3.3.3   Assertions

The previous section described a useful proof method, and demonstrated correctness proofs for some short algorithms. These ideas can be extended to prove correctness of large algorithms in a practical manner which does not consume too much programmer effort.

The major obstacle to proofs of correctness of larger programs is that it is difficult for a human to visualize the entire operation of a large algorithm at one time. In other words, the understanding of the algorithm which is so essential to a correctness proof cannot be brought to bear simultaneously on all parts of a large algorithm. Fortunately, this obstacle has already been met in another setting and a remedy proposed. The same problem arises in the *design* of large algorithms. The remedy is modularization (recall Section 2.8). The task at hand is divided into more or less independent pieces, or *modules*, which can be designed separately. The independence of the modules, sometimes referred to as *clean interfaces* between modules, is of prime importance. If the interaction between modules were too complex, then the ability to design them in isolation would be lost.

Modularization similarly aids program certification. As each module is designed, an informal proof of correctness is simultaneously produced. The proof certifies that the module matches its specifications, which describe the inputs provided to the module, and the outputs which are expected.

Just as one tries to design a module independently of the modules which it calls (i.e. "lower level" modules), one tries to make its proof of correctness independent of the correctness proofs of the lower level modules. During the design it is not necessary to understand *how* the lower level modules operate. The only requirement is the specifications, which describe *what* the modules do. Similarly, the only requirement for the correctness proof of the original module is confidence that the lower level modules meet their specifications.

The specifications of any module consist of two parts. The first is a specification of the range of *inputs* upon which the module is expected to operate. For example, Euclid's *GCD* algorithm (Section 3.3.2) was required to work only for non-negative integers x and y. The second part is a specification of the desired *effect* of the module. For example, it must be stated that the module computes the *GCD* of its inputs, or that it reserves an airline seat, or whatever. The two main parts of a module's specifications are known as *pre-conditions* and *post-conditions* respectively. Essentially, the pre-conditions describe the state of the computation before the module is executed, and the post-conditions give the state afterwards. Pre- and post-conditions are also known as *assertions*, since they assert the truth of some condition.

Complicated pieces of an algorithm are sometimes too interrelated and intertwined to allow them to be modularized. Nevertheless, they must be designed, understood and proved correct. In such cases, assertions can be placed in the middle of a piece of the algorithm, in order to document the state of the computation at that point. Indeed, a number of examples of this practice were presented in Section 3.3.2. In both the *exponentiate* algorithm and in Euclid's algorithm assertions were placed at the points marked ∗∗∗. Such an assertion represents an understanding of the algorithm as seen from that point. It provides a bridge in understanding between the input assertion (pre-condition) and the output assertion (post-condition).

The more complex a single module is, the more assertions will be required in order to bridge the gap between the input and output assertions of the module. In the extreme, a very complex module is difficult to understand and difficult to prove correct. It will probably be incorrectly designed, and will contain bugs.

In addition to the pre- and post-conditions, a complex algorithm should contain assertions at key points. The points chosen should be logically related to the functioning of the algorithm. A good choice might be just before or just after a piece of program which performs some well-defined task. In Euclid's algorithm, for example, the assertion was placed just after a sequence of statements which computed two new values of x and y with an important and easily stated property.

In order to properly bridge the gap between the pre- and post-conditions, it is necessary to have a good understanding of how each assertion can be reached from nearby assertions. In other words, the assertions should be so placed that it is easy to understand the flow of control from one assertion to the next. In practice, this usually means placing at least one assertion inside each loop of the program.

Consider the following sketch of an algorithm:

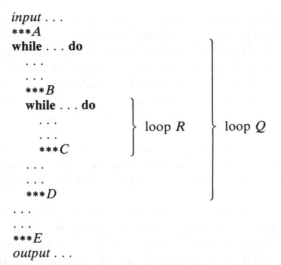

```
input . . .
***A
while . . . do
  . . .
  . . .
  ***B
  while . . . do
    . . .          ⎫
    . . .          ⎬ loop R    ⎫
    ***C           ⎭           ⎬ loop Q
  . . .                        ⎪
  . . .                        ⎪
  ***D                         ⎭
. . .
. . .
***E
output . . .
```

The exact placement of the assertions (labelled ***A through ***E)
depends upon the key points of understanding of the algorithm. The placement shown is fairly typical, and follows the guideline that each loop contains at least one assertion.

With the placement as shown, it is necessary to prove that if assertion A
is true, and the statements between A and B are executed, then B is true.
Similarly, from B to C, C to C (once around loop R), C to D, D to B (once
around loop Q), D to E, A to E (if loop Q is never entered), and B to D (if
loop R is never entered). It then follows that if the pre-condition A is true
initially, and the output statement is ever reached, then the post-condition E
will be true at that point. This use of assertions is a convenient way of proving
partial correctness.

An example of an algorithm with two nested loops occurs in the following problem. There is a box full of various multicolored balls. It is desired to
know the maximum number of balls which have a matching color. The
following algorithm suffices.

```
module balls
{Calculates the maximum number of balls which have a
  matching color}
set max to 0
repeat for each color                              ⎫
  set count to 0                                   ⎪
  repeat for each ball              ⎫              ⎬ loop Q
    if the ball has that color      ⎬ loop R       ⎪
      then add 1 to count           ⎭              ⎪
  if count > max                                   ⎪
    then set max equal to count                    ⎭
output max                                              (3.20)
```

In order to prove this algorithm correct, it is necessary to read through and understand it. It appears that when the inner loop R has been executed n consecutive times, *count* will equal the number of balls out of the first n balls which have the given color. When the loop is finished, *count* will be the total number of balls with the given color. When the outer loop Q has been executed m times, *max* will be equal to the maximum number of balls which have the same color, out of the first m colors.

Once this type of understanding has been achieved, the corresponding assertions can be inserted in the form of English comments:

module *balls*
{Calculates the maximum number of balls which have a
  matching color}
{(A) A number of multicolored balls are given as input}
set max to 0
repeat *for each color*
  set count to 0
  repeat *for each ball*
    if *the ball has that color*
      then *add* 1 *to count*
        {(B) When this point has been reached n consecutive times,
          count will equal the number of balls, out of the first n balls,
          which have the given color}
  {(C) *count* now equals the total number of balls with the given color}
  if *count* > *max*
    then *set max equal to count*
  {(D) When this point has been reached m times, *max* will equal the
    maximum number of balls which have the same color, out of the first
    m colors}
{(E) *max* now equals the maximum number of balls which have the
  same color}
output max   (3.21)

To prove the program correct, we may assume the truth of the pre-condition A and try to prove the post-condition E. Our assertions B, C and D may be used as stepping stones.

Now B may be reached after A, or after D. It is easy to see that in either case, B is correct. This may be proved by induction if a more formal proof is required.

The assertion C is reached if and when the inner loop terminates. Since B is true, C is obviously true. It is also possible that the inner loop is never executed (if there are no balls), in which case control passes from A to C. It is straightforward to check that C is true in this case as well.

D can be proved from the truth of C and knowledge of the previous value of *max*. If $m = 1$, the previous value of *max* must be ascertained by studying the program and noting that initially *max* was set to zero. If $m > 1$, the previous value of *max* is given by D itself. Thus D is proved by induction. This induction is easy enough to see in one's head, or it can be written down if desired.

Finally, the post-condition E can be reached from D if the outer loop terminates. Clearly the truth of E follows. Alternatively, E could be reached from A if the outer loop was never executed. In this case, there are no colors, and E is true.

We have proved that if A is true and E is ever reached, then E is true. Thus the algorithm is partially correct (in fact it is not difficult to show that the algorithm is also totally correct). For an algorithm such as this an adequate informal proof would consist of the assertions, coupled with a careful reading of the algorithm to assure oneself that each assertion follows from its neighbors in the way described above.

Only a more formal proof would actually require all the steps to be written down, as we have done above. Remember that the aim of correctness proofs is to increase one's confidence in an algorithm's correctness. Complete confidence of correctness is infeasible. The golden rule remains: the best proof is the clearest and shortest proof which is adequate to convince one's colleagues.

3.3.4   Termination

A proof of partial correctness gives reasonable confidence in the results produced by an algorithm. Provided a result is output, we can be reasonably confident that it will be correct. However, as indicated in Section 3.3.1, a proof of partial correctness does not guarantee that a result *is* output: if one wants such a guarantee one needs a proof of *total* correctness. In other words, one must also prove that the algorithm terminates, or reaches its output statement.

Recall algorithm 3.3 for testing the truth of Fermat's last theorem:

module *Fermat*(n)
{Tests Fermat's last theorem on input n}
repeat *for* $a = 1,2,3, \ldots$ {for ever}
  repeat *for* $b = 1,2,3, \ldots, a$
    repeat *for* $c = 2,3,4, \ldots, a+b$
    if $a^n + b^n = c^n$
      then *output a,b,c and n, and halt*   (3.22)

This algorithm is easy to prove partially correct, since if anything is ever output for $n > 2$ it will obviously be a counter-example to Fermat's last theorem.

However, proving total correctness in this case seems considerably more difficult. Indeed, no proof of termination of this algorithm is known at the present time. As with proofs of partial correctness, creativity is required to determine whether or not an algorithm halts. We know from Section 3.1.3 that there is no mechanical method of deciding the issue.

A fundamental technique for understanding why a loop must terminate (or for proving that the loop terminates, which amounts to the same thing), is to observe some value which *decreases significantly* (or alternatively which increases significantly) every time the loop is executed.

Consider Euclid's *GCD* algorithm once again.

> **module** *Euclid(x,y)*
> {Outputs the greatest common divisor of the non-negative integers x
> and y}
> **while** $y \neq 0$ **do**
> *calculate remainder of* x/y
> *set x equal to y*
> *set y equal to remainder*
> {at this point $GCD(x,y)$ equals the GCD of the original inputs}
> *output x*   (3.23)

Partial correctness of this algorithm was proved in Section 3.3.2, but that proof gave no indication that the algorithm would terminate. The proof showed only that $GCD(x,y)$ remained constant, so that if the output statement is ever reached, the correct result is produced. However, the same is true of the following algorithm, which clearly never terminates.

> **module** *funnyEuclid(x,y)*
> {Does nothing, and never terminates}
> **while** $y \neq 0$ **do**
> *do nothing*
> {at this point $GCD(x,y)$ equals the GCD of the original inputs}
> *output x*   (3.24)

Therefore, there must be some sense in which the loop of Euclid's algorithm makes significant progress. In fact, y decreases by a least 1 each time around the loop. This is true because y is set equal to the remainder of something divided by y. The remainder is a number between zero and $y - 1$. Thus y is set equal to a value between zero and $y - 1$, and therefore y eventually becomes zero and the loop terminates.

In general, in order to prove that a loop makes progress, one can show that the state of the computation steadily changes towards some goal each time around the loop. What actually is changing, the direction in which it is changing, and the goal towards which it is heading depend on one's understanding of the algorithm at hand.

This point is illustrated by a function devised by Ackermann:

module $A(x,y)$
{Ackermann's function $A(x,y)$ has two inputs x and y which must be non-negative integers}
if $x = 0$
   then answer is $y + 1$
   else if $y = 0$
       then answer is $A(x-1,1)$
       else answer is $A(x-1,A(x,y-1))$ (3.25)

The interested reader might like to try to understand this algorithm. It is not an easy task. Try tracing the execution of $A(2,2)$ or $A(3,1)$.

For the purpose of this discussion, we need only understand enough about the algorithm to see that it terminates for any non-negative integers x and y. There is no explicit loop, but we need to worry whether there is an infinite loop of recursive calls.

Our aim is to find something which is steadily decreasing, because when x is zero, no recursive call is made. Note that on two of the recursive calls, x is decreased by 1, so progress is being made. On the remaining recursive call, x is unchanged but y is decreased by 1. This represents progress too, albeit slow progress, because when y eventually reaches zero the recursive call $A(x-1,1)$ causes x to be decreased. Thus all three recursive calls either immediately decrease x, or cause x to be decreased eventually. Either way, the algorithm steadily grinds towards its terminating condition, $x = 0$.

An easier recursive algorithm is the tree outputting algorithm 3.18.

module *outputtree(T)*
{Outputs all the nodes of binary tree T in left to right order}
if *T is not empty*
   then *outputtree(left subtree of T)*
      output root of T
      outputtree(right subtree of T)   (3.26)

To see that this algorithm terminates, note that the size of the tree decreases by at least one on every recursive call (since the subtree of a tree does not contain the root of the tree). Thus progress is made on every recursive call, and the terminating condition, which checks for a tree of size zero, must always be reached.

Proofs of termination are often straightforward, provided that one understands the algorithm. Here is an algorithm which appears simple, but which no-one yet understands.

> **module** *tricky(x)*
> {This algorithm expects one input *x* which is a positive integer}
> **while** $x > 1$ **do**
>   **if** *x is even*
>   **then** *set x to x/2*
>   **else** *set x to $3x + 1$*   (3.27)

Tracing the execution of this algorithm shows that it terminates for many values of *x*. However, no-one can yet see whether or not it terminates in every case.

3.3.5   Resource Bounds

As indicated in Section 3.3.1, the partial and total correctness of an algorithm may not be the only ways in which it must satisfy its specifications. One further requirement concerns the resources used by the algorithm. A proper understanding of an algorithm should include an understanding of whether or not the algorithm can feasibly be executed within the environment for which it is intended.

In Section 3.2.2 we described a technique for proving resource bounds for algorithms developed by the divide and conquer approach. This is the technique of recurrence relations. For the matrix multiplication algorithm, for example, we obtained a recurrence relation expressing the time required to multiply $n \times n$ matrices in terms of the time needed to multiply $n/2 \times n/2$ matrices. The relation is

$$T(n) = 7T(n/2) + cn, \text{ and } T(1) = k$$

The solution is

$$T(n) = (2c/5 + k)n^{\log 7} - 2cn/5$$

which can be proved by induction as follows.

Inductive hypothesis: The solution is $T(n) = (2c/5 + k)n^{\log 7} - 2cn/5$
Basis: When $n = 1$, $T(1) = (2c/5 + k) - 2c/5 = k$, as expected.
Inductive step: Assume the inductive hypothesis holds for a particular n.
  Then from the recurrence relation,
  $$T(2n) = 7T(n) + 2cn$$
  Now by the inductive hypothesis
  $$\begin{aligned} T(2n) &= 7((2c/5 + k)n^{\log 7} - 2cn/5) + 2cn \\ &= 7(2c/5 + k)n^{\log 7} - 4cn/5 \\ &= (2c/5 + k)(2n)^{\log 7} - 2c(2n)/5 \end{aligned}$$

Therefore the inductive hypothesis holds for $2n$ as well.

Conclusion: The inductive hypothesis holds for $n = 1,2,4,8, \ldots$

Note that we have proved something about the execution time $T(n)$ only for $n = 1, n = 2, n = 4, n = 8$, and so on. In other words, n must be a power of 2. This is reasonable, since our particular algorithm was defined only for matrices whose size is a power of 2. Some modifications to the algorithm, and the proof of correctness, are required if n may be any positive integer.

In general, proof by induction and the judicious use of assertions are useful methods of proving resource bounds—as indeed they are for proving other aspects of correctness. As before, it is the understanding of the algorithm which is critical. From a good understanding, an informal proof will automatically follow.

For example, it is possible to show that Euclid's *GCD* algorithm requires only time proportional to the logarithm of its inputs (i.e. proportional to the lengths of x and y when these numbers are written as a sequence of decimal or binary digits). To see this, we need an even greater understanding of the algorithm than we needed for the proof of partial correctness (Section 3.3.2) and the proof of total correctness (Section 3.3.4). As before, let $x = my + r$, so that r is the remainder of x/y. If $x \geqslant y$ then $m \geqslant 1$, and so $y + r \leqslant x$. Since $r < y$ it follows that $r + r < x$, and thus $r < x/2$. Now on any two consecutive executions of the loop, y is set equal to the remainder (which is less than $x/2$) and then x is set equal to y. Therefore the key observation is that every second time around the loop x will be at least halved.

The argument in the previous paragraph assumes that $x \geqslant y$. This may not be true initially, but must hold after at most one execution of the loop. Since $y > r$ and x is set to y and y is set to r, it is clear that $x > y$ after any execution of the loop. (Note that this argument holds for the first execution as well. In particular, if $x < y$ then the effect of the loop is to exchange the values of x and y.) The appropriate assertions can now be added to the algorithm:

> **module** *Euclid*(x,y)
> {Outputs the greatest common divisor of the non-negative integers x and y}
> **while** $y \neq 0$ **do**
>   *calculate remainder of* x/y
>   {When this point *** has been reached $2n + 1$ times,
>   the remainder cannot exceed the largest original input divided by 2^n}
>   *set x to y*
>   *set y to remainder*
>   {whenever this point is reached, $x > y$}
> *output x*   (3.28)

Proofs of both assertions were sketched above. We conclude this section with a more detailed proof of the first assertion. Let w be equal to the largest original input (i.e. the larger of the original values of x and y).

Inductive hypothesis: For every $n \geq 0$, if the point marked *** is reached $2n + 1$ times, then the remainder is less then $w/2^n$.

Basis: Let $n = 0$. The first time *** is reached, the remainder is less than y and so is certainly less than w.

Inductive step: Assume the inductive hypothesis is true for a particular value of n. If *** is reached $2n + 3$ times, $x > y$ by the second assertion. So by an argument given above, the remainder $r < x/2$. Therefore r is less than half of what the remainder was when *** was reached for the $(2n + 1)$th time. By the inductive hypothesis, that remainder was less than $w/2^n$. So r is less than $w/2^{n+1}$.

Conclusion: The inductive hypothesis holds for every value of $n \geq 0$.

It follows that if the loop in Euclid's *GCD* algorithm is executed $2 \log w + 1$ times, the remainder will be less than $w/2^{\log w} = w/w = 1$. Since the remainder is a non-negative integer it must be equal to zero and so the loop will not be executed again. Thus the execution time is no worse than proportional to the logarithm of the largest input.

EXERCISES

1   As evidence for the Church–Turing thesis:
   (a)   Show that it is possible to perform addition even if "add 1" is the only arithmetic operation available to an algorithm designer (*Hint*:   use iteration);
   (b)   Repeat (a) for subtraction;
   (c)   Show that it is possible to transform any algorithm using recursion into an algorithm without recursion (*Hint*:   use iteration and the *stack* data structure of Section 2.11).

2   Do you believe the Church–Turing thesis? Discuss.

3   Consider the execution of algorithm 3.3 when $n = 2$ (i.e. Fermat (2)). What is output by the algorithm? If the algorithm continued executing instead of halting, what would be output next?

4   Explain to a friend why the halting problem is non-computable. Has this helped you to understand the proof?

5   Show that any proposed algorithm for the halting problem must fail on infinitely many inputs. (*Hint*:   consider the use of a finite look-up table.)

6   Design an algorithm which finds where any proposed algorithm for the halting problem fails. (*Hint*:   given the text of any proposed *halttester*, your algorithm should construct the text of the corresponding algorithm called *funny*.)

7   Consider the problem of deciding whether the set of possible outputs of an algorithm is finite or infinite. Prove that this problem is not computable.

8   Show that if a problem (which requires only a "YES" or "NO" answer) has a proof system, then it is partially computable. (*Hint*:   consider an algorithm which generates all the possible proofs of the proof system and then make it halt at the appropriate time.)

9   The *complement* of a problem can be obtained by exchanging the "YES" and "NO" answers. Prove that if both a problem and its complement are partially computable, then they are also computable. (*Hint*:   interleave the executions of the two algorithms).

10   Using Exercise 3.9, write down as much as you know about the complement of the halting problem.

11   Write a program which prints its own text using a real programming language. Figure 3.4 can be used as a guide.

12   Use the recursion theorem to show that there are two distinct algorithms which print each other. Start by designing an algorithm which constructs the text of a program to print an arbitrary sequence of characters *D*, and then outputs the text which it constructed.

13   How much time will algorithm 2.10 use in the worst case as a function of the size of its input?

14   How much time will algorithm 2.41 use in the worst case as a function of the size of its input? How much time will it use in the best case? What do you think will happen in the average case?

15   Write a recursive module which represents the integer multiplication algorithm of Fig. 3.8.

16   Write a recursive module which represents the matrix multiplication algorithm of Fig. 3.12.

17   Prove by induction that
  (a) $T(n) = cn\log n + kn$ is the solution to the recurrence relation resulting from algorithm 3.12.
  (b) $T(n) = (2c + k)n^{\log 3} - 2cn$ is the solution to the recurrence relation resulting from the integer multiplication algorithm of Fig. 3.8.

18   Show that the following problems are in the set NP:
  (a)   travelling salesperson;
  (b)   time-tabling;
  (c)   non-primality (*Hint*:   every number which is not prime has factors).

19   Discuss the claim that "if there were an easy method of finding solutions to problems in NP, then the method would be most useful for human survival."

20 Consider the following proposed algorithm for the bin-packing problem. Arrange the trucks in a circle, and moving around the circle repeatedly load the largest remaining crate onto the next truck. Find an example in which this algorithm fails.

21 Design an algorithm for the bin-packing problem which always works correctly. Show that your algorithm uses exponential time in the worst case.

22 Sketch the fastest parallel algorithms you can think of for the following tasks:
(a) addition of two n-digit numbers;
(b) multiplication of two n-digit numbers;
(c) the connectivity problem.
Write down the amount of time and the number of processors used by your algorithms.

23 Investigate the behavior of *tricky(x)*—algorithm 3.27—for different values of x.

24 Prove the correctness of some of the algorithms in Chapter 2 (e.g. algorithm 2.11 or algorithm 2.41).

25 Use induction to prove the following properties of the Towers of Hanoi algorithm (2.30):
(a) no larger disk is ever placed on top of a smaller one
(b) the number of disks moved is $2^N - 1$.

BIBLIOGRAPHY

More detailed treatments of computability may be found in

R. Bird, *Programs and Machines: An Introduction to the Theory of Computation*, Wiley, London, 1976.

J. M. Brady, *The Theory of Computer Science: A Programming Approach*, Chapman and Hall, London, 1977.

K. L. Clark, and D. F. Cowell, *Programs, Machines, and Computation*, McGraw-Hill, London, 1976.

N. J. Cutland, *Computability: An Introduction to Recursive Function Theory*, Cambridge University Press, Cambridge, 1980.

M. Davis (ed.), *The Undecidable*, Raven, N.Y., 1965.

H. R. Lewis and C. H. Papadimitriou, *Elements of the Theory of Computation*, Prentice-Hall, N.J., 1981.

M. Machtey and P. Young, *An Introduction to the General Theory of Algorithms*, North-Holland, N.Y., 1978.

M. L. Minsky, *Computation: Finite and Infinite Machines*, Prentice-Hall, N.J., 1967.

The complexity of algorithms is discussed in

A. V. Aho, J. E. Hopcroft and J. D. Ullman, *The Design and Analysis of Computer Algorithms*, Addison-Wesley, Massachusetts, 1974.

S. Baase, *Computer Algorithms: Introduction to Design and Analysis*, Addison-Wesley, Massachusetts, 1978.

M. R. Garey and D. S. Johnson, *Computers and Intractability: A Guide to the Theory of NP-Completeness*, Freeman, 1979.

S. E. Goodman and S. T. Hedetniemi, *Introduction to the Design and Analysis of Algorithms*, McGraw-Hill, N.Y., 1977.

D. E. Knuth, *The Art of Computer Programming*, Vols. 1–3, Addison-Wesley, Massachusetts.

H. R. Lewis and C. H. Papadimitriou (as above)

M. Machtey and P. Young (as above)

Correctness proofs of algorithms are treated in

S. Alagić and M. A. Arbib, *The Design of Well-Structured and Correct Programs*, Springer-Verlag, N.Y., 1978.

R. Bird (as above)

J. M. Brady (as above)

E. W. Dijkstra, *A Discipline of Programming*, Prentice-Hall, N.J., 1976.

Z. Manna, *Mathematical Theory of Computation*, McGraw-Hill, N.Y., 1974.

4   THE EXECUTION OF ALGORITHMS: COMPUTER ARCHITECTURE

In the previous chapters, we have investigated the design and the theory of algorithms. For an algorithm to be useful, there must be available a *processor* which can read, understand, and execute the instructions comprising the algorithm. A *computer* is a general purpose processor which can execute a large range of different types of algorithms. This chapter discusses the design of computers.

4.1   THE STRUCTURE OF COMPUTERS

Recall from Chapter 1 (see Fig. 1.2) that a computer consists of a central processing unit (CPU), a memory, and some input and output devices. The *memory* is used to hold the program currently being executed, as well as any data associated with it. The *CPU* is that part of the computer which is responsible for executing the operations specified by the program. The *input* and *output devices* are provided for communication between the computer and the outside world.

After designing algorithms in the way we have discussed in Chapter 2, computer programmers must write them in a *programming language* so that they can be executed by the computer. Unfortunately, high level programming languages, while convenient for human use, are unsuitable for direct execution by computers because the construction cost of such computers turns out to be prohibitive. Computer manufacturers have therefore built computers to execute programs which are written in far simpler languages called *machine languages*. It follows that some mechanism must be provided for the translation of high level programming languages into machine languages. The translation process is described in Chapter 5, whilst this chapter discusses the design of computers capable of executing programs written in a machine language.

Figure 4.22 gives a simple example of a machine language. The details of that language are explained in Section 4.5.1. For the moment, it will suffice to look briefly at the various types of instruction in order to get a feel for machine languages.

The LOAD and STORE instructions are typical instructions for transferring information to and fro between the memory and the CPU. ADD, SUBTRACT, MULTIPLY and DIVIDE instruct the CPU to perform the appropriate arithmetic operation. The four JUMP instructions, together with RETURN, are used to control the order in which the instructions comprising a program are executed.

In the early days of computing, computers were built which could execute machine language programs directly. However, it was soon realized that the various instructions of any given machine language have many similarities with each other. It is possible to isolate a small number of fundamental operations, called *microinstructions*, and to express every machine language instruction as a small set of these microinstructions. For example, every machine language instruction involves the transfer of data from one place to another inside the computer. This is obvious in the case of LOAD and STORE because their entire purpose is to transfer information. The arithmetic operations (ADD, SUBTRACT, MULTIPLY and DIVIDE) also involve transfer of data from place to place inside the CPU. We will see (in Section 4.5.2) that the JUMP and RETURN instructions too involve the transfer of information inside the computer, and that all the machine language instructions of Fig. 4.22 can be expressed in terms of a number of such fundamental operations.

For reasons of economy, modern computers are designed to execute the microinstructions rather than directly executing machine language programs. Computer manufacturers also supply a program, called an *interpreter* (written in terms of microinstructions), which instructs the computer on how to read, understand and execute each machine language instruction. Therefore, the computer and the interpreter together are capable of executing programs written in machine language. Computers which are constructed in this manner are called *microprogrammed computers*, and they are described in greater detail in Section 4.4.

Two further terms which are often used in relation to computers are *software* and *hardware* (recall Section 1.3). Software refers to all programs associated with a computer. Hardware refers to physical equipment from which a computer is constructed. Programs which are written using micro-instructions are sometimes given the special name *firmware*, or *micro-*

programs. For example, the interpreter discussed in the preceding paragraph is a microprogram, or a piece of firmware.

The hardware of modern computers is almost entirely electronic, although it is also possible to build computers from other types of hardware. The first computer conceived, the Analytical Engine designed by Charles Babbage over a hundred years ago, was purely mechanical. The first computers which were actually built were electromechanical. Fluid driven machinery, such as pneumatic apparatus, could include computers which are built entirely from pneumatic devices so that they can be powered from the same source as the machinery they control. However, most computers are built from electronic components for reasons of cost, speed, reliability, and the ability to function in a harsh environment. These factors are those mentioned in Chapter 1 as being responsible for the computer's rapid proliferation.

Electronic computer hardware is described in the following sections, beginning with principles of physics and culminating in the design of a complete microprogrammed computer. The discussion will concentrate upon the design of the memory and the CPU. Input and output devices by their very nature must sometimes contain mechanical components since they need to interact with the outside world (e.g. closing a valve in a chemical plant). Input and output devices are described in Section 4.6.

Computers which are currently commercially available can be categorized into three groups. *Large computers*, costing hundreds of thousands of dollars, are very fast at performing calculations, have large amounts of memory, and can be simultaneously connected to many input and output devices. *Minicomputers*, costing thousands of dollars, are slower and smaller. *Microcomputers* are extremely compact, relatively slow, and they have little memory and few facilities for input and output devices. However, their prices may be as low as a few dollars. The computer design principles of this chapter apply equally to all these categories of computers. No matter where in the cost–size spectrum a computer lies, the same fundamental concepts of computer design are used for its construction. In particular, all the above types of computers may be microprogrammed computers (a term not to be confused with microcomputers).

4.2 PHYSICS AND ELECTRONICS

4.2.1 Semiconductors

If one were to open the back of a computer, one would see a set of rectangular boards plugged together in a rack. Each board contains a collection of plastic packs wired together. Inside each plastic pack we find a tiny

Fig. 4.1 (a)   A complete computer system. (Courtesy Intel Corporation).

Fig. 4.1 (b)   Chip of silicon inside its plastic pack. (Courtesy Intel Corporation).

chip of silicon, typically about a quarter of the size of a human fingernail (Fig. 4.1). In order to understand what is happening in the chip, we need to look extremely closely at a small portion of it. The chip is predominantly crystalline silicon, the main constituent of sand. Near the surface, some areas of the crystalline structure contain traces of phosphorus, and others contain traces of boron. There are also some thin layers of silicon dioxide, and thin strips of aluminum.

It would be hard to understand a chip without realizing that it is the *electrical* characteristics of the chip which are all important. Aluminum, like most metals, is a good conductor of electricity, because its electrons can move about freely. Pure silicon, on the other hand, is a poor conductor because all its electrons are tightly bound inside the crystalline structure. Silicon with traces of phosphorus has some extra free electrons and is called an *n-type semiconductor*. It has a limited ability to conduct negative electric charge. Conversely, silicon with traces of boron lacks some electrons in its crystalline structure, and thus has a limited ability to conduct positive electric charge. It is called a *p-type semiconductor*. Finally, silicon dioxide is a poor conductor (i.e. a good electrical insulator).

Fig. 4.1 (c)   Close-up of a silicon chip. (Courtesy Intel Corporation).

4.2.2   Transistors

Our next step in understanding computers comes when we notice that the different semiconducting materials occur in a regular pattern throughout the chip. The smallest unit of the pattern is called a *transistor* (Fig. 4.2). There can be over 10 000 such transistors on a single chip.

As can be seen in Fig. 4.2(b), there are three places in each transistor where aluminum conductors touch the surface of the silicon. They are called the *collector*, the *base*, and the *emitter* of the transistor. The electrical characteristics of the semiconductors cause a transistor to act as an *electrical switch*. When the correct voltage is applied to the base, an electric current can flow from the collector to the emitter. In the absence of such a voltage on the base, no current can flow.

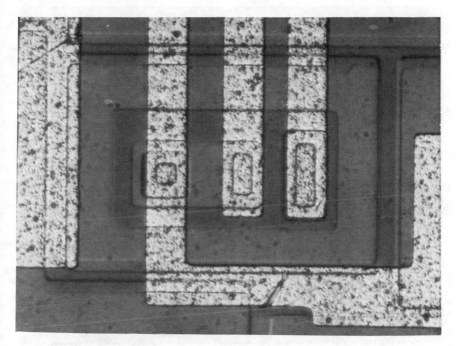

(a)   Photomicrograph of a portion of a chip containing one transistor.
      (Courtesy AWA Microelectronics).

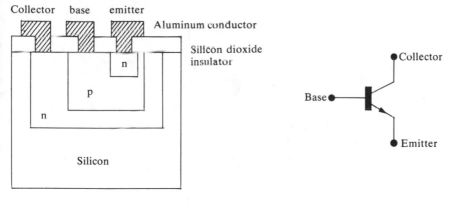

(b) transistor made
     from n-type and
     p-type semiconductors

(c) symbol for
     transistor

Figure 4.2

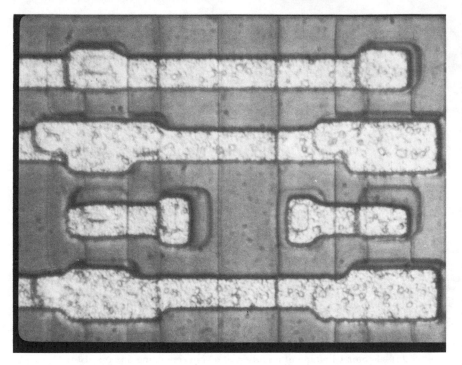

(a) Photomicrograph of a portion of a chip containing two transistors. (Courtesy AWA Microelectronics).

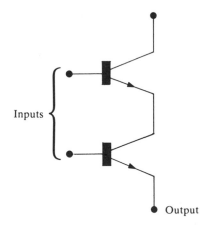

Inputs

Output

(b) One AND gate made from two transistors (highly idealized).

Figure 4.3

4.2.3 Gates

A larger pattern can be observed on the chip in the way *groups of transistors* are interconnected by the aluminum strips (Fig. 4.3(a)). Each group of transistors is called a *gate*. Figure 4.3(b) shows (in a highly idealized manner) two transistors connected together in such a way that an electric current can flow from the collector of one to the emitter of the other only when the appropriate voltage is applied to the bases of both. Such a design can be used as the basis of an AND gate, defined in a moment.

An important feature of gates is that they distinguish only between two different electrical voltages, which we call 0 and 1. Although the voltages to which transistors can be subjected can vary over a continuous range of values, gates regard any input voltage as either "low" or "high" (i.e. 0 or 1). When designing machines, computer scientists focus almost exclusively on discrete or *digital* quantities such as 0 and 1, and for this reason the type of computer discussed in this book is often called a digital computer.

A gate has some *inputs*, each of which can independently have the voltage corresponding to either 0 or 1, and one *output* which is either 0 or 1 depending on the values of the inputs. Three common gates, AND, OR and NOT, are shown in Fig. 4.4. Note that the AND gate will output 1 only when both of its inputs are 1. OR will output 1 when one or the other (or both) of its inputs are 1. The NOT gate has only one input. Its output is 1 when its input is 0.

Because it is convenient to build gates which operate only on 0s and 1s, almost all digital computers represent their data with codes consisting solely of 0s and 1s. Numbers are therefore expressed in the *binary* system (Fig. 4.5) rather than the decimal notation we use in everyday life. Similarly characters (e.g. the letters A to Z), and even the instructions of which an algorithm consists, are represented by sequences of 0s and 1s.

Inputs	Output		Inputs	Output		Input	Output
0 0	0		0 0	0		0	1
0 1	0		0 1	1		1	0
1 0	0		1 0	1			
1 1	1		1 1	1			

| (a) AND gate | (b) OR gate | (c) NOT gate |

Figure 4.4   Symbols and definitions of AND, OR and NOT gates.

$10^3 = 1000$	$10^2 = 100$	$10^1 = 10$	$10^0 = 1$
1	9	0	4

(a) Decimal number system uses base ten. The number represented is
$1 \times 1000 + 9 \times 100 + 0 \times 10 + 4$ which is equal to one thousand nine hundred and four.

$2^3 = 8$	$2^2 = 4$	$2^1 = 2$	$2^0 = 1$
1	1	0	1

(b) Binary number system uses base two. The number represented is
$1 \times 8 + 1 \times 4 + 0 \times 2 + 1$ which is equal to thirteen.

Figure 4.5

4.3 COMPONENTS

As there can be a few thousand gates on one chip, and many chips in a computer, it is too difficult to understand computers only in terms of gates. The vast number of gates and the complexity of their interconnections make it impossible to visualize all of the gates in a computer at once. To aid visualization, computer scientists have organized groups of gates into larger components, and it is these components which can be pieced together to make a complete computer. Important components include *memories*, *adders*, *buses*, *clocks* and *control logic*.

4.3.1 Memories

It is essential for computers to be able to remember data, whether for a short period of time (e.g. intermediate results obtained part way through a calculation), or for longer periods. A component which can store either 0 or 1 is called a *flip-flop* and can be constructed as shown in Fig. 4.6.

Note that a flip-flop has two inputs, *control* and *data-in*, and one output, *data-out*. The reader can verify from Fig. 4.6 that when control is turned on (i.e. set equal to 1), then data-out = data-in. Now when control is turned off (i.e. set equal to 0), data-out cannot change, no matter how often data-in changes. Therefore after control is turned off the flip-flop remembers the last value which data-in had while control was equal to 1.

Anything which can equally have either 0 or 1 as its value is said to hold one *bit* (*binary digit*) of information. Thus a flip-flop can store one bit of

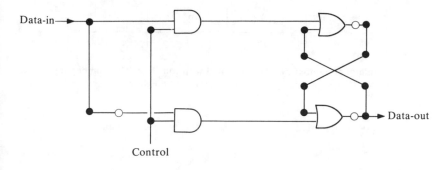

Control

Figure 4.6   Flip-flop.

information. As another example, if a person tosses a fair coin and announces the outcome—either "heads" or "tails"—he is communicating one bit of information. Eight bits are often called one *byte*.

Naturally, computers need to remember more than a single bit of information. For example, a number may have many digits all of which need to be stored. Computers usually handle data in fixed-size chunks called *words*, though the size of the word may vary from one computer to another. The word size in a microcomputer may be 8 bits, a minicomputer might have a word size of 16 bits, while a large computer could have a word size of 60 bits. If the word size is N bits, then N flip-flops are needed to store one word of data. Such a set of flip-flops is called a *register*.

Many different types of data can fit into one word. If only non-negative integers are required, they can be represented using the binary number system (Fig. 4.5(b)). If the word size is N bits this scheme allows any number between 0 and $2^N - 1$ to be represented. In general the rightmost bit (called the *least significant* bit) is the units column, and columns further to the left have progressively greater weights until the leftmost (or *most significant*) bit, which has a weight of 2^{N-1}.

Negative numbers can be represented in a similar manner. The only change is to let the most significant bit have a weight of -2^{N-1}. An example is given in Fig. 4.7. A little thought shows that any number between -2^{N-1} and $2^{N-1} - 1$ can be represented by this method, which is called the *twos complement* representation. A feature of this representation is that negative and non-negative numbers may easily be distinguished by inspecting the most significant bit. When this bit is 1 the number is negative; when it is 0 the number is zero or positive.

As well as numbers it is also desirable to represent characters inside a computer. Several standard methods of representation have been estab-

-2^3	2^2	2^1	2^0
1	0	1	1

(a) Twos complement number system illustrated with four bits. The number represented is $1 \times (-8) + 0 \times 4 + 1 \times 2 + 1 \times 1$ which is equal to minus five.

twos complement	decimal equivalent
1000	-8
1001	-7
1010	-6
1011	-5
1100	-4
1101	-3
1110	-2
1111	-1
0000	0
0001	1
0010	2
0011	3
0100	4
0101	5
0110	6
0111	7

(b) Table of four-bit twos complement numbers.

Figure 4.7   Twos complement number system.

lished, one common method being the ASCII representation shown in Fig. 4.8. This convention uses seven bits to represent a character, so that a word of N bits can be used to represent up to $N/7$ characters.

There are also standard methods of representing fractional numbers, and numbers of very high precision with more digits than can be fitted into a single word. These methods use a few words to represent each number.

Registers, which can hold one word of data, are usually constructed from the fastest available technology. This makes them quite expensive, and so they are kept few in number and are used mainly to hold information which is required very frequently. However, computers also need to store large amounts of information such as the instructions of the algorithm being executed, and the bulk of the data on which the algorithm is working. Computers therefore have a very large memory made from slightly slower but cheaper technology. This is called the *main memory*, and it often contains between 10^4 and 10^6 *cells*, each with a capacity equal to the word size of the computer. It is convenient to think of these cells as being numbered

Character	ASCII representation
⋮	⋮
>	0111110
?	0111111
@	1000000
A	1000001
B	1000010
C	1000011
D	1000100
E	1000101
F	1000110
G	1000111
H	1001000
I	1001001
J	1001010
K	1001011
L	1001100
M	1001101
N	1001110
O	1001111
P	1010000
Q	1010001
R	1010010
S	1010011
T	1010100
U	1010101
V	1010110
W	1010111
X	1011000
Y	1011001
Z	1011010
[	1011011
\	1011100
⋮	⋮

Figure 4.8   ASCII representation of some characters.

consecutively, starting from zero. That is, the cells are numbered 0,1,2,3,....
These numbers are called *addresses*, and each cell has a unique address.

In order to store information in the main memory, it is necessary to
present the memory with an address, as well as the information to be stored.
The memory will then store the information in the memory cell which has the
given address. Conversely, information can be retrieved by presenting an
address to the main memory. The memory will then retrieve the information
stored at the given address.

As well as being able to store a large number of simple items of
information, such as integers and characters, the memory can also store
more complicated data structures. These include sequences and trees as
described in Section 2.11. A sequence of integers, for example, can be
represented by a set of *consecutive* memory cells, each cell holding one of the

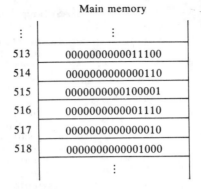

(a) The sequence of integers (28, 6, 33, 14, 2, 8) represented by memory cells 513 through 518.

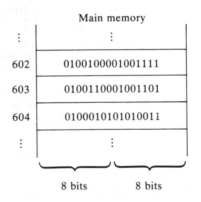

(b) The sequence of characters (H, O, L, M, E, S) represented by memory cells 602 through 604. There are two characters per memory cell.

Figure 4.9 Representation of sequences.

integers in the sequence (Fig. 4.9(a)). A sequence of characters can be similarly represented, each memory cell holding as many complete characters as the word size of the computer will permit. A sequence of characters in a machine with a word size of 16 is illustrated in Fig. 4.9(b).

In order to store an arbitrary tree in the memory of the computer it is necessary to use some memory cells for holding the *data* contained in the tree, and other memory cells for storing addresses which represent the *relationships* between the data. Consider the representation shown in Fig. 4.10(b) for the tree of Fig. 4.10(a). In this example each node of the tree requires three memory cells for its representation. The first memory cell

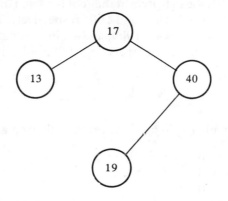

(a) A tree with an integer at each node

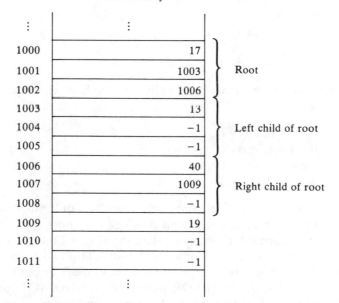

(b) A representation of the tree starting at memory cell 1000. For clarity, numbers have been shown in decimal rather than binary notation.

Figure 4.10   Representation of trees.

holds the data, while the remaining two cells store the addresses at which the left and right subtrees of the node may be found. Thus the three memory cells representing the root of the tree contain the numbers 17, 1003, and 1006, indicating that the data item at the root is 17 and that the left and right subtrees are stored at cells 1003 and 1006 respectively. The right subtree is represented by the numbers 40, 1009, and –1, indicating that its data item is 40, its left subtree is stored at memory cell 1009, and it has no right subtree.

4.3.2 Adders

In the decimal number system we have the following addition table:

$0 + 0 = 0$, carry 0
$0 + 1 = 1$, carry 0
$0 + 2 = 2$, carry 0
$0 + 3 = 3$, carry 0
$\vdots$
$4 + 5 = 9$, carry 0
$4 + 6 = 0$, carry 1
$4 + 7 = 1$, carry 1
$4 + 8 = 2$, carry 1
$\vdots$
$9 + 9 = 8$, carry 1

Similarly, in the binary number system we have the addition table shown below.

$0 + 0 = 0$, carry 0
$0 + 1 = 1$, carry 0
$1 + 0 = 1$, carry 0
$1 + 1 = 0$, carry 1

Notice that a carry is necessary only when both of the digits are 1. This is the exact circumstance in which an AND gate outputs 1, and an AND gate is therefore perfect for computing the carry (Fig. 4.11(a)). The binary addition table shown above also shows that the sum of the two digits is 1 exactly when one digit is 1 and the other is 0. Thus the sum can be obtained by (first digit AND NOT second digit) OR (second digit AND NOT first digit). This is illustrated in Fig. 4.11(b). We have just constructed a component called a *half-adder* (Fig. 4.11(c) and (d)), which adds two digits and produces one sum and one carry.

A computer must of course be able to add large numbers with many digits. If the word size is N, then an N-digit adder is required. A multi-digit

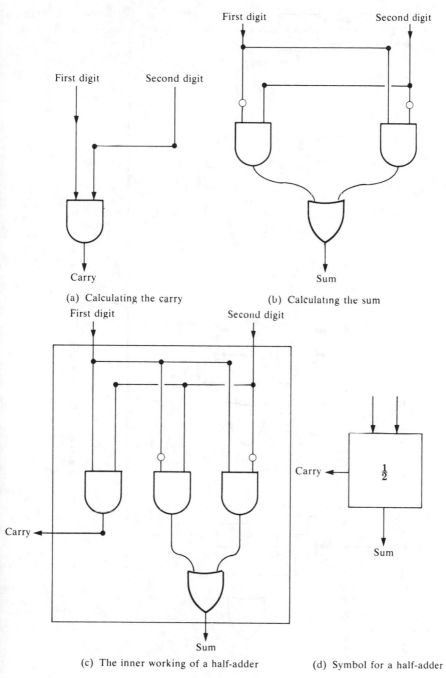

(a) Calculating the carry

(b) Calculating the sum

(c) The inner working of a half-adder

(d) Symbol for a half-adder

Figure 4.11

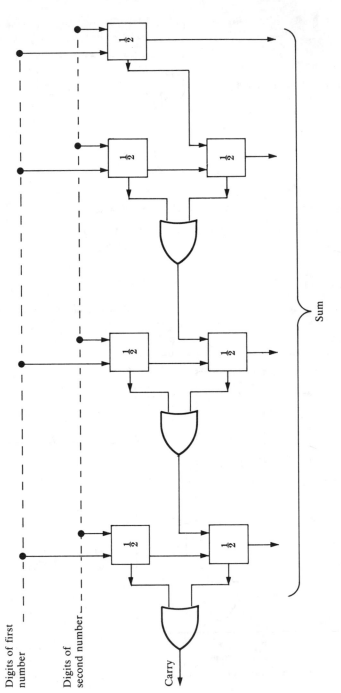

Figure 4.12 Complete adder for two 4-bit numbers.

adder can be constructed from many half-adders as shown in Fig. 4.12. Although this diagram may look complicated at first, the algorithm it illustrates is really quite straightforward. For every column of the numbers being added (except the least significant), the appropriate digit of the first number is added to that of the second number, giving a sum and a possible carry. The sum is then added to the carry from the previous column, giving the final sum for that column and another possible carry. The two possible carries are ORed together to give the carry out of that column.

4.3.3 Data Buses

Because a computer is built from a number of components, it is essential to be able to move information back and forward between them (e.g. between the memory and the adder). This movement of information can be achieved by *data buses*.

A data bus is basically a collection of wires which connects the different components together. The number of wires in a data bus is usually equal to the word size of the computer, so that data can be transferred in chunks of the same size as that which the components are built to handle. For example, if the adder can add numbers which are 16 bits long, and the cell size of the memory is 16 bits, it is clearly desirable for the data bus to be able to transfer 16 bits of data back and forth between the adder and the memory.

Since a data bus can transfer only one word of data at once, it is necessary to determine which components are permitted to use the bus at any given time. This can be done by connecting each component to the bus via an AND gate whose other input is a control signal (Fig. 4.13). Note that when control signal one is turned on, the data from component A will appear on the bus, and will therefore be transferred to components X, Y and Z. Similarly if control signal two is turned on, then the data from component B will appear on the bus.

4.3.4 Clocks and Control Logic

We have seen that a computer consists of various components connected together by data buses. The components often need *control* signals to regulate their activity. For example, a control signal determines when a flip-flop stores its data-in input (recall Fig. 4.6). Similarly, control signals determine which component transfers its data onto a bus (Fig. 4.13).

Control signals emanate from a computer component known as the *control logic*. The control logic is responsible for transferring the correct data at the appropriate time from component to component, and for ensuring that appropriate operations on the data are carried out.

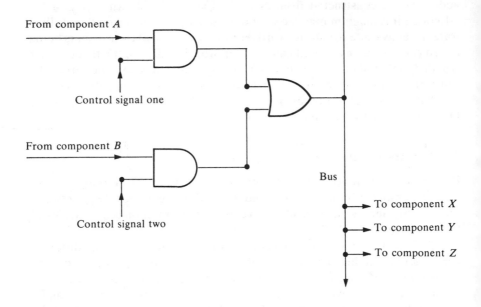

Figure 4.13   One wire of a computer's data bus.

An important part of the control logic is the *clock*, which produces signals at a regular rate. These signals are used by the control logic to ensure that all the computer's components remain synchronized with one another, and that each component is allowed enough time to complete its operation.

The clock shown in Fig. 4.14, for example, repeatedly produces five signals, called phases 1,2,3,4 and 5. It would first set PHASE1 = 1, then PHASE2 = 1, and so on until PHASE5 = 1; then again PHASE1 = 1, etc. The time between its changes might be 40 nanoseconds ($= 40 \times 10^{-9}$ seconds), which is typical of many computers. Thus the time to complete an entire cycle of 5 phases would be 200 nanoseconds.

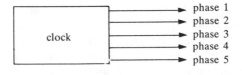

Figure 4.14   Clock.

4.4 MICROPROGRAMMED COMPUTERS

We now know enough about the components of a computer to put together an entire working computer (Fig. 4.15). This is a more detailed description of the CPU and main memory of the computer of Fig. 1.2. It has the capability of executing programs which are expressed in terms of extremely simple instructions called *microinstructions*. As mentioned in Section 4.1, microinstructions are very fundamental computer operations. For the sake of definiteness, a word size of 16 has been chosen.

4.4.1 Components of the Computer

The computer of Fig. 4.15 has three data buses, two of which are used as inputs to the adder, and the third is the adder's output. Each of these buses contains 16 wires. The machine also has a number of registers called A, B, C, D, MPC, MIR, MDR, and MAR. The latter four denote *microprogram counter*, *microinstruction register*, *memory data register*, and *memory address register* respectively. The meaning of these names will become clear shortly. Each register (except MIR) is 16 bits long. Information can be transferred to and from these registers by turning on the appropriate control signals (recall Fig. 4.13). For example, if control signals 1, 6 and 14 are turned on, the contents of registers A and MDR will be added, and the result placed in register MAR. If control signal 11 is turned on as well, then the result will also be placed in register C. The old contents of register MAR and register C will be lost, being replaced by the new result. If control signal 7 is turned on, the adder subtracts the contents of bus 2 from bus 1 instead of adding. Turning on control signal 8 causes the result from the adder to be shifted left one binary position before being placed onto bus 3. The effect of shifting left is to move each bit one place to the left, thereby losing the leftmost bit and automatically setting the rightmost bit to zero. (This is the same as multiplying by 2.)

The computer of Fig. 4.15 also contains two memories. The *micromemory* is used to hold the instructions of a program for this computer. These instructions are called *microinstructions* and the whole program is called a *microprogram*. Each cell of the micromemory contains 22 bits (the reason will be explained in Section 4.4.2), and there can be up to 1024 cells altogether. Therefore the cells have addresses in the range 0,1,2, ..., 1023. The micromemory can be operated by placing an address in the MPC register. The contents of the corresponding cell in the micromemory will then be available, and can be moved into the MIR register when the gate leading into MIR is opened. MIR is therefore 22 bits long, instead of the 16 bits of the other registers.

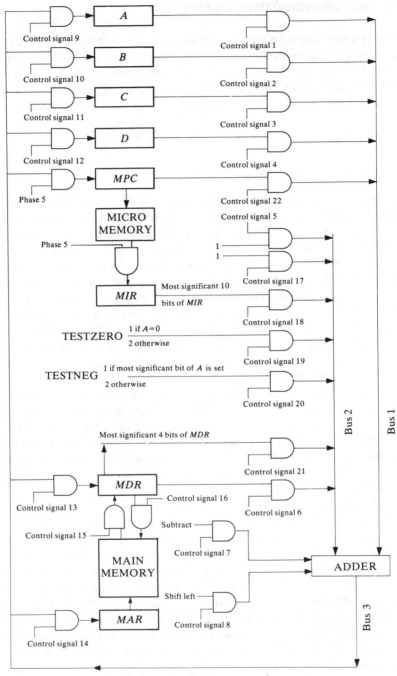

Figure 4.15 A microprogrammed computer.

The second memory is the *main memory*. It is used to hold the data upon which a microprogram operates. Each cell contains 16 bits. The main memory is typically considerably slower than the micromemory, so that it can be built from cheaper components to keep the computer's construction costs down. We will see that information is retrieved from the micromemory more frequently than from the main memory, thereby justifying the extra expense necessary to build a relatively fast micromemory. A further justification is that the micromemory is relatively small and so its cost does not contribute as substantially to the total cost of the computer.

The main memory takes the contents of the *MAR* register as the address of one of the cells in the memory. In our machine we will consider this address as a number in the range 0 to 4095. Since 4095 is $2^{12} - 1$, only the 12 least significant bits of *MAR* need be used as the address. (Typically the main memory would be much larger: for example, one million words of main memory is not unusual.) If control signal 15 is turned on, then the content of the cell whose address is in the *MAR* register is copied into the *MDR* register. Alternatively, if control signal 16 is turned on, then the content of *MDR* is copied into the appropriate cell of main memory (replacing whatever was stored there before). The reader can now see why *MAR* and *MDR* stand for *memory address register* and *memory data register* respectively.

Because the main memory can be used both to store and retrieve data, it is called a *read/write* memory. Gate 15 causes a *read* from main memory into *MDR*; gate 16 causes a *write* of the contents of *MDR* into main memory. In contrast, the micromemory is a read-only memory. While the microprogram is being executed, its microinstructions will need to be read, but not changed. Of course, some mechanism must be provided for initially placing the program into the micromemory. Various possible mechanisms for this task can be found through the bibliography.

Before seeing how a microprogram is executed by this computer, we will mention a few further details concerning Fig. 4.15. The rationale behind these details will become apparent in Section 4.5. Setting control signal 5 or 17 causes the constant value 1 to be placed on bus 2. Control signal 19 places 1 onto the bus if register *A* contains the value zero (i.e. all bits equal 0), and 2 is placed onto the bus otherwise. Similarly, control signal 20 places 1 on the bus if the most significant bit of *A* is 1, and 2 is placed on the bus otherwise. Control signal 21 will place the most significant four bits of *MDR* onto the least significant four bits of the bus. Similarly, control signal 18 transfers the most significant 10 bits of *MIR* onto the bus.

4.4.2 Microinstructions

An important outstanding question is what causes the various control signals in the computer to be turned on and off at the appropriate times. The answer

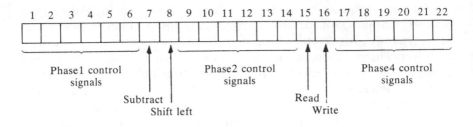

Figure 4.16   One microinstruction.

is that the control signals are directly governed by the microprogram being executed. More specifically, at any given time, the register *MIR* contains some microinstruction. Hence its name: *microinstruction register*. The register contains 22 bits, each one governing one control signal in the computer, as shown in Fig. 4.16. For example, if bit 3 of the microinstruction is "set" (i.e. if it equals 1), then control signal 3 will be turned on. Similarly, bit 7 of the microinstruction tells the adder to subtract instead of adding (Fig. 4.15).

However, if all the control signals whose corresponding bits are set were turned on at once, the computer would not work properly. Consider what would happen, for example, if the microinstruction had bits 2, 5 and 10 set. The effect should be to add one to register *B*. However, there is nothing to stop the contents of register *B* travelling around and around, adding an extra one every time through the adder. Therefore, the control signals which can be turned on at any time are regulated by a *clock* (see Section 4.3.4). Each microinstruction corresponds to one cycle of the clock, from PHASE1 to PHASE5. During each phase, only certain control signals are allowed to turn on, as shown in Table 4.1.

Table 4.1

Clock phase	*Control signals which can be turned on*
1	1–8
2	9–14
3	15–16
4	17–22
5	the control signals marked "PHASE5"

Now the operation of the entire computer can be understood by referring back to Fig. 4.15. During phases 1 and 2 the contents of registers can be added or subtracted (and possibly shifted left), and the result stored in some register. Phase 3 is used for reading or writing into main memory. The adder may again be used during phase 4, and the result obtained will always be stored into MPC in phase 5. Also during phase 5, the micromemory reads one of its cells into MIR, according to the address stored in MPC. Thus MIR will contain the next microinstruction, ready to be executed during phases 1–5 of the next clock cycle.

The reader can see from the discussion above that the MPC register, or *microprogram counter*, plays a very special role. It contains the address of the microinstruction currently being executed. Similarly, the MIR register contains the actual microinstruction being executed.

There is one exception to the rule that each bit of the MIR governs one control signal. When bit 18 is set, control signals 1–10 will remain turned off. The reason that this exception is necessary is that bit 18 causes the most significant ten bits of MIR to be transferred onto a bus, as mentioned earlier. This allows a microinstruction to move those ten bits into the MPC, thereby causing a jump to the microinstruction specified by those bits.

4.4.3 A Sample Microprogram

We have discussed many details of the computer sketched in Fig. 4.15. Now let us look at a simple program to see how all the parts of the computer work together to execute the program.

The machine can add and subtract, but how can we make it multiply two numbers? The following algorithm multiplies register C by register A, and places the result in main memory cell 1.

> **module** *multiply*
> {Multiplies the contents of register C by the contents of register A and
>   places the result in main memory cell 1}
> *set MDR to 0*
> **repeat** A *times*
>   *add C to MDR*
> *move 1 to MAR and tell main memory to write*   (4.1)

This algorithm simply adds C into the MDR register, A times. The answer, of course, is A times C, provided that MDR is large enough to hold the product. If the contents of A and C were very large, then their product might need more than the 16 bits available in MDR. In this case, the algorithm above would be incorrect (see Exercise 4.14).

As discussed in Chapter 2, if we want a computer to execute an algorithm, we must first express the algorithm as a program using only the instructions available. For our machine, this means we have to write a

Microinstruction

Micromemory address	1	2	3	4	5	6	7	8	9	10	11	12	13	14	15	16	17	18	19	20	21	22
0														1			1					1
1																			1			1
2							1	1									1					
3			1		1								1				1					1
4	1				1	1											1					
5			1												1	1	1					1

Figure 4.17   A microprogram for multiplication (blanks represent zero).

microprogram consisting of a sequence of microinstructions, each one 22 bits long. The microprogram for multiplication is shown in Fig. 4.17.

Figure 4.17 illustrates the fact that writing microprograms is a tedious task. Therefore, in this chapter we will usually only sketch microprograms, instead of writing out the 22 bits of each microinstruction. For example, a sketch of the above multiplication microprogram is shown in Fig. 4.18. The reader can check that each line corresponds to exactly one microinstruction in Fig. 4.17.

Micro-memory address	Microinstruction	Explanation
0	$0+0 \rightarrow MDR; MPC+1 \rightarrow MPC$	Initialize MDR
1	$MPC+ TEST\,ZERO \rightarrow MPC$	Check if A is zero
2	$5 \rightarrow MPC$	Yes: exit from loop
3	$C+MDR \rightarrow MDR; MPC+1 \rightarrow MPC$	No: add C to MDR
4	$A-1 \rightarrow A \quad ; 0+1 \rightarrow MPC$	Decrease A and go to top of loop
5	$0+1 \rightarrow MAR; write; MPC+1 \rightarrow MPC$	Write product into cell 1

Figure 4.18   Sketch of a microprogram for multiplication.

The astute reader will have noticed that although our algorithm for multiplication is short, it is terribly time-consuming. The reason is that the loop is executed A times, and A can be a very large number. Because the A register contains 16 bits, its contents could be as large as $65\,535$ (i.e. $2^{16}-1$), and the loop can therefore be executed up to $65\,535$ times. Execution of the loop body involves three microinstructions, and hence three clock cycles. Thus the multiplication algorithm may use almost $200\,000$ clock cycles, or 0.04 seconds, in the worst case. This is a long time for multiplication in a machine which can carry out five additions every millionth of a second.

Is there a faster algorithm to multiply C by A? Yes: the following algorithm takes time proportional to the number of bits in the A register. It will require at most 16 additions of C, rather than $65\,535$ as before. The idea behind the algorithm is always to shift C appropriately before adding it. This idea is based on the standard long multiplication method taught in school. Fig. 4.19 gives a simple example. (Recall Fig. 3.7, which illustrates the same method used to multiply decimal numbers.)

				0	0	0	1	1	1		$= C$
×				0	0	0	1	1	0		$= A$
				0	0	0	0	0	0		
			0	0	0	1	1	1			$= C$ shifted once
		0	0	0	1	1	1				$= C$ shifted twice
	0	0	0	0	0	0					
0	0	0	0	0	0						
0	0	0	0	0	0						
				1	0	1	0	1	0		$=$ product

Only a fixed number of bits
are available to hold product

Figure 4.19   Standard long-multiplication method.

The faster multiplication algorithm below differs slightly from the long-multiplication method. We start looking at the bits in A from the left. Instead of shifting C, the partial sum in MDR is shifted left once every time around the loop. In order to terminate the algorithm, an "artificial 1" is initially placed on the rightmost end of the A register. The eventual arrival of this "artificial 1" at the left end of the A register signals that the multiplication is complete. The algorithm is as follows:

module *multiply*
{Multiplies the contents of register *C* by the contents of register *A* and
leaves the result in register *MDR*}
set MDR to zero
if *leftmost bit of A is* 1
  then *add C to MDR*
shift MDR left one bit position
shift A left one bit position
add 1 to A
while *A has some bit other than the leftmost set to* 1 **do**
  if *leftmost bit of A is* 1
    then *add C to MDR*
  shift MDR left one bit position
  shift A left one bit position   (4.2)

A sketch of the faster multiplication microprogram appears in Fig. 4.20, and the actual microprogram in Fig. 4.21. It is not hard to check that this program will execute at most 84 microinstructions. At 200 nanoseconds per clock cycle, the program will take no longer than 17 microseconds (17 millionths of a second) in order to multiply two numbers. This is more than 2000 times faster than the previous multiplication algorithm we looked at.

Micro-memory address	Microinstruction		Explanation
0	$0 + 0 \rightarrow MDR$;	$MPC + TESTNEG \rightarrow MPC$	Set *MDR* to 0; check if most sig. bit of *A* is 1.
1	$C + MDR \rightarrow MDR$;	$MPC + 1 \rightarrow MPC$	Yes: add *C* to *MDR*
2	$0 + MDR \overset{shift}{\rightarrow} MDR$;	$MPC + 1 \rightarrow MPC$	Shift *MDR*
3	$A + 0 \overset{shift}{\rightarrow} A$;	$MPC + 1 \rightarrow MPC$	Shift *A*
4	$A + 1 \rightarrow A$;	$MPC + 1 \rightarrow MPC$	Set end marker on *A*
5		$MPC + TESTNEG \rightarrow MPC$	Check if most sig. bit of *A* is 1
6		$10 \rightarrow MPC$	Yes: jump ahead
7	$0 + MDR \overset{shift}{\rightarrow} MDR$;	$MPC + 1 \rightarrow MPC$	No: shift *MDR*
8	$A + 0 \overset{shift}{\rightarrow} A$;	$MPC + 1 \rightarrow MPC$	Shift *A*
9		$5 \rightarrow MPC$	Go to top of loop
10	$A + 0 \overset{shift}{\rightarrow} A$;	$MPC + TESTZERO \rightarrow MPC$	Shift *A*; test if *A* is zero
11		$14 \rightarrow MPC$	Yes: we've finished
12	$C + MDR \overset{shift}{\rightarrow} MDR$;	$MPC + 1 \rightarrow MPC$	No: add *C* to *MDR*
13		$5 \rightarrow MPC$	Go to top of loop

Figure 4.20 Sketch of a faster microprogram for multiplication.

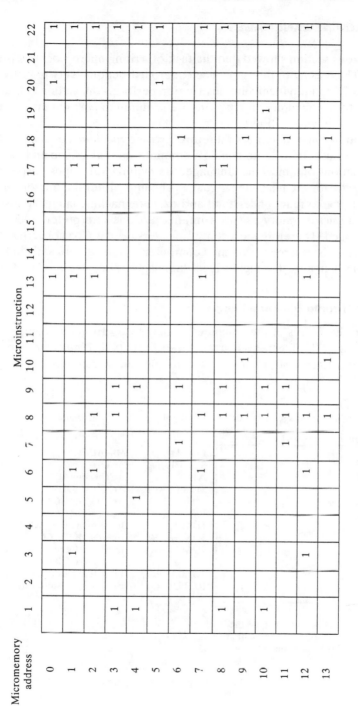

Figure 4.21 A faster microprogram for multiplication.

4.5   MACHINE LANGUAGES

The previous section showed that the task of writing microprograms is very tedious. The reason for this is that each microinstruction is very primitive. In other words, an individual microinstruction performs only a tiny operation, and therefore many microinstructions are required to perform even a small job like multiplying two numbers.

Computer manufacturers therefore provide *machine languages* which are easier to use. In order to enable a computer to understand and execute the instructions of a machine language, the manufacturer must also supply an *interpreter* for the machine language. The interpreter is a microprogram whose job it is to read, understand and execute machine language instructions. The micromemory usually contains just one interpreter, and this is never changed. Therefore most computer users need not be concerned with the details of the microprogrammed computer, but need think only in terms of machine language (or higher level languages, discussed in Chapter 5).

4.5.1   A Simple Machine Language

Although the details of the machine language vary from one computer to another, Fig. 4.22 illustrates a small set of fairly typical machine language instructions. Each instruction in this example can be represented using 16

Machine language instruction		Symbol	Explanation
4 bits	12 bits		
0001		LOAD	$M{\rightarrow}ACC$
0010		STORE	$ACC{\rightarrow}M$
0011		ADD	$ACC+M{\rightarrow}ACC$
0100		SUBTRACT	$ACC-M{\rightarrow}ACC$
0101		MULTIPLY	$ACC*M{\rightarrow}ACC$
0110		DIVIDE	$ACC/M{\rightarrow}ACC$
0111		JUMP	Jump to memory cell M
1000		JUMPZERO	Jump to M if ACC is zero
1001		JUMPMSB	Jump to M if most significant bit of ACC is set
1010		JUMPSUB	Jump to the subroutine at M
1011		RETURN	Return from subroutine at M

These 12 bits give the
address of some cell M in
the main memory.

Figure 4.22   A simple machine language.

bits. The most significant four bits (called the *operation code* of the instruction) identify which operation is intended. The remaining twelve bits give an address of a cell in main memory. In general, each instruction specifies an operation which is to be carried out on the contents of the given cell.

The LOAD operation can be used to move a value from main memory into one of the registers of our computer, which traditionally is called the *accumulator*. STORE achieves the opposite effect: that is, the value in the accumulator is moved into a main memory cell. In both cases the memory cell referred to is the one whose address is given in the least significant twelve bits of the instruction. The four arithmetic operations ADD, SUBTRACT, MULTIPLY and DIVIDE combine some number from the main memory with the accumulator, and leave the answer in the accumulator.

The remaining operations cause a *transfer of control* in the machine language program. All machine language programs, and the data they operate upon, are stored in the main memory of the computer. Ordinarily, the interpreter executes one instruction after another in sequential order. However, when a JUMP operation is encountered the interpreter next executes the instruction at the given address, instead of continuing in sequential order.

The JUMPZERO operation causes a jump if the number stored in the accumulator is equal to zero. Otherwise, execution of the program continues in the normal sequential manner. JUMPZERO is useful for testing for various conditions, such as termination of a loop. Similarly, JUMPMSB causes a jump if the most significant bit of the accumulator is set. Such an instruction is particularly useful when dealing with negative numbers, since it tests whether a number is negative or not (recall Fig. 4.7). However, we

Main memory address	Machine language instructions	Explanation
946	LOAD 958	
947	STORE 957	Set y to 1 initially
948	LOAD 956	
949	JUMPZERO 959	If $x = 0$ we have finished
950	SUBTRACT 958	
951	STORE 956	Subtract 1 from x
952	LOAD 957	
953	ADD 957	
954	STORE 957	Double y
955	JUMP 948	
956		This cell holds x initially
957		This cell ends up with the answer y
958	1	This cell holds the value 1
959		

Figure 4.23   An example machine language program which calculates $y = 2^x$

will make the simplifying assumption that all numbers to be dealt with are positive.

A sample machine language program is shown in Fig. 4.23. This program takes the number x stored in memory cell 956 and calculates 2^x, storing the result in memory cell 957.

Notice that both the machine language program and the data it operates on are stored in the main memory. This arrangement allows the programmer flexibility in designing programs and their data, since it allows either a large program with a small amount of data or a small program with a large amount of data to fit into the main memory. However, the arrangement can lead programmers to confuse a program with its data, so some modern computers have moved away from this flexible arrangement.

The remaining two machine language operations can be used to achieve modular structure in a program. JUMPSUB causes the interpreter to begin executing the module (often called a *subroutine*) which can be found at the given address. The RETURN operation tells the interpreter to return from the module back to the original program.

For example, suppose the interpreter is currently executing the instruction in memory cell 307 which is "JUMPSUB 945". The effect is to place the

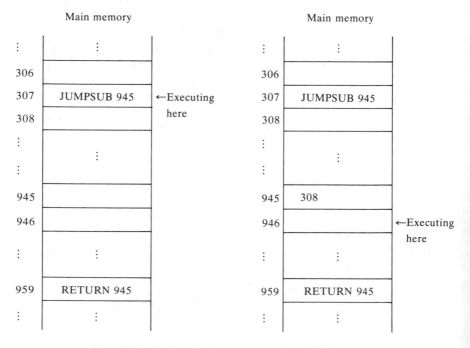

Figure 4.24 Before and after executing a JUMPSUB.

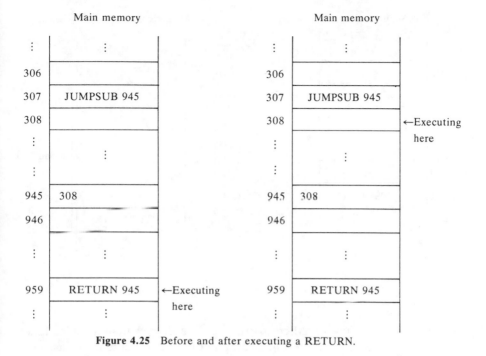

Figure 4.25   Before and after executing a RETURN.

number 308, called the *return address*, into memory cell 945, and then jump to cell 946. The situation is shown in Fig. 4.24. The module whose first instruction is at cell 946 will now be executed. Suppose that the interpreter eventually encounters a "RETURN 945" instruction. This instruction tells the interpreter to look in cell 945 and use the number stored there as a return address. In our example, the interpreter will therefore jump to cell 308, and continue executing the program stored there. Fig. 4.25 illustrates the situation before and after the RETURN instruction is executed.

We have seen how the JUMPSUB and RETURN operations can be used to *call a module* and to *return from a module*. Using these operations, it is easy to call the same module from different places in a program and to always return to the correct place (Fig. 4.26). Thus modules are particularly useful for performing the same type of task at different points in a program.

4.5.2   A Microprogrammed Interpreter

Although in the early days computers were built to execute machine language instructions directly, this leads to an expensive computer design as

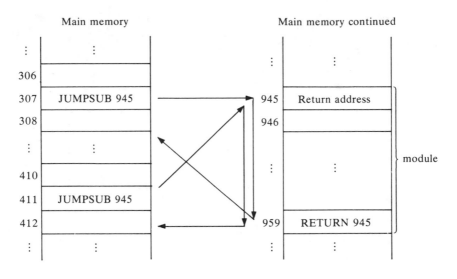

Figure 4.26   Calling one module from two different places.

mentioned in Section 4.1. Microinstructions are simpler than machine language instructions, and therefore a computer built to execute microinstructions requires fewer components than a computer built to execute machine language instructions directly. It is more economical to build a microprogrammed computer, and to write an interpreter for the machine language instructions.

The basic action of an interpreter is to repeatedly fetch a machine language instruction from the main memory, discover the intent of the instruction, and then execute the appropriate steps. For the interpreter to carry out its job, it must remember the address of the next instruction to be executed. We will use register B to hold this address (refer to Fig. 4.15). B is usually called the *program counter* register. Register A is the accumulator. The interpreter algorithm can be stated as follows.

module *interpreter*
{Repeatedly fetch and execute machine language instructions from
  main memory}
repeat
    fetch next machine language instruction
    add 1 *to B*
    decode the instruction
    execute the instruction
forever   (4.3)

Micromemory address	Microinstruction		Explanation
0	$B+0{\rightarrow}MAR$,read	; $MPC+1{\rightarrow}MPC$	Fetch next instruction into MDR
1	$B+1{\rightarrow}B$	; $MPC+MDR$top bits${\rightarrow}MPC$	Add 1 to program counter and decode instruction
2		$13{\rightarrow}MPC$	Load
3		$15{\rightarrow}MPC$	Store
4		$17{\rightarrow}MPC$	Add
5		$19{\rightarrow}MPC$	Subtract
6		$21{\rightarrow}MPC$	Multiply
7		$38{\rightarrow}MPC$	Divide
8		$55{\rightarrow}MPC$	Jump
9		$56{\rightarrow}MPC$	Jumpzero
10		$59{\rightarrow}MPC$	Jumpmsb
11		$62{\rightarrow}MPC$	Jumpsub
12		$65{\rightarrow}MPC$	Return
13	$0+MDR{\rightarrow}MAR$,read	; $MPC+1{\rightarrow}MPC$	Execute LOAD
14	$0+MDR{\rightarrow}A$	; $0+0{\rightarrow}MPC$	mem${\rightarrow}$acc
15	$0+MDR{\rightarrow}MAR$	; $MPC+1{\rightarrow}MPC$	Execute STORE
16	$A+0{\rightarrow}MDR$,write	; $0+0{\rightarrow}MPC$	acc${\rightarrow}$mem
17	$0+MDR{\rightarrow}MAR$,read	; $MPC+1{\rightarrow}MPC$	Execute ADD
18	$A+MDR{\rightarrow}A$	; $0+0{\rightarrow}MPC$	acc + mem${\rightarrow}$acc
19	$0+MDR{\rightarrow}MAR$,read	; $MPC+1{\rightarrow}MPC$	Execute SUBTRACT
20	$A-MDR{\rightarrow}A$	; $0+0{\rightarrow}MPC$	acc-mem${\rightarrow}$acc
21			Execute MULTIPLY (similar to Fig. 4.20)
⋮	⋮	⋮	⋮
38			Execute DIVIDE (as in Exercise 4.12)
⋮	⋮	⋮	⋮
55	$0+MDR{\rightarrow}B$	; $0+0{\rightarrow}MPC$	Execute JUMP
56		$MPC+TESTZERO{\rightarrow}MPC$	Execute JUMPZERO
57	$0+MDR{\rightarrow}B$	; $0+0{\rightarrow}MPC$	$A=$zero: jump
58		$0+0{\rightarrow}MPC$	$A{\neq}$zero: continue
59		$MPC+TESTNEG{\rightarrow}MPC$	Execute JUMPMSB
60	$0+MDR{\rightarrow}B$	; $0+0{\rightarrow}MPC$	Most sig. bit of A is 1
61		$0+0{\rightarrow}MPC$	Bit is zero: continue
62	$0+MDR{\rightarrow}MAR{\rightarrow}C$	; $MPC+1{\rightarrow}MPC$	Execute JUMPSUB
63	$B+0{\rightarrow}MDR$,write	; $MPC+1{\rightarrow}MPC$	Save return address at top of module
64	$C+1{\rightarrow}B$	; $0+0{\rightarrow}MPC$	Jump into module
65	$0+MDR{\rightarrow}MAR$,read	; $MPC+1{\rightarrow}MPC$	Execute RETURN
66	$0+MDR{\rightarrow}B$	; $0+0{\rightarrow}MPC$	Jump to return address

Figure 4.27   A microprogrammed interpreter.

The point of adding 1 to the B register, of course, is to cause the interpreter to step through the machine language program sequentially. But what if the machine language instruction is a jump? Then, while executing the instruction, the interpreter must change the B register appropriately. The complete interpreter is sketched in Fig. 4.27, and is intended to be studied in conjunction with Fig. 4.15.

The idea of the interpreter is to fetch the next machine language instruction from main memory, its address being given by the program counter register B. Then 1 is added to B so that B will contain the address of the *next* instruction. The instruction which has been read from main memory is contained in MDR, and its most significant four bits must be examined in order to determine the operation code of the instruction. The interpreter performs this examination by adding the four bits into MPC. This causes the microprogram to jump ahead to one of the microinstructions from 2 to 12. The microinstruction reached in this manner causes the microprogram to jump to a set of microinstructions appropriate for executing the machine language instruction which is in MDR. Microinstructions 2–12 are called a *jump table*.

Each set of microinstructions for executing one machine language instruction can now be studied independently. For example, ADD is executed by the two microinstructions 17 and 18. Since the least significant bits of MDR are the address of the memory cell whose content should be added to the accumulator, MDR is moved into MAR and the main memory is instructed to read. The number read from the main memory is then added to the A register, which we are using to represent the accumulator. Finally, MPC is set equal to zero, so that the interpreter returns to the beginning of its loop in order to fetch, decode and execute the next machine language instruction.

Let us look at one more piece of the interpreter: microinstructions 56–58 which execute JUMPZERO. In order to test whether or not the number in the accumulator is zero, $TESTZERO$ is added into MPC. Recall that $TESTZERO$ is equal to either 1 or 2 depending on whether A is zero or not. Thus if A contains zero a 1 is added to MPC and so microinstruction 57 is executed. This microinstruction copies MDR into the program counter register B, so that the interpeter will next fetch, decode and execute the machine language instruction at the given address. Alternatively, if A does not contain zero, then 2 is added to MPC and thus microinstruction 58 will be executed. This does not affect the program counter B, and so no jump will take place. The interpreter will simply fetch, decode and execute the next machine language instruction in sequence.

The reader can check that the interpreter as given will execute most machine language instructions in one microsecond. The exceptions are

JUMP which takes 0.8 microseconds, JUMPSUB which requires 1.2 microseconds, and MULTIPLY and DIVIDE which each use about 17 microseconds.

4.5.3 More Complex Machine Languages

The machine language we have discussed in Section 4.5.1 is much simpler than many of the machine languages which are commercially available. Some machine languages have hundreds of different instructions. It is not difficult to imagine the expense and difficulty of designing a computer to execute such languages. Even with the microprogrammed interpreter approach, the interpreter needs to be very long and complex to handle such complicated languages.

The justification for large machine languages has always been that a wide variety of instructions is useful to programmers. In fact most programs are now written in much higher level languages than machine language. (The reasons for this were mentioned briefly in Chapter 1 and will be discussed in more detail in Chapter 5.) Ironically, the use of complex machine languages enormously complicates the task of translating high level languages into machine language. Thus large, complex machine languages have proven to be a double curse, impeding the implementation of higher level languages and being difficult to implement themselves.

However, there are some features which can be added to our machine language which really would facilitate translation of higher level languages to machine language. An example is the inclusion of instructions which operate on stacks (recall Section 2.11). This considerably eases translation of arithmetic expressions. A stack can also be used to provide a better mechanism for calling and returning from modules, particularly when modules may call themselves recursively.

Another feature which could improve our machine language is more sophisticated *addressing*. Our instructions include 12 bits which represent some address in main memory. This simple use of addresses is called *direct* addressing. However, it is sometimes convenient to regard the 12 bits as a constant which can itself be added or loaded into an accumulator. This is called *immediate* addressing.

Indexed addressing (outlined in Exercise 4.19) is useful for stepping through sequential data structures, and is particularly suitable for handling arrays in high level languages (Section 2.11). Another method of addressing which is frequently useful is *indirect* addressing. Indirect addressing treats the 12 bits as the address of a memory cell which itself contains an address. Indirect addressing is helpful when dealing with complicated data structures which may contain addresses of other data structures within them. Figure 4.28 illustrates these various forms of addressing.

Main memory

"Index" register D

	3

512	514
513	17
514	23
515	289

(a) Contents of main memory and "index" register D

Type of addressing	Sample instruction	Value loaded into accumulator
immediate	LOAD 512 immediate	512
direct	LOAD 512 direct	514
indirect	LOAD 512 indirect	23
indexed	LOAD 512 indexed	289

(b) Illustration of the effect of different types of addressing

Figure 4.28   Various forms of addressing.

One further feature which is essential in computers that are used for scientific calculations is a special set of machine language instructions to perform arithmetic on fractions and on high precision numbers which require many more significant digits than can be represented with only 16 bits. If the available arithmetic operations operate only on 16-bit integers, as in our machine language, then scientific calculations would be very tedious indeed.

4.6 COMMUNICATING WITH THE OUTSIDE WORLD

Our discussion in this chapter so far has centered on the central processor (CPU) and the main memory of computers. Of course, computers must also exchange information with the outside world. As mentioned in Section 4.1, computers need to *input* their data and programs, and to *output* their results.

4.6.1 I/O Devices

The devices with which computers can communicate are many and varied. Collectively, they are called *input/output* (*I/O*) *devices*, or *peripherals*. Examples of peripherals which are used for input are:

keyboard (similar to a typewriter) for entering typewritten characters;
optical reader for written text;
punched card reader, which typically can input a few hundred cards per minute;
sensors for temperature, pressure, position etc. (these are often used in scientific experiments and in industrial machinery);
microphone to allow sound to be input directly into the computer;
electronic clock to tell the time of day;
magnetic ink reader for bank cheques;
power-fail equipment to tell the computer that the electrical power has failed, and thus only a small amount of stored power remains with which to save any critical data.

Peripheral devices which are used by computers for output include:

video screen (as in a TV) to display written text or diagrams;
high speed line printer (these can print up to a few thousand lines of text per minute);
effectors to operate valves, turn machinery on or off, apply a force, etc.;
plotter to draw graphs and other pictures;
loudspeaker to allow the computer to output sounds such as spoken words or music.

There are also some devices which can be connected to computers and used for both input and output. For example:

other computers;
magnetic disks used for cheap storage of vast amounts of information;
magnetic tapes, which are even cheaper than disks but slower;
other devices which are an electronic equivalent to magnetic disks.

Devices for the cheap storage of vast amounts of information, such as magnetic disks and tapes, are collectively called *secondary storage*.

In order to communicate with I/O devices, machine languages can include special instructions which send information to peripherals and receive information from peripherals. These instructions usually include a number of bits which specify the peripheral for which the communication is intended. An alternative method of I/O communication is to regard each peripheral as part of main memory, each with its own address. Information can then be exchanged with the device by using the ordinary LOAD and STORE machine language instructions.

4.6.2 I/O Techniques

One of the many difficulties which programmers face when programming in machine language is that each peripheral device is unique. Each has its own conventions and peculiarities regarding the sequence and format of the information which must be exchanged between it and the computer. This problem is considerably eased for the high level language programmer, as will be seen in Chapter 5.

To make the discussion more concrete, consider a simple input device such as a punched card reader. A punched card is a piece of cardboard with 80 columns. Each column can have some holes punched in it to represent one keyboard character. The purpose of a card reader is to read a deck of cards, one card at a time, and communicate the characters punched into each card to the computer.

Let us suppose that a card reader has two associated registers, which are regarded as main memory cells. One is called the *buffer register* and is used to transfer characters from the punched cards. The other, called the *status register*, is used to control the card reader, and to find out the status of the card reader at any time.

The possible status conditions of the card reader are

card reader busy;
card hopper empty (i.e. no card left to be read);
card reader malfunctioning;
character read successfully.

A simple algorithm for reading one card from the card reader is

module *readacard*
{Attempts to read one card from the card reader}
check card reader not busy and hopper not empty
instruct card reader to read one card
while *card reader busy* **do**
    wait until status register changes
    if *malfunction*

    then *alert operator*
    else {character has been read successfully}
       move character from buffer register to
         somewhere else in main memory
       clear bit in status register which
         indicated successfully read character
{card has now been read successfully and card reader
is no longer busy}   (4.4)

The main problem with this algorithm is that it occupies the CPU for the length of time required to read a card. Because a card reader is a mechanical device it is relatively slow, and it may take as much as a tenth of a second to read a card. During this time the CPU could execute 100000 machine language instructions. Instead, it spends most of the time waiting for the card reader's status register to change. Thus I/O which is based on an algorithm such as this is very wasteful of the CPU. Furthermore, since the CPU is fully occupied in handling each peripheral, only one peripheral can be active at once.

A more sophisticated I/O technique is to allow the CPU to continue performing some other task after starting the card reader. When finally a character has been read successfully, the program being executed must be temporarily *interrupted* while the successfully read character is stored away or otherwise handled. Then the interrupted program can be resumed until interrupted again by the arrival of the next character. The advantage of this *interrupt driven* I/O technique is that the physical job of reading a card is overlapped with the computer's other tasks.

Interrupts can be incorporated in a computer as follows. Whenever the status register of some peripheral changes, the CPU executes a JUMPSUB instruction to some fixed main memory address. A special module which can handle the interrupt begins at the fixed address. When the module, usually called an *interrupt handler*, has finished, it can simply execute a RETURN instruction so that the interrupted program will be resumed.

The only remaining problem is how to make the CPU execute the JUMPSUB instruction at the appropriate times. The solution is to add a further register to the computer, and to arrange that each peripheral sets a bit in this register whenever the peripheral's status changes. The micro-programmed interpreter checks this register from time to time (usually at the beginning of each cycle) to see whether any bit has been set. If so, the interpreter executes the JUMPSUB instruction; if not, it continues as normal with the next machine language instruction of the program being executed.

The interrupt driven I/O technique we have described still suffers from the defect that the computer must take some action for every character which is transferred to or from a peripheral. This can be unacceptably time consuming when characters are being transferred very frequently. Therefore a third method of I/O is available on many computers. The idea is to have a special I/O processor which shares its memory with the main computer. The CPU tells the I/O processor what I/O operation to perform. The I/O processor then performs the operation and interrupts the CPU only when the entire I/O transfer has been completed.

For example, in order to read a card, the main computer might instruct the I/O processor to read 80 characters from the card into memory cells 2001–2080. The main computer then continues with some other task, while the I/O processor reads the card. When all 80 characters have been transferred to the correct destination, the I/O processor interrupts the computer to announce completion. I/O processors are sometimes called *Direct Memory Access* (DMA) devices, or *channels*. They provide an example of an effective use of parallelism in order to speed up a computation.

EXERCISES

1   Convert the following numbers from binary notation to decimal notation:
(a)   000101   (b)   011111   (c)   000000   (d)   001000.

2   Convert the following numbers from six-bit twos complement notation to decimal notation:
(a)   110011   (b)   001101   (c)   100000   (d)   011111.

3   Convert the following numbers from decimal notation to six-bit twos complement notation:
(a)   18   (b) -18 (c) -1 (d)   0.

4   The following is an ASCII representation of a sequence of characters:
1000010100000110000101000010100000110001111000101
What is the sequence of characters?

5   (a)   Add the binary numbers 000101 and 000011;
(b)   multiply these two numbers.
In both cases, perform the arithmetic in binary and then check your answers by converting everything to decimal.

6   Show that in a twos complement representation, if each 0 and each 1 is changed to 1 and 0 respectively and then the number 1 is added, the result is the negation of the original number. (Colloquially, we say "complement and increment gives negation".)

7   Present some examples which illustrate that the complete n-digit adder designed in Section 4.3.2 works correctly even if the input numbers are represented in twos complement notation.

8 Describe some simple checks which could be incorporated into the complete n-digit adder to decide if it is possible to represent the result of the addition using only n digits. Assume firstly that all numbers are represented in binary notation. Repeat for twos complement representation.

9 How many gates (AND, OR and NOT) are used by the complete n-digit adder designed in Section 4.3.2?

10 Redraw Fig. 4.13 assuming that there are *three* components A, B and C which are connected onto the bus.

11 Write down a single microinstruction which causes the computer of Fig. 4.15 to perform an infinite loop.

12 Sketch a microprogram for division.

13 Sketch a microprogram which counts the number of bits in register A which are set equal to 1.

14 Describe some simple checks which could be incorporated into the multiplication microprogram of Fig. 4.20 to decide if it is possible to represent the result of the multiplication using only 16 bits.

15 When the computer of Fig. 4.15 is first switched on, its components may be in random states and anything could happen. Discuss what could be added to the computer to start it in a sensible manner. You may assume that the micromemory permanently contains a microprogram, whether the computer is switched on or off.

16 Write down a single machine language instruction (i.e. 16-bit number) which causes the interpreter of Fig. 4.27 to perform an infinite loop.

17 If the interpreter of Fig. 4.27 is presented with a machine language instruction whose operation code is greater than 1011 unexpected actions occur. Describe what happens in each case and suggest a modification which will cause the interpreter to ignore all undefined operation codes.

18 Write a machine language program using the instructions of Fig. 4.22 for any algorithm of Chapter 2.

19 Assume the machine language of Fig. 4.22 is changed as follows.

(a) A new instruction SETINDEX (operation code 1100) is added which copies the least significant 12 bits of the instruction into register D, and

(b) The first six instructions (from LOAD to DIVIDE) use *indexed* addressing instead of direct addressing. In other words, rather than the least significant 12 bits representing an address of main memory, those 12 bits plus the contents of register D give a main memory address.

Modify the interpreter of Fig. 4.27 accordingly.

20 Write a program using the modified machine language of Exercise 19 to compute the total of a sequence of integers. You may assume that the sequence is terminated by a zero.

BIBLIOGRAPHY

Introductions to computer architecture:

C. C. Foster, *Computer Architecture*, Van Nostrand Reinhold, N.Y., 1970.

C. W. Gear, *Computer Organization and Programming*, 3rd edn, McGraw-Hill, Tokyo, 1980.

G. W. Gorsline, *Computer Organization: Hardware/Software*, Prentice-Hall, N.J., 1980.

V. C. Hamacher, Z. G. Vranesic and S. G. Zaky, *Computer Organization*, McGraw-Hill, Tokyo, 1978.

H. M. Levy and R. H. Eckhouse, Jr, *Computer Programming and Architecture: The VAX-11*, Digital Press, 1980.

H. S. Stone, *Introduction to Computer Organization and Data Structures*, McGraw-Hill, N.Y., 1972.

A. S. Tanenbaum, *Structured Computer Organization*, Prentice-Hall, N.J., 1976.

P. Wegner, *Programming Languages, Information Structures, and Machine Organization*, McGraw-Hill, N.Y., 1968.

More advanced material:

C. G. Bell and A. Newell, *Computer Structures: Readings and Examples*, McGraw-Hill, N.Y., 1971.

G. G. Boulaye, *Microprogramming*, Macmillan Press, London, 1975.

Y. Chu, *Computer Organization and Microprogramming*, Prentice-Hall, N.J., 1972.

R. W. Doran, *Computer Architecture: A Structured Approach*, Academic Press, N.Y., 1979.

G. J. Myers, *Advances in Computer Architecture*, Wiley, N.Y., 1978.

5 THE EXECUTION OF ALGORITHMS: SYSTEM SOFTWARE

5.1 INTRODUCTION

The last chapter described how a typical computer is constructed, and how it executes programs which are written in machine language. The computer we described is not by itself particularly useful, for a variety of reasons.

(1) There is no easy way of getting a program into the computer's memory, or for initiating the program's execution.

(2) The input/output (I/O) facilities are difficult to use, since the programmer must be aware of the peculiarities of each peripheral. He must also ensure that his program inspects the status registers of peripherals to see when input or output is complete, or alternatively he must provide interrupt handling modules. The detailed organization of I/O transactions diverts substantial programming effort from the more important task of implementing the algorithm in question.

(3) There is no easy way for a program or its data to exceed the size of the computer's main memory.

(4) All the computer's resources are devoted to executing a single program. This program might occupy only a small fraction of the main memory and might use only one or two peripherals, but the rest of the memory and the other peripherals are unused until the program is completed. If the computer is expensive the under-utilization of its resources is bad economics.

(5) The computer must be programmed in machine language. For reasons to be explained shortly, machine language is quite inappropriate for most programming tasks.

The conclusion to be drawn from these points is that computer hardware, such as that described in Chapter 4, is of little use by itself: it

requires additional facilities to allow its easier and more economical exploi-
tation. These facilities are provided by a range of programs which are usually
supplied by the computer manufacturer. The programs are regarded as
being as much a part of the computer system as the computer hardware itself,
and are often referred to as *system software* or *systems programs*. In this
chapter we shall describe the major components of system software, concentrating on two items in particular.

(1)   *The Operating System*
      A computer is equipped with a single operating system (though a
      manufacturer may offer several to choose from) which performs three
      major functions:

      (a)   it makes it unnecessary for the user to be aware of some of the
            more awkward features of the computer, such as its limited
            memory size and the idiosyncrasies of its I/O facilities;

      (b)   it provides facilities for manipulating programs and data, so that a
            user can request, for example, that a particular program be
            executed with a particular set of data as input, and that the output
            be produced on a line printer;

      (c)   it allows the sharing of the computer's facilities by several simul-
            taneous users.

      Operating systems will be described in detail in Section 5.5.

(2)   *Language Translators*
      Language translators do what their name implies: they translate pro-
      grams written in high level languages (such as Pascal, Fortran
      and Cobol) into the machine language of the computer concerned.
      A separate translator is needed for each high level language used.
      Language translators fall into two main classes—*interpreters* and
      compilers—both of which will be discussed in Section 5.2.

   The advantages of writing a program in a high level language rather
than in a machine language need some discussion. We saw in Chapter 2 that
algorithms are naturally expressed in terms of control constructs such as
sequence, selection, iteration and recursion. We also saw that the data
manipulated by an algorithm usually has some logical structure, such as a
record, sequence, or tree. Very few of these control constructs and data
structures are directly available in machine language. Most of the control
constructs must be built from primitive operations such as JUMP, while the
data structures must be tediously constructed through primitive operations
on addresses.

The lack of adequate control constructs and data structures implies that an algorithm needs far more refinement to express it in machine language than it does to express it in a higher level language. The effort required, and hence the probability of mistakes, is far greater for machine language programs than for equivalent high level language programs. Furthermore, the human effort required to understand a machine language program is much greater than that for a high level language program.

A further disadvantage of machine languages is that each one is peculiar to a particular kind of computer. This means that the transfer of a machine language program from one kind of computer to another is very tedious, since the program must be rewritten in a different machine language. The term *portability* is used to denote the ease with which programs can be moved between different computers: the portability of machine language programs is very low.

One defense of machine language is that a programmer can usually produce a faster and more compact machine language program than can a language translator working from a high level program. However, the skill and effort required to do this is often considerable, and the cost in manpower is generally far greater than the savings resulting from more efficient execution. In the relatively few cases where it is important (e.g. the time-critical applications mentioned in Section 3.2.1), high efficiency can be achieved by *tuning* the machine language program produced by a translator. Tuning consists of identifying those parts of a program which are executed most often (e.g. the bodies of inner loops), and replacing them with machine language modules which are hand written to make execution more efficient.

A further defense of machine language is that it allows the programmer access to hardware components such as CPU registers and device status registers (see Chapter 4). Such access is not required in most applications, and therefore most high level languages do not provide it. Sometimes, however, it is essential, particularly in certain portions of the operating system. The use of machine language in these cases is unavoidable.

Summarizing, high level languages should be used in almost all situations. Machine language should be used only for tuning, or for essential access to parts of the computer which are otherwise hidden.

Other major items of system software, which we shall not describe in detail, include

(3)   *Editors*
During program development it is usually necessary to make frequent alterations to the program – correcting errors, adding modules, and so on. To avoid massive retyping it is customary to keep the program in secondary storage (Section 4.6.1) and to perform the alterations in

situ. The systems program used to make the alterations is called an *editor*. In fact an editor can be used not only to alter programs, but also to alter any other pieces of textual information which might be kept in secondary storage. The nature of such information varies according to the computer's applications: examples are program documentation, user manuals, form letters, bibliographies, catalogs, and the draft of this book.

The facilities provided by an editor allow a user to locate, delete, or replace specific pieces of text, and to insert new pieces of text where required. Most editors are used *interactively*—that is, the user issues commands to the editor from a terminal, and inspects the alterations as they are made. Video terminals are particularly suitable for editing, since the editor can display the portion of text being worked on, and the user can easily see the effect of his alterations. (An editor and a video terminal form part of the *word processing systems* described in Chapter 7.)

(4) *Loaders*
As we shall see in Section 5.2, certain language translators place translated programs in secondary storage until they are required for execution. The systems program responsible for moving the translated programs back into memory is called a *loader*. Most loaders are also capable of combining program modules translated on separate occasions into a single machine language program. This facility is particularly useful for incorporating commonly used "library" modules into a program without repeatedly having to translate them.

5.2 PROGRAMMING LANGUAGE TRANSLATORS

The function of a programming language translator is, as indicated in the last section, to translate programs written in a high level language into equivalent programs expressed in machine language. The programs can then be executed by a microprogrammed interpreter such as that of Chapter 4. In this section we shall examine how the translation of high level programs into machine language is effected.

There are two kinds of entity in a high level program which need translation: the statements (instructions) and the data structures. The statements of a high level language are generally more powerful than those of machine language: that is, it takes several machine language statements to describe the same process as a single high level language statement. Thus each high level statement is typically translated into a number of machine level statements, a process which can be viewed as further refinement of the high level statement. The data structures which can be manipulated in a high level language (e.g. lists, sequences of characters, trees) are not directly available in machine language. Instead such structures have to be represented in terms of bits, numbers and addresses, and the translator must transform the high level data structures into some machine level representation. (For example, we saw in Chapter 4 that a sequence of items might be represented by a number of adjacent cells in memory; any reference in the high level program to a particular item in the sequence must be translated into a reference to the appropriate cell in memory.)

Broadly speaking there are two separate strategies that can be adopted in the translation of high level programs. These are called *interpretation* and *compilation*, which we discuss further below.

5.2.1 Interpretation

The strategy of interpretation is to translate and execute a high level program statement by statement, execution of each statement preceding translation of the next. Interpretation is performed by a program known as an *interpreter*, which executes the following algorithm.

> *start at the beginning of the high level program*
> **repeat**
> > *translate the next high level statement*
> > *arrange for the result to be executed*
> **until** *the end of the high level program*   (5.1)

In most cases the interpreter is equipped with a set of ready made modules, each of which consists of a sequence of machine language statements corresponding to a particular type of high level statement. Thus to translate each high level statement the interpreter simply examines the statement to see what type it is and hence which module should be called. The data items manipulated by the high level statement (i.e. the statement's *operands*) are passed to the module as parameters. When the module has been executed control returns to the interpreter, which then repeats the cycle on the next high level statement.

The interpreter determines the type of each high level statement by using the syntax rules of the language concerned (recall Section 2.2). We shall explain later how this is done, but the reader should note here that translation relies on each statement being syntactically correct. If a statement contains a syntax error the interpreter will detect and report it, but since the error will probably render the statement ambiguous no attempt will be made to execute it.

Summarizing, the action of the interpreter is described by algorithm 5.2, which is a refinement of algorithm 5.1.

> *start at the beginning of the high level program*
> **repeat**
>   *syntactically analyze the next statement to determine its type and operands*
>   **if** *no syntax error*
>   **then** *call the module for this statement type, with the statement's operands as parameters*
>   **else** *report error*
> **until** *the end of the high level program or*
>   *a syntax error occurs* (5.2)

Note that the microprogrammed interpreter of Chapter 4 is a simple version of that described above. The microprogrammed interpreter interprets machine language statements in terms of microinstructions, while the interpreter described above interprets high level language statements in terms of machine language. The structure and purpose of each interpreter is the same: it is only the levels at which they operate which differ. Algorithm 5.2 is the basic algorithm executed by all interpreters.

The speed of translation depends largely on the syntax of the language being translated: the more complex the syntax the slower the translation. Since an interpreter translates each high level statement every time it is executed it is advantageous to keep the syntax of the language as simple as possible, and this is a major design goal of many high level languages which are normally translated by interpretation. In the Basic language, for example, which was designed with interpretive translation in mind, the type of each statement is determined solely by its first word. The microprogrammed interpreter of Chapter 4 also gains speed from the very simple syntax of the machine language it interprets. The type of a machine language statement is determined by its operation code, and its single operand is the data stored in the memory cell indicated by its address field.

The alert reader may by now have asked himself the following question. If a high level language is interpreted in terms of machine language, and machine language is interpreted in terms of microinstructions, why cannot the middle step be omitted and high level languages be interpreted directly by microprogram? The answer is that they can—at least in principle. However, there are several arguments against doing so.

(1)   A microprogrammed interpreter for a high level language would be far more complex than that for machine language, since a high level language is much richer in both syntax and semantics. As we saw in Chapter 2, there is a significant design advantage in breaking down a complex process into a number of simpler stages.

(2) A practical benefit of two-stage interpretation is that for each high level language used only the first stage (high level language in terms of machine language) need be rewritten. The second stage (machine language in terms of microinstructions) remains the same.

(3) Because of its complexity a microprogrammed interpreter for a high level language would be quite large and would require a considerable amount of (relatively expensive) micromemory to hold it.

(4) In an attempt to reduce the size of the interpreter the power of each microinstruction would need to be increased beyond that of the examples in Chapter 4. This could be achieved only by increasing the number of bits in each microinstruction (and hence in each word of micromemory), and by adding complexity to the microprogram control logic.

These considerations imply that the direct microprogrammed interpretation of high level languages is not usually a viable proposition. The result is the almost universal adoption of two stage interpretation via machine language.

5.2.2 Compilation

It is apparent from algorithm 5.1 that when a high level program is translated by an interpreter the translation proceeds hand in hand with execution. This implies that if a program statement is to be executed several times (in a loop, for example) it must also be translated several times, as the execution and translation of each statement are inextricably bound together. This can be a source of unnecessary overhead since retranslation of statements is clearly redundant. The overhead of retranslation may be unacceptable, particularly in any of the following circumstances:

(1) the time taken to translate a program statement outweighs the time taken to execute it;

(2) the program is executed frequently without change (e.g. a payroll program);

(3) execution speed is paramount (e.g. when responses must be given quickly, as in an airline reservation system or a system controlling industrial machinery).

The way to avoid such overhead is to adopt a different strategy of program translation and execution. This strategy separates translation from execution by insisting that the entire program be translated before execution commences (in sharp contrast to interpretation, where execution of each statement precedes translation of the next). The translation and execution of a program under this strategy is described by algorithm 5.3, which the reader should compare with algorithm 5.1 describing interpretation.

start at the beginning of the high level program
repeat
    translate the next high level statement
until *the end of the high level program*
arrange for the entire translated program to be executed   (5.3)

The translation of the high level program, as described by the first four lines of algorithm 5.3, is called *compilation*; it is carried out by a systems program called a *compiler*. Execution commences only when the entire high level program has been compiled. The original high level program is often referred to as the *source program*, and the machine language program which is the result of compilation is called the *object program*. It is the object program which is ultimately executed.

Since compilation and execution are separate processes, an object program, once produced by a compiler, can be executed an arbitrary number of times without recompilation of the source program. The only facility required is a means of storing the object program until execution is requested. The computer's secondary storage is usually used for this purpose, and the object program is transferred by a loader into memory when execution is required.

Like an interpreter, a compiler analyzes the syntax of the source program by using the syntax rules of the high level language concerned. We shall describe how this is done later in this chapter, when we shall also indicate how the appropriate machine language statements are generated. In the meantime we mention one further consequence of the distinction between interpretation and compilation.

An interpreter has the source program available while each translated statement is being executed. If an error occurs during execution the interpreter can readily provide information about the location of the error and the current state of the computation. Moreover, this information can be expressed in terms of the high level program itself—which statement is being executed, what the values of various data items are, and so on. In contrast, when a compiled program is being executed the source program may no longer be available. This means that when an error occurs meaningful information is difficult to obtain. Because of its superior error diagnostic capability, interpretation is particularly suited to program development and debugging. Once the program has been debugged, however, it will execute more quickly if it is compiled—an advantage which increases the more often the program is used.

Interpreters tend to be used in situations where the same program is not used very often, where execution speed is relatively unimportant, or where insufficient memory or secondary storage is available to hold an object program (e.g. in home computers). Compilers are used where the same program is executed repeatedly, or execution speed is paramount. In some cases a switch from interpretation to compilation is made when program development is complete and productive use commences. The switch depends on the availability of both an interpreter and a compiler for the language concerned.

5.3 SYNTAX DEFINITION

It is apparent from the last section that program translation is crucially dependent on the syntax of the language concerned. In this section we shall look briefly at how the syntax of programming languages can be specified, before proceeding in subsequent sections to describe the process of translation in more detail.

The pioneering work on the syntax of programming languages was carried out in the late 1950s, culminating in the publication of the Algol 60 Report in 1960. Algol 60 was the first commonly used programming language to have a formally defined syntax: the report describing the language contained a complete and precise syntax definition. The notation used in the report is called *Backus-Naur Form* (BNF) after its two principal originators: the same notation, with various minor modifications, has subsequently been used in defining the syntax of many other programming languages. The notation we shall use here is a minor variation.

We start by recalling that a program consists of a sequence of elementary symbols, such as the names of data items, certain punctuation characters, and various special words like **if** and **repeat**. The elementary symbols permitted in a particular language are called the *terminal symbols* of the language. The terminal symbols can be combined in various ways to form more complex constructs, such as conditions, statements, and programs themselves. Each kind of construct which can be built in this way is called a *syntactic category*, or *non-terminal symbol*, of the language. (There is a similarity with natural language, whose terminal symbols are words and punctuation marks, and whose syntactic categories include phrases, clauses and sentences.) The basic idea behind syntax definition is to specify precisely how the syntactic categories of a language are constructed.

This is done by formulating a set of rules, or *productions*, each of which defines how a particular syntactic category can be built from

(1)   members of other syntactic categories; and/or
(2)   terminal symbols of the language.

The set of terminal symbols, the set of syntactic categories, and the set of productions together define the syntax of a language.

As an example we shall consider the syntax definition of telephone directory entries which detail subscribers' names, addresses and numbers in more or less conventional fashion. A typical directory entry is

Smith John B. 97 Main   51374

The syntax of an entry can be defined by the BNF production

entry → *person-name address* number

where syntactic categories are shown in italics and terminal symbols are in ordinary type. This production can be read as "an entry is defined to be a person-name, followed by an address, followed by a number".

The categories *person-name* and *address* now need to be defined. Starting with the former, we can write

person-name → *surname forename {forename}*

Curly brackets mean that the enclosed category or symbol is repeated zero or more times, so the above production can be read as "a person-name is defined to be a surname followed by at least one forename". Since a forename may be abbreviated to an initial, we define

forename → *proper-forename* | *initial*

The vertical bar in BNF means "or", so this production reads "a forename is defined to be a proper-forename or an initial."

The definition of an initial is

initial → *letter*

meaning that an initial is a letter followed by a period (which is a terminal symbol). The definition of a letter is of course

letter → A | B | C | ... | Z

Definition of the remaining syntactic categories proceeds similarly, giving the complete syntax of a directory as shown in Fig. 5.1. The reader should note how every syntactic category is ultimately defined in terms of terminal symbols (names, numbers, letters, and period). The terminal symbols themselves need no further definition, and therefore do not appear on the left-hand side of any production.

It is worth mentioning that for simplicity the syntax definition of Fig. 5.1 does not include any specification of format (e.g. that various symbols should be separated by spaces). If format specification is required then "space" characters must be added to the set of terminal symbols and included in the appropriate productions (see Exercise 5.4).

entry→person-name address number

person-name→surname forename{forename}

surname→ name

forename→proper-forename|initial

proper-forename→ name

initial→letter.

address→ number *street-name*

street-name→ name

letter→ A|B|C|....|Z

Figure 5.1   The syntax of a simple telephone directory entry.

statement→conditional|loop|assignment

conditional→ **if** *condition* **then** *statement*

loop→ **while** *condition* **do** *statement*

assignment→ set name to *expression*

expression→ name *operator* name

operator→ +| −

condition→ name *relation* number

relation→ =| ≠

Figure 5.2   The syntax of a programming language fragment.

The syntax of a programming language is of course more complex than that of our telephone directory example, but it can be defined in exactly the same way. (A language such as Pascal needs about 100 productions.) Figure 5.2 gives the flavor of such a definition. The figure shows the syntax of part of a hypothetical language, based on the constructs we introduced in Chapter 2. The language contains three kinds of statement:

(1)   a *conditional*, which expresses selection
(2)   a *loop*, which expresses iteration
(3)   an *assignment*, which expresses how to calculate a value and assign it to a data item. Examples of an *assignment* are

> *set X to Y + Z*

and

> *set NET to GROSS − TAX*

Both a *conditional* and a *loop* include a *condition*, which is a test on the value of some data item. Examples of a *condition* are

$$X \neq 5 \quad \text{and} \quad GROSS = 0$$

Hence an example of a *conditional* is

if $X \neq 5$
  then *set X to Y + Z*

and an example of a *loop* is

while $X \neq 0$ **do**
  set X to X − Y

Note that the definition of a *statement* is recursive, since it involves syntactic categories which are themselves defined in terms of *statement*. Thus, for example, a *statement* can be part of a *loop*, which is itself a form of *statement*. This implies that a statement can consist of an arbitrary number of nested loops, each of which is a statement in its own right. Similarly, a statement can contain an arbitrary degree of nested selection, or an arbitrary combination of nested loops and selection. Thus the following is a valid statement:

if $X \neq 0$
  then while $Y \neq 0$ **do**
    set Y to Y − X

Recursive definition is a very powerful feature of BNF, since it allows arbitrarily complex programs to be constructed from a grammar with relatively few productions. Note, however, that recursive productions must contain at least one non-recursive alternative—otherwise the definition would be tautologous (cf. the "escape route" from recursive algorithms discussed in Section 2.9). In the example above, *assignment* is the non-recursive alternative definition of *statement*.

We shall not deal with syntax definition in any further detail here: the interested reader is referred to the bibliography, or to any modern programming language manual, which should include a formal definition of the language's syntax. The use of syntax definition in the syntax analysis of a program will be discussed in Section 5.4.2.

5.4   COMPILERS

Section 5.2 gave an overview of the language translation process carried out by interpreters and compilers: this section fills in some of the details. The material presented can be regarded as a refinement of the step *translate the next high level statement*

which is the third line, and the heart, of both algorithm 5.1 (the basic algorithm for interpreters) and algorithm 5.3 (the basic algorithm for compilers). The discussion will be conducted in the context of compilers, but much of it is also applicable to interpreters.

The process of compilation can be viewed as having three major phases, as shown in Fig. 5.3. The three phases are

(1) *Lexical Analysis*   The string of characters comprising the source program is broken up into a sequence of separate symbols, or *tokens*, much as the characters comprising a piece of English text can be separated into a sequence of words and punctuation marks. The symbols in the source program are typically the names of data items manipulated by the program, operators such as + and − , and special *reserved words* such as **if** and **while**.

(2) *Syntax Analysis*   The program is *parsed*—that is, its syntactic structure is determined by using the grammatical rules of the language concerned to analyze the sequence of tokens produced during lexical analysis. This phase is similar to (but much easier than) the parsing of English text, given the sequence of words and punctuation marks comprising it.

(3) *Code Generation*   Appropriate machine language statements are generated for each syntactic element of the program. These machine language statements are often referred to as *object code*; the final set of such statements is the translated program, or *object program*.

Many compilers have a fourth phase, called *optimization*, which follows code generation. Its purpose is to make the object program smaller or quicker to execute (by techniques such as detection and elimination of redundant statements, making loop bodies as short as possible, and using registers instead of memory cells whenever feasible). The improvements are often only marginal, and are gained at the expense of additional complexity in the compiler and extra time during compilation. The extent to which it is used should therefore be governed by how often the object program is to be executed.

The reader should not interpret Fig. 5.3 as implying that the entire source program must be processed by each phase before the next phase begins. In some compilers this may indeed be the case, particularly when the computer on which the compiler runs has a main memory which is too small to hold the entire compiler at once. (Compilers tend to be large programs, occupying 10000–100000 memory cells.) In such circumstances the three

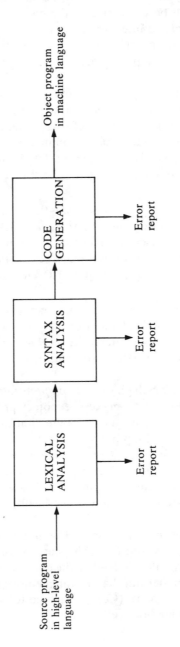

Figure 5.3 The three phases of compilation.

phases are performed by distinct components of the compiler: each component resides in the computer's secondary memory until the corresponding phase is to be carried out.

In general, however, the three phases are interleaved, so that, for example, the modules responsible for syntax analysis might call the lexical analysis modules to obtain the next token and might call the code generation modules to produce object code for the statement just analyzed. If more than one processor is available the phases can be overlapped, providing a practical example of parallel computation.

5.4.1 Lexical Analysis

Lexical analysis is the first phase of compilation (recall Fig. 5.3). Its main function is to reduce the source program to a sequence of terminal symbols for the syntax analysis phase to work on.

The program text is processed character by character, and the analyzer

(1)   determines whether each character is a terminal symbol in its own right (e.g. + and −) or whether it must be grouped with its neighbors to form a "bigger" terminal symbol such as a name, a number, or a reserved word;
(2)   removes syntactically redundant characters such as multiple spaces and comments intended for human readers;
(3)   rejects spurious characters as errors in the source program.

Terminal symbols are passed from the lexical analyzer to the syntax analyzer in the form of *tokens*. Each token represents a particular terminal symbol. A token has two components:

(1)   its *type*, indicating what kind of terminal symbol the token represents (e.g. **if**, +, number)
(2)   its *value*, indicating the value, if any, of the terminal symbol the token represents. For example, the value of a number token is simply the number it represents, and the value of a name token is the name it represents. (In fact name and number tokens are the only ones we shall mention which have meaningful values: the values of other tokens can be regarded as undefined.)

As an example of lexical analysis, consider the program statement

if $X \neq 1$
   then *set* Y *to* $X + Y$

in the language defined in Fig. 5.2. The lexical analyzer might transform this statement into the token sequence

if *name* ≠ *number* **then** *set name to name + name*
  (*X*)   (1)   (*Y*)   (*X*)   (*Y*)

where the value of each token (where applicable) is shown beneath its type. The sequence is then passed to the syntax analyzer.

For the convenience of the programmer most lexical analyzers print the source program exactly as presented, though printing can usually be suppressed if not required. Any errors detected during lexical analysis are reported in the program printout or on the programmer's terminal (or both). In some cases a programmer may wish analysis to cease as soon as an error is detected (so that he can correct it without further ado). In other cases he may want analysis to proceed despite the occurrence of errors (so that he can correct all outstanding errors at once). In the latter cases the analyzer must report each error, ignore the offending character, and continue analysis at the next symbol it can recognize.

5.4.2 Syntax Analysis

Syntax analysis is the second phase of compilation. Its function is to parse the source program—that is, determine its syntactic structure—so that the code generation phase can subsequently produce machine language statements appropriate to each syntactic element. (The reader will recall from Section 3.1.4 that parsing an arbitrary program expressed in a BNF grammar is indeed a computable problem; fortunately it is also feasibly computable.)

The syntactic structure of any valid sequence of terminal symbols can be represented by its *parse tree*, which has the terminal symbols as its leaves and the syntactic category to which the sequence belongs as its root. For example, the parse tree of the directory entry

    Smith John B. 97 Main 51374

is shown in Fig. 5.4. (The parse tree is constructed according to the syntax of Fig. 5.1.) The parse tree indicates that this particular sequence of symbols is a valid directory entry, and the tree also contains complete information about the sequence's syntactic structure. Figure 5.5 shows another parse tree, this time of the statement

    if $X \neq 1$
       then *set* Y *to* $X + Y$

in the language defined in Fig. 5.2.

In general, the parse tree of a valid program has leaves which are the terminal symbols comprising the program text and a root which is the syntactic category *program*. The major task of a syntax analyzer is to

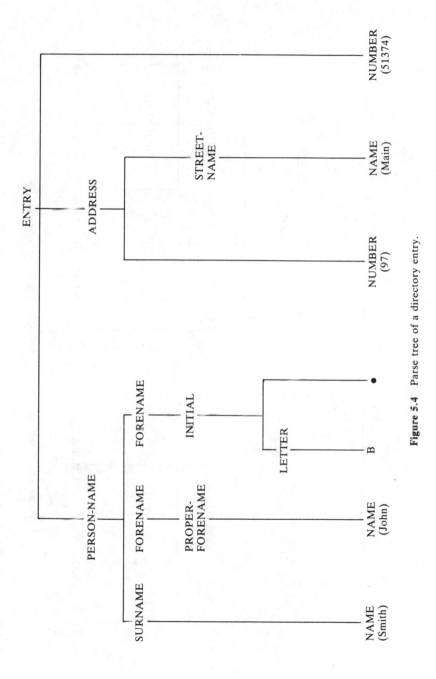

Figure 5.4 Parse tree of a directory entry.

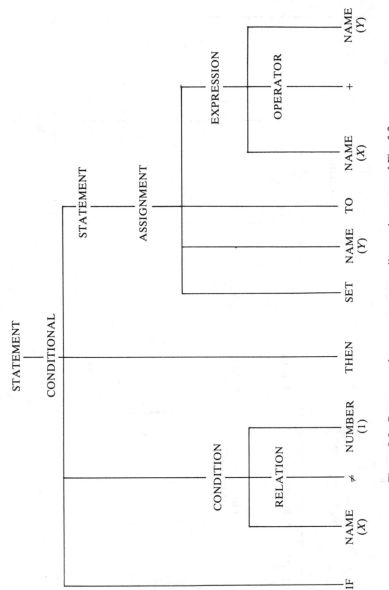

Figure 5.5 Parse tree of a statement, according to the syntax of Fig. 5.2.

construct the parse tree from the program text (more strictly, from the sequence of lexical tokens representing the program text). There are many algorithms for doing this, each designed to meet different objectives. Some algorithms are applicable only to languages with a particular type of syntax (i.e. whose productions satisfy certain restrictions); some are designed to minimize parsing time, some to minimize memory requirements, and some to provide sophisticated error-handling capabilities. The algorithm chosen for a particular compiler depends on the syntax of the language concerned and on the overall design objectives of the compiler writer.

There are, however, two main approaches to parsing. The first, called *bottom-up* parsing, is to start with the leaves of the parse tree and work up towards the root. (Remember, trees in computer science grow upside down!) The syntax analyzer tries to combine neighboring tokens in the source program to form elements of simple syntactic categories. These elements are then combined to form elements of more complex categories, and so on. Analysis is complete when successive combinations result in the entire source text being identified as a member of the category *program*. Note that at any stage several combinations may be possible, but if the syntax is unambiguous only one will ultimately lead to a complete parse tree. The analyzer may therefore try several unsuccessful combinations before hitting on the one which makes further progress possible. This process of controlled trial and error is an instance of *backtracking*—the exploration of a particular avenue and the return to explore other avenues if the first proves unsuccessful.

As an example of bottom-up parsing consider analysis of the telephone directory entry of Fig. 5.4. The analyzer might first recognize that Smith can be a surname and that John can be a forename, and might therefore try to combine Smith and John into a person-name. The combination is legitimate, but it leads to a dead end, since there is no production which allows the initial B. to be combined with the preceding person-name or with the following number. The analyzer must therefore backtrack and try a different combination, perhaps this time of all four symbols Smith, John, B and the period at once. This combination into a person-name is successful, as the following symbols can be combined into an address and a number, and the parse tree is readily completed.

The other principal method of parsing is *top-down*. As the name implies, this method starts with the root of the parse tree and works down towards the leaves. The analyzer starts with the hypothesis that the source text is indeed a valid program, and seeks to verify this hypothesis by looking for subunits of the text which are members of syntactic categories occurring at the first level of the parse tree. Recognizing such first level subunits involves looking for second level subunits which can possibly form them, and this in turn involves looking for third level subunits, and so on. As an example, analysis of the text shown in Fig. 5.4 would start with the hypothesis that the text is a valid directory entry. Verification of this hypothesis involves looking in the text for a person-name, an address, and a number, which are syntactic elements at the first level of the tree. Recognition of a person-name involves looking for a surname and possibly an initial, and so on. If occurrences of all the appropriate categories and symbols can be found, then the string is indeed a valid directory entry, with a parse tree constructed during the search. Note that some backtracking may be required; for example, in looking for a forename the analyzer might first try to find a proper-forename but eventually have to backtrack and look for an initial instead.

Top-down analysis is interesting in that algorithms to perform it can often be derived very simply from the productions of the language. Such an algorithm contains a number of modules, each of which corresponds to a particular syntactic category and whose function is to parse character sequences which are members of that category. As explained above, such parsing involves the parsing of members of simpler categories, so the body of each module consists of calls to other modules which perform this lower level parsing. The modules called are those which correspond to the categories on the right-hand side of the defining production.

As an example, consider the syntactic category *statement* in the programming language syntax of Fig. 5.2. This category has an associated module *parse-statement* whose function is to parse any sequence of symbols which is a valid statement. Since *statement* is defined by the production

statement → *conditional* | *loop* | *assignment*

the body of *parse-statement* consists of calls to the modules *parse-conditional*, *parse-loop*, and *parse-assignment*, each of which parses members of the corresponding syntactic category. These modules in turn call other modules appropriate to the right-hand sides of their defining productions.

Module *parse-statement* can be sketched as follows:

module *parse-statement*
{Outline of module to parse a statement in our simple language}
parse-conditional
if *not successful*
　then *parse-loop*
　　if *not successful*
　　　then *parse-assignment*
　　　　if *not successful*
　　　　　then *report failure*　　　　　　　　　　　　　(5.4)

The algorithm for *parse-assignment* is

> **module** *parse-assignment*
> {Outline of module to parse an assignment. Failure of any step implies
> failure of the module to perform the parse}
> *check that the type of the next token is "set"*
> *check that the type of the next token is "name"*
> *check that the type of the next token is "to"*
> *parse-expression*   (5.5)

The other modules can be defined in the same way. Note that the structure of each module reflects the structure of the defining production. For example, if the right-hand side of the production is a sequence then so is the body of the corresponding module (e.g. *parse-assignment*). Similarly, alternative definitions in the production are reflected by selective execution in the module (e.g. *parse-statement*). Recursive productions are reflected by recursive calls: for example, *parse-statement* calls *parse-conditional* which in turn calls *parse-statement*. (Escape from the recursion occurs when *parse-conditional* fails, forcing *parse-statement* to try its other alternatives.) Finally, if the defining production contains iteration the corresponding module contains a loop. The close correspondence between the parsing modules and the productions make it possible to generate parsing algorithms automatically. We shall discuss this point further in Section 5.4.4.

As mentioned earlier, both top-down and bottom-up parsing may involve backtracking. Since backtracking implies "wasted" processing, the degree to which it occurs in parsing a particular program largely determines how long the parse will take. If rapid parsing is one of the design goals of a language, then backtracking should be eliminated. This means that when faced with a number of options the analyzer must know the correct one to take. This can be accomplished by designing the syntax in such a way that the correct option at any stage is defined by the next few symbols in the program text. The analyzer need then look only a few symbols ahead in order to determine the option it should follow. This approach can be taken to the limit by designing the syntax so that only a single symbol lookahead is required. (Pascal, among other languages, has a syntax defined in this way.)

For example, the syntax of our hypothetical programming language (Fig. 5.2) is defined so that the type of each statement can be determined from its first symbol (**if**, **while**, or *set*). Thus when trying to parse a statement the analyzer need look only at this symbol in order to determine which of the three possible options to follow. The module *parse-statement* can therefore be re-written as follows.

module *parse-statement*
{Parses a statement, using single symbol lookahead to eliminate back-
  tracking}
if *the type of the next token is "***if***"*
  then *parse-conditional*
  else if *the type of the next token is "***while***"*
    then *parse-loop*
    else if *the type of the next token is "***set***"*
      then *parse-assignment*
      else *report failure*   (5.6)

The costs of eliminating backtracking are the additional constraints on the
language: overall design objectives will determine whether or not they are
worth paying.

Up to this point we have implicitly assumed that the source program is
syntactically correct. As any programmer will testify, this assumption is
unrealistic: a compiler must therefore be able to deal with any syntax errors
which occur. Detection of an error is relatively simple, since construction of
the parse tree will fail at some stage. However, it may not be obvious why the
failure has occurred, since the error may be hidden in part of the tree which
has already been built. For example, suppose that the telephone directory
entry

    Jones Mary 42 High 67431

is erroneously written

    Jones Mary High 67431

The syntax of directory entries (see Fig. 5.1) is such that the symbol High will
be interpreted as a forename and the number 67431 will be interpreted as
the first component of an address. A syntax error will be detected when the
rest of the address cannot be found: at this stage the partially completed
parse tree (assuming top-down analysis) will be as shown in Fig. 5.6.
Although the error is not detected until the end of the entry, it actually
occurs much earlier.

This kind of problem can be tackled by designing the syntax of a
language in such a way that errors become apparent almost immediately,
before parsing has continued very far. One way of doing this is to use certain
terminal symbols to separate pieces of text which belong to different syntactic categories. (Semi-colons and commas are popular choices.) For example,
we could modify our directory entry syntax by adding a comma as an extra
terminal symbol and by using it to separate the name, address, and telephone

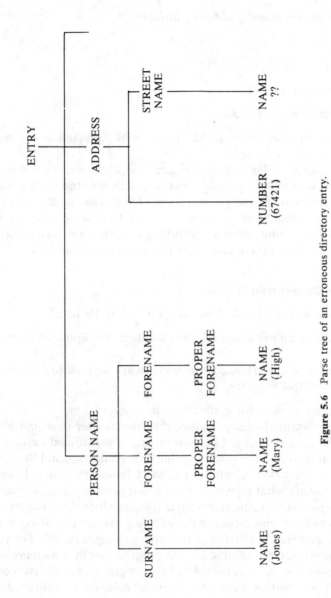

Figure 5.6 Parse tree of an erroneous directory entry.

number of each subscriber. In other words we could modify the production defining an entry to be

entry → *person-name* , *address* , number

If the entry

Jones Mary, 42 High, 67431

is now erroneously written

Jones Mary, High, 67431

(i.e. the same error as before), the error can be detected at the point it occurs.

As with lexical analysis, there are occasions when detection of an error should not prevent further parsing. On these occasions the syntax analyzer must report the error to the programmer, abandon as small a part of the parse tree as possible, and continue at the next syntactic category it can recognize. This procedure allows any further errors to be detected, but since the parse tree is incomplete code generation need not continue.

5.4.3 Code Generation

Code generation is the third phase of compilation. Its functions are

(1)   to allocate memory space for the data items manipulated by the program;
(2)   to generate machine language statements appropriate to each syntactic element of the program.

We shall discuss each of these functions in turn.

All programming languages allow the programmer to invent his own names for the data items used in a program. As mentioned earlier, these names are transformed into tokens during lexical analysis, and the value of each token is the name it represents. Most languages compel the programmer to specify what type of item (e.g. integer, character, sequence of characters) a particular name refers to: languages which do not insist on this often have a built-in convention of defaults (e.g. names beginning with the letters I–N are treated in Fortran as referring to integer items). The type of item each name refers to is defined by the programmer in certain *declarative information* which appears at the start of the program, or at the start of each module. This information is stored in a *symbol table* during syntax analysis.

The code generator uses the declarative information as a basis for allocating a portion of memory to each data item in the program. The address of the allocated portion is placed in the symbol table entry for the corresponding name. Each symbol table entry therefore contains the name of a data item, the type of the data item, and its address in memory.

Once memory has been allocated the code generator can proceed to produce machine language statements for each syntactic element of the program. These syntactic elements are such things as loops, conditions, and statements, and the code generator produces object code appropriate to each.

As an example we shall consider code generation for various syntactic categories of the simple language we defined earlier (Fig. 5.2). In that language an *expression* has the form

N1 *operator* N2

where N1 and N2 are the names of data items, and the operator can be "+" or "−". The code generated for an *expression* (in the machine language of section 4.5) should be

either	or
LOAD A1	LOAD A1
ADD A2	SUBTRACT A2

respectively, where A1 and A2 are the addresses of the data items N1 and N2. (We are using the symbols LOAD, ADD, SUBTRACT, and so on for clarity: the code generated is actually the binary equivalent of these operations.) This code leaves the value of the expression in the accumulator. An algorithm to generate the code is

> **module** *generate-expression(T)*
> {Generates code for an expression in our simple language.
> The parameter T is the parse tree of the expression concerned}
> *set A1 to the address of the data item whose name is in the left subtree of T*
> *generate "LOAD A1"*
> *set A2 to the address of the data item whose name is in the right subtree of T*
> **if** *the operator in T is "+"*
> **then** *generate "ADD A2"*
> **else** *generate "SUBTRACT A2"*   (5.7)

The addresses A1 and A2 are found in the symbol table entries for the corresponding data items.

An *assignment* in our language has the form

> *set N to expression*

where N is the name of some data item. Recall that the code for *expression* leaves the value of the expression in the accumulator, and that the STORE instruction transfers the value in the accumulator to a specified memory cell. The code generated for an *assignment* should therefore be the code for the *expression*, followed by

> STORE A

where A is the address of the data item N. The net effect is to place the value of the expression in the memory cell which represents N. Hence an appropriate algorithm is

> **module** *generate-assignment(T)*
> {Generates code for an assignment in our simple language. T is the parse tree of the assignment concerned}
> *set A to the address of the data item whose name is on the left of T*
> *generate-expression(right subtree of T)*
> *generate "STORE A"*   (5.8)

Other code generation modules can be constructed in the same way: for instance the module for a *statement* is

> **module** *generate-statement(T)*
> {Generates code for a statement in our simple language. T is the parse tree of the statement concerned}
> **if** *the statement is a conditional*
> **then** *generate-conditional(subtree of T)*
> **else if** *the statement is a loop*
>   **then** *generate-loop(subtree of T)*
>   **else** *generate-assignment(subtree of T)*   (5.9)

To make the example concrete, we shall describe what happens during compilation of the statement

> **if** $X \neq 1$
>   **then** *set* Y *to* $X+Y$

We saw in Section 5.4.1 that the lexical analyzer transforms the statement into the following sequence of tokens:

> **if** *name* $\neq$ *number* **then** *set name to name + name*
> (X)   (1)   (Y)   (X)   (Y)

The syntax analyzer recognizes this as a valid statement, constructing the parse tree shown in Fig. 5.5. The code generator uses declarative information in the program to allocate memory cells for the data items X and Y, and for the number 1. The resulting symbol table entries are shown in Fig. 5.7.

To generate code for the statement the code generator calls the module *generate-statement* sketched above. The parse tree indicates that the state-

ITEM NAME	ITEM TYPE	ADDRESS
X	integer	1456
Y	integer	1457
1	integer	100

Figure 5.7 Symbol table entries for code generation example.

ment is a *conditional*, and *generate-statement* therefore calls *generate-conditional*. This in turn calls *generate-condition*, and *generate-statement* again. On this second call the parse tree indicates that *generate-statement* should call *generate-assignment*. *Generate-assignment* operates in the way described earlier, and produces the following code.

```
LOAD  1456
ADD   1457
STORE 1457
```

The operation of *generate-condition* is similar (we shall not give the details), and the code generated for the complete statement is shown below. (We are assuming that the object code is to occupy memory from cell 1000 onward.)

Address	Instruction	
1000	LOAD	1456
1001	SUBTRACT	100
1002	JUMPZERO	1006
1003	LOAD	1456
1004	ADD	1457
1005	STORE	1457
1006	. . . .	

The first three instructions are the object code for the *condition* "$X \neq 1$", and the other three instructions are the code for the *assignment* "set Y to $X + Y$".

The reader may have realized that the modules for code generation and syntax analysis are very similar. Both kinds of module reflect the structure of the defining productions. For certain types of syntax which require no backtracking (such as that of our simple language) the correspondence is so close that code generation and syntax analysis can be combined. For example, the modules *parse-assignment* and *generate-assignment* (5.5 and 5.8) can be combined as follows:

> **module** *parse-and-generate-assignment*
> {Parses an assignment in our simple language, and generates code for it}
> *check that the type of the next token is "set"*
> *check that the type of the next token is "name"*
> *set A to the address of the item this token represents*
> *check that the type of the next token is "to"*
> *parse-and-generate-expression*
> *generate "STORE A"*   (5.10)

Once the object code has been generated it is sometimes *optimized*. Optimization can be regarded as a postscript to code generation or as an optional extra phase of compilation. Its purpose is to make the object program more efficient in some sense, usually by increasing its execution speed or sometimes by decreasing its memory requirements. As an example of what can be done, consider again the object code generated for the statement

> **if** $X \neq 1$
> **then** *set Y to X + Y*

If the statement is altered so that $X \neq 1$ is replaced by $X \neq 0$, the generated code is identical (but memory cell 100 contains 0 instead of 1). However, the instruction

> SUBTRACT   100

is now redundant, since subtraction of zero has no effect. The second occurrence of

> LOAD   1456

is also redundant, since the content of cell 1456 is already in the accumulator. The code can therefore be optimized to

Address	Instruction	
1000	LOAD	1456
1001	JUMPZERO	1004
1002	ADD	1457
1003	STORE	1457
1004	. . . .	

Optimization can be a time consuming process, since it involves inspection of the object code and the application of quite complex algorithms. In general there is a tradeoff between the time spent in optimization and the time gained during program execution. Detailed optimization is worthwhile only if the program is to be executed frequently or if it forms part of a time-critical application (e.g. control of a nuclear power station).

5.4.4 Compiler-writing Tools

In our discussion of syntax analysis (Section 5.4.2) we pointed out that the construction of a top-down parsing algorithm can be quite straightforward, provided the syntax of the language concerned can be defined by a set of BNF productions. Indeed, derivation of the parsing algorithm from the syntax definition is so straightforward that the derivation itself can be readily described by an algorithm, and implemented as a program. Such a program is called a *parser-generator*, since it generates a parsing algorithm from a syntax definition. (Our discussion has been limited to top-down parsing, but parser-generators also exist for bottom-up parsing.) A parser-generator is a very useful tool, as it can largely automate the construction of the syntax analysis phase of a compiler.

With some extensions a parser-generator can construct not only the syntax analysis phase, but the entire compiler itself. For historical reasons a parser-generator extended in this way is called a *compiler-compiler*, though compiler-generator would be a more accurate description. A compiler-compiler generates a compiler for a language L on a computer C from a specification of

(1) the syntax of L and
(2) the machine language instructions of C corresponding to statements in L.

The first of these is used to generate a parser, the second to produce appropriate code generation modules.

Since a compiler-compiler is intended to produce a compiler for any language on any computer there is little chance that the compiler it generates in any particular case will be as good as a similar compiler produced by hand. However, a compiler-compiler can be an effective tool for the rapid implementation of a new language, or an existing language on a different computer. In these cases a rough and ready compiler can be generated with little programming effort, and a more efficient compiler can be produced later if necessary.

We should point out that a compiler-compiler is not a piece of system software, but a tool for writing system software. As such it does not figure largely (or at all) in most manufacturers' product lines, since most computer users do not write their own compilers. It is, however, very valuable in those environments where language implementation and innovation are carried out.

5.4.5 Assemblers

A simple example of a language translator is the *assembler*, which translates programs written in an *assembly language* into machine language. An assembly language can be regarded as a slightly higher form of machine language: each statement in an assembly language usually corresponds to a single machine language instruction. Like machine language, an assembly language is peculiar to the computer for which it is designed: programs written in an assembly language cannot be transferred to other computers without rewriting them.

The major difference between assembly language and machine language lies in the way that memory cells may be referred to. In a machine language program a memory cell must be referred to by its address. In an assembly language program, on the other hand, a cell can be referred to by a name chosen by the programmer. The correspondence between names and addresses must, however, be specified in the program. (The way this is done is not important here; the interested reader is referred to the bibliography.)

The syntax of a typical assembly language statement (for a computer such as that described in Chapter 4) is

statement → *operation address*
operation → LOAD | STORE | ADD | ...
address → name | number | *address op* number
op → + | −

Examples of valid statements are

ADD A LOAD $A+1$ STORE $A-3$

where A is the name given by the programmer to a particular memory cell. The address $A+1$ is the address of the cell following A; $A-3$ is the cell three before A.

Because most assembly languages have a simple syntax (like that above), the tasks of lexical and syntactic analysis are very straightforward. During syntax analysis information is gathered about the correspondence between the names and addresses of memory cells, and this information is entered in a symbol table (cf. Section 5.4.3). Code generation, too, is straightforward. The assembler generates one machine language instruction for each assembly language statement. The *operation* in each statement is translated into the corresponding operation code in machine language (e.g. for the machine language of Section 4.5, ADD is translated into 0011). Using information in the symbol table, the *address* in each statement is translated into the numerical address of the corresponding memory cell. Thus if A is the name given to cell 42, the assembly language statement

ADD $A + 1$

is translated into

0011 000000101011

It will be apparent from this discussion that assembly languages are little more than a convenient form of machine language. Assembly languages therefore suffer from the same defects as machine languages (discussed in Section 5.1), and are unsuitable for the expression of complex algorithms or for writing programs which may be used on several different computers. Although widely used in the past, the advent of higher level languages has reduced their role considerably. Their use is now normally restricted to tuning, or to a few programs which are extremely machine dependent, such as the handling of interrupts and the control of I/O devices (see Section 4.6).

5.5   OPERATING SYSTEMS

5.5.1   Overview

An operating system is perhaps the most important piece of system software accompanying a computer, and is usually the most complex. Its broad purpose is to provide facilities which make the computer easier and more economical to use. All computers (except possibly some primitive micro-computers) have an operating system which is usually supplied by the manufacturer, and in many cases the operating system is the product of a design and development effort comparable to that of the computer hardware itself. The reasons why operating systems are so complex—sometimes comprising hundreds of thousands of program statements—will become apparent as this section progresses.

An operating system fulfills many detailed functions, which can be broadly categorized as follows (cf. Section 5.1).

(1)   Making it unnecessary for the user or other system software to be aware of awkward features of the computer hardware. Some of the most awkward features are concerned with handling input and output (I/O), and the operating system plays a major role in making the I/O facilities easier to use.

(2)   Provision of facilities for the manipulation of programs and data. The user needs to be able to instruct the computer system to do such things as "Compile my program called CHESS", or "Amalgamate the two sets of data called RURAL and URBAN, and use the result as input to my previously compiled program called SURVEY ANALYSIS." The operating system is responsible for interpreting these commands and organizing the complex set of actions necessary to carry them out.

(3)   Sharing the computer's resources among several simultaneous users. The aim is to increase the availability of the computer to its users, and at the same time to maximize the utilization of such resources as the central'processor, the memory, and the peripherals. The importance of resource utilization depends on the cost of the resources concerned: the recent rapid decline in hardware costs has led to decreased emphasis on resource utilization, to the extent that many microcomputers are dedicated to a single function and never shared at all. Large computers, however, are still expensive enough to warrant considerable effort in sharing their resources.

Perhaps the best way to appreciate these functions is to consider how one might use a computer if it had no operating system at all. Suppose, for example, that the purpose of the computer is to execute a variety of jobs for a number of users. (A *job* can be thought of as the sequence of actions necessary to execute a user program; in a simple case it might involve compilation of the source program, followed by the loading and execution of the object program.) If the computer has no operating system, then in order to have a job executed each user must go through a sequence of steps something like the following:

(1)   present the source program to an appropriate input device (e.g. if the source program is punched on cards, place the cards in a card reader);

(2)   initiate a compiler to read the source program from the input device, compile it, and place the resulting object program in secondary storage;

(3)   initiate a loader to transfer the object program from secondary storage to main memory;

(4)   place any data required by the program in the appropriate input device;

(5)   initiate execution of the object program;

(6)   collect the output from whatever output device the program uses (e.g. a printer).

Under this procedure the *throughput* of the computer (i.e. the number of jobs it executes in a given time) is limited by the speed at which each user can press the appropriate buttons and handle the I/O devices employed by his program. Such human activities are tediously slow when compared with the execution speed of the central processor, so it is apparent that the computer is not being effectively utilized.

A first step toward increasing the throughput is to delegate the manipulation of buttons and I/O devices to a skilled operator, but in view of the great disparity between human and computer speeds the improvement is only marginal. A more significant step is to automate the sequence of operations involved in executing a job, so that human intervention is reduced to a minimum. This can be done by introducing a small control program whose purpose is to initiate the compiler, the loader, and the object program at the appropriate times. The operator's role is then reduced to handling I/O devices.

Unfortunately not all jobs require the same sequence of operations. They may, for example, require the use of different compilers, and those which involve previously compiled programs require no compiler at all. The control program must therefore be able to distinguish between different jobs, and invoke the operations appropriate to each. Hence each job must have some associated *job control information* (supplied by the user) detailing what sort of job it is and what the user requires. The control program must be able to interpret this information and act accordingly. Furthermore, an error in one job should not affect subsequent jobs, and so the control program must be able to handle errors in some rational way. Thus the control program is responsible for the interpretation of job control information, the initiation of appropriate operations, and error handling. It is, in fact, an embryonic operating system.

With human intervention reduced to a minimum, the throughput of the computer is now limited by the speed at which it can perform I/O. (Remember from Chapter 4 that the speed of I/O devices is usually far less than that of a central processor.) An increase in throughput can be achieved only by removing the I/O limitation. This can be done by making use of *interrupts*—the signals from I/O devices to the central processor which indicate that a transfer of data is complete (see Section 4.6). An interrupt facility allows the processor to initiate an I/O transfer, to continue processing while the transfer takes place, and to receive notification by means of an interrupt when the transfer is complete.

The ability to overlap I/O transfers with processing can be exploited only if the processor has something else to do while each I/O transfer takes place. One way of ensuring this is by *multiprogramming*—that is, by having the programs and data for several jobs in main memory at the same time. While one job waits for input or output to take place the processor can execute another job instead. The end of the I/O transfer is notified by an interrupt, and the waiting job can then be resumed, either immediately or when the second job requests some input or output of its own. The idea is illustrated in Fig. 5.8, which shows the execution of three jobs in a multiprogrammed system. For simplicity the three jobs in the example are identical, each requiring a period of execution lasting 1 millisecond (i.e. thousandth of a second, abbreviated ms) before and after an I/O transfer which also lasts 1 ms. Figure 5.8(a) shows execution of the three jobs in sequence, as in a non-multiprogrammed system; Fig. 5.8(b) shows the effect of multiprogramming. Note that in Fig. 5.8(b) the processor is busy all the time and that the three jobs are completed in 6 ms; in Fig. 5.8(a) the processor is idle for 3 ms and the jobs take 9 ms to complete. Multiprogramming in this case increases the throughput from an average rate of 333 jobs per second (1 job every 3 ms) to 500 jobs per second (1 job every 2 ms)—an increase of 50%. In general, of course, one cannot expect that the processing and I/O requirements of the different jobs will complement each other as conveniently as in our example. However, the more jobs there are in memory the higher is the chance that one of them is ready to be executed.

As well as increasing throughput, multiprogramming has other advantages. One of these is improved utilization of resources such as peripherals, since the jobs in memory at any time can be chosen so that their resource requirements complement each other and together account for all (or nearly all) the resources available. A second advantage is that it creates the possibility of several users having access to the computer simultaneously. Each user can initiate jobs from his own terminal, and the jobs can be executed at the same time as jobs initiated by other users at other terminals. The progress of each job, and any results it produces, can be reported immediately to the originating terminal. This mode of operation is called *multi-access* or *time-sharing* (the latter term derives from the sharing of processor time among the users).

The implementation of multiprogramming requires significant additions to the embryonic operating system described earlier. In particular, modules are needed to perform the following functions.

(1)   *Dispatching*   Switching the processor from one job to another as appropriate.

(2)   *Interrupt handling*   Interpreting each interrupt as a signal that an I/O transfer is complete and hence that the job which requested the transfer can now resume execution.

(3)   *Resource allocation*   Allocation of the computer's resources to jobs as required. The resources include memory, I/O devices, and the processor itself. However, the latter is sufficiently important to be considered separately (under (1) above).

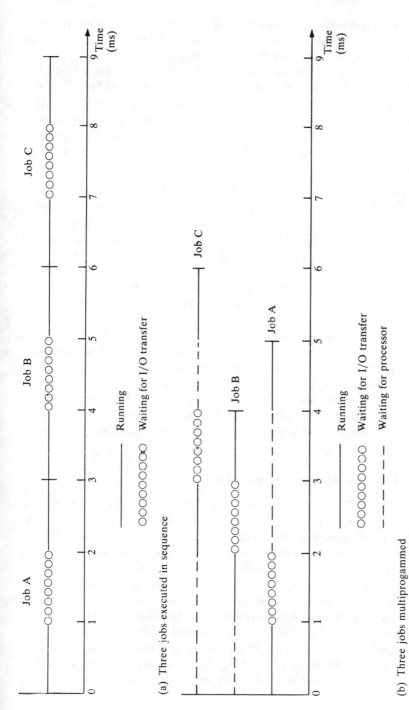

Figure 5.8 The effect of multiprogramming.

(4)   *Resource protection*   Ensuring that no job can access any resource which has not been allocated to it. This is essential if jobs are to be protected against the effects of error or malice in others.

(5)   *Scheduling*   Deciding which job (or jobs) to select for execution when some other job finishes. The programs and data of jobs awaiting execution are normally held in secondary storage and transferred into main memory immediately before execution commences. The decision about which job(s) to start is based on such factors as the urgency of each job, the resources currently available, and the resources each job requires.

We shall discuss these functions in more detail later, but it will already be apparent that the increased throughput and resource utilization obtained through multiprogramming are achieved only at the expense of considerably increasing the complexity of the operating system. Such complexity is not warranted if the computer is inexpensive enough to be dedicated to a single user (as in a home computer) or to a single function (as in a microcomputer which controls a piece of industrial machinery). Multiprogramming is, however, the common mode of operation for larger and more expensive computers.

Summarizing the discussion so far, our desire to increase the throughput of the basic computer hardware has led us to introduce an operating system with a large number of functions. Some of these functions also make the computer easier to use. For example, the handling of interrupts relieves the programmer from the task of writing pieces of program to detect when I/O transactions are complete. In the next few sections we shall look at how some of these functions can be implemented, and at the algorithms involved in doing so.

5.5.2   Processor Allocation: the Dispatcher

We saw earlier that execution of a job may involve execution of a number of different programs, such as a compiler, a loader, and a compiled object program. Provision of operating system functions also involves execution of a number of different programs—programs which are part of the operating system. The execution of a program is called a *process* (recall Chapter 2), and the operating system is responsible for initiating and coordinating the variety of processes which need to be carried out. Some of these processes perform operating system functions (such as scheduling and I/O handling), while others (such as compilation) are initiated on behalf of users.

The simultaneous existence of a number of processes implies that the computer's central processing unit (CPU) must be shared among them. This is the case even when the computer has only a single user, since processes initiated on behalf of the user must still share the CPU with processes which are part of the operating system. When multiprogramming is in force the degree of sharing is correspondingly increased. Sharing is effected by repeatedly switching the CPU from one process to another, so that each process is executed for a short time before it loses the CPU to some other process. The switching is usually done so rapidly (every fiftieth of a second or so) that all the processes appear to be executed simultaneously, though the CPU can of course be allocated to only one process at a time.

If more than one CPU is available, then some processes really can be executed concurrently. However, there are generally far fewer CPUs than processes, and so the CPUs must still be switched from one task to another. Computers with sufficient CPUs to allocate one to every process are not yet commercially available, though several are in the experimental design and construction phase. In the following paragraphs we shall assume that CPU switching is necessary, but we shall not restrict the discussion to single CPU machines.

Once a process is initiated it can be in any of the following three states (see Fig. 5.9).

(1) *Running*   The process is being executed by a CPU.
(2) *Ready*   The process is executable, and is waiting for a CPU to be allocated to it. All ready processes are candidates for allocation of a CPU.

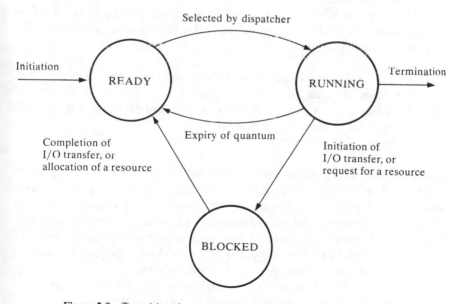

Figure 5.9   Transitions between the three possible states of a process.

(3) *Blocked*   The process cannot proceed until some event, such as the completion of an I/O transfer, occurs. Blocked processes are not candidates for allocation of a CPU.

A running process becomes blocked when it requests an I/O transfer, and it remains blocked until the transfer is complete. At this point the process becomes ready, and eventually runs again when a CPU is allocated to it. Thus processes which alternate computation with I/O repeatedly cycle through the running, blocked, and ready states.

In some operating systems the initiation of an I/O transfer is the only occasion on which a CPU is switched away from a process. However, such an arrangement can lead to the monopolization of a CPU by a single process which performs I/O only rarely. To achieve more equitable sharing of CPUs it is necessary to limit the length of time for which a process can execute continuously, and to switch the CPU away from any process which reaches its limit. The amount of time allowed to a process for continuous execution is called its *quantum* (or *time-slice*)—a process which uses up its quantum moves from the running to the ready state, yielding its CPU to some other ready process. The process is given a fresh quantum when it is next selected to run. The choice of quantum size depends on a variety of complex factors, such as the amount of time the process has already used, the overhead incurred by switching, and the constraints of equity. Typical values fall in the range $1/50-1/4$ second.

The responsibility of switching CPUs among processes lies with an operating system module called the *dispatcher* (or *low-level scheduler*). The dispatcher is normally invoked whenever

(1) a running process requests an I/O transfer or some resource, thus becoming blocked; or
(2) the quantum of a running process expires, indicating that the corresponding CPU should be reallocated; or
(3) a running process terminates.

In each of these cases the dispatcher must select one of the ready processes to run next. The selection criteria are usually aimed at ensuring an equitable share of the CPUs for all processes, but in some cases selection is biased toward those processes which are deemed to have a high priority (perhaps because they perform important system functions, or because they are associated with jobs of some urgency). Selection by the dispatcher causes a process to move from the ready to the running state.

The preceding discussion is summarized in Fig. 5.9, which shows the three states of a process and the transitions between them.

5.5.3 Memory Management

One of the most important functions of an operating system is the management of the memory resources of the computer. Memory management has three major aspects:

(1) *Allocation*   For a process to be executed it must be allocated sufficient memory to hold its program and data.

(2) *Protection*   It is important that no process can access any portion of memory not allocated to it. Protection against such illicit access is essential if programming errors in a process are to be prevented from affecting other processes. Protection is also essential in preventing unauthorized inspection of another process's data, or malicious interference in another process's execution.

(3) *Utilization*   Memory is a valuable resource since it is the only place in which the programs of executing processes can reside. It is therefore important to use it to best advantage, by allocating as much as possible at any time and by trying to ensure that there are always processes in memory which are ready to be executed.

It should be clear that in order to achieve high utilization the operating system must be free to allocate to a process whatever portion of memory is currently available. Moreover, the operating system may need to move a process's program and data from one area of memory to another so that, for example, several small unallocated areas may be amalgamated into a larger more usable area. This means that when a program is written and compiled neither the programmer nor the compiler can know whereabouts in memory the program will reside during execution. We saw in Section 5.4 that part of the process of compilation is the generation of addresses in the object program, so the question which naturally arises is the following. How can a compiler (or other language translator) generate appropriate addresses when it does not know which area of memory the object program will occupy during execution?

The answer to this question lies in a clear distinction between the *program addresses* generated by a language translator and the *memory addresses* of the cells in which the object program eventually resides. The language translator assumes that the whole of memory is available, and generates program addresses ranging from zero upwards: these addresses must subsequently be transformed into corresponding memory addresses for the area of memory allocated to the object program by the operating system. The transformation from program addresses to memory addresses is usually performed by the CPU at the time the object program is executed. There are several ways of doing this, all of them requiring some modification of the CPU hardware and microprogram we described in Chapter 4 (where we assumed that only one program resided in memory at once), and all of them using information maintained by the operating system. Two commonly used methods, and the memory management policies that can be based on them, are described in the following subsections.

Base and limit registers

The first method of transforming program addresses into memory addresses requires the provision of a further register in the CPU. This register, known variously as a *base*, *datum*, or *relocation* register, contains the *base address* of the currently executing process—that is, the address of the first cell of memory allocated to the process. The CPU transforms each program address used by the process into the appropriate memory address simply by adding the content of the base register to it. This can be done by means of a minor modification to the microprogram.

As an example, suppose that two processes A and B are allocated areas of memory as shown in Fig. 5.10. Process A has program addresses in the range 0–1199 and is allocated memory cells 1500–2699; process B has program addresses in the range 0–799 and is allocated memory cells 2800–3599. When the dispatcher selects process A to run it loads the base address 1500 into the base register (Fig. 5.10(a)). The CPU computes the appropriate memory addresses by adding the content of the base register to each program address used during execution: each memory address is therefore 1500 greater than the corresponding program address, correctly reflecting the position of process A in the memory. Similarly, when process B is selected to run, the base register is loaded with the base address 2800 (Fig. 5.10(b)), and each program address used during execution of B has 2800 added to it to produce the appropriate memory address. Note that processes A and B can use the same program addresses, but that these will be appropriately transformed into different memory addresses. Thus the program address 135, say, will be transformed into the memory address 1635 when A is running and into the memory address 2935 when B is running.

The use of a base register allows the program and data for each process to be located in any available portion of memory, and to be moved by the operating system at will. The only burden on the operating system is to remember the base address of each process and to load the base register accordingly when the process is selected to run. The base register is not, however, sufficient to protect a process against intrusions into its allocated memory by some other process, whether through error or malice. For example, if process A of Fig. 5.10 uses the program address 2000, this will be transformed by the CPU into memory address 3500. Memory cell 3500 is, however, allocated to process B, and should therefore not be accessible to process A. Some means of preventing such access is called for.

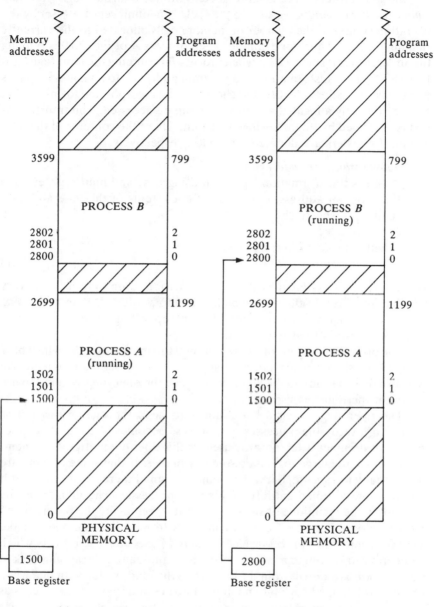

(a) Process *A* running   (b) Process *B* running

Figure 5.10   Address transformation by a base register.

Suitable protection can be provided by adding a further register, called a *limit register* or *length register*, to the CPU. The limit register is set by the operating system to the number of memory cells allocated to the currently running process. Thus, for example, when process A of Fig. 5.10 is running the limit register is set to 1200; when process B is running the limit register is set to 800. The transformation of a program address into a memory address is basically the same as before, but checks can be incorporated to ensure that only legitimately allocated memory cells can be accessed. The transformation is described by the following algorithm, where the contents of the base and limit registers are denoted by b and l respectively.

> **module** *transform-address(a)*
> {Address transformation algorithm using base and limit registers. a is the program address; b and l are the contents of the base and limit registers respectively}
> **if** $a < 0$ *or* $a \geq l$
>   **then** *indicate addressing error*
>   **else** *set memory address to* $a + b$ (5.11)

This algorithm is executed by the CPU's microprogram to transform every program address into the corresponding memory address. If an addressing error occurs, then control is returned to the operating system, which normally aborts the offending process.

The preceding paragraphs have outlined the mechanisms by which base and limit registers provide hardware support for memory management. We now turn our attention to the algorithms which the operating system can use to exploit these mechanisms.

The operating system's basic aim is to keep the memory as full as possible of executable processes. If a process becomes blocked the area of memory it occupies is temporarily useless: this does not matter if the memory is sufficiently large to contain so many processes that some of them are always ready to execute, but if the memory is small there is a danger that it may become occupied entirely by blocked processes. The danger can be reduced by the technique of *swapping*—that is, removing the program and data of a blocked process from main memory to secondary storage to make room for some other process which is ready to execute. The process which has been swapped out of memory becomes a candidate for swapping back in again as soon as it moves from the blocked to the ready state. Note that when a process is swapped back into memory it need not occupy the same cells as before it was swapped out: the operating system simply loads the base register with the new base address when the process is selected to run. Decisions about which processes to swap are based on such criteria as a process's priority, the amount of memory it occupies, the length of time for which it is expected to be blocked, and the length of time for which it has already occupied memory. Swapping can greatly increase the effective use of memory, but only at the cost of the time taken to move programs and data to and from secondary storage.

On termination of a process the area of memory it occupies can be allocated to a new process. Since it is unlikely that the new process will require exactly the same amount of memory as the old one, a small area of memory may be left unused, as shown in Fig. 5.11. After a time, when several

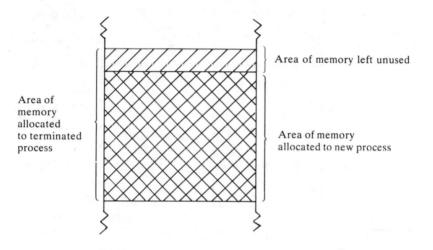

Area of memory left unused

Area of memory allocated to terminated process

Area of memory allocated to new process

Figure 5.11   Memory fragmentation.

cycles of termination and reallocation have occurred, the memory may become *fragmented*—that is, a substantial proportion of it may be taken up by a large number of unallocated areas, each of which is too small by itself to accommodate a process. Excessive fragmentation implies low memory utilization, and the operating system must therefore strive to keep fragmentation to a minimum. This can be done by careful allocation (several algorithms exist, but are beyond the scope of this book) and by amalgamating adjacent areas of unused memory to form larger more usable areas. If all else fails the entire content of memory can be moved downward, creating a single unallocated area at the top. This process, called *compaction*, is illustrated in Fig. 5.12. The overhead of moving everything in memory and resetting all the base addresses is considerable, and compaction is therefore regarded as a last resort.

One disadvantage of memory management schemes which rely on base and limit registers is that the whole of a process's program and data must be

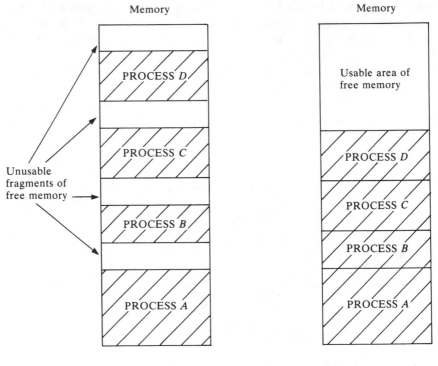

(a) Before compaction   (b) After compaction

Figure 5.12   The effect of compaction.

simultaneously present in memory when the process is executed. This means
that

(a)   space must be found for the entire program and data, even though the
      process may use only a small part of it during any particular period of
      execution; and

(b)   the size of the program and data is limited by the capacity of the
      computer's memory.

In the following paragraphs we describe a memory management mechanism
which avoids this disadvantage.

Paging
Paging is a memory management technique which allows a process to be
executed when only a portion of its program and data is resident in main

memory. It therefore allows a process to be executed even when all its program and data cannot be fitted into memory at once. (It is not the only such technique: others may be found through the bibliography.)

When paging is employed the program and data of each process are regarded as being partitioned into a number of *pages* of equal size, and the computer's memory is similarly divided into a number of *page frames* of the same size. Each page frame is capable of holding a single page of any process. Page frames are allocated among processes by the operating system, so that at any given time each process may have a few pages which occupy page frames in memory while the rest are held in secondary storage.

The division of a process's program and data into pages is quite simple. If the page size is 1000, say, then page 0 comprises all program and data with program addresses in the range 0–999; page 1 comprises all program and data with program addresses 1000–1999, and so on. Note that it is only the computer hardware and the operating system which regard a process as being divided in this way: the mechanics of paging are both irrelevant and invisible to programmers and language translators.

The CPU transforms a program address into a memory address by

(a)   calculating from the program address which page, and which cell within the page, is being referred to; and

(b)   using information maintained by the operating system to determine which page frame the page currently occupies.

The first of these steps is straightforward, requiring only division of the program address by the page size. For example, if the program address is 2764 and the page size is 1000, then the reference is to cell 764 of page 2. In practice the page size is chosen to be a power of 2 (usually 512, 1024, or 2048), making the division (in binary) trivial.

The second stage of address transformation is performed by means of a *page table*, which is a table indicating which page frame, if any, is occupied by each of a process's pages. The operating system maintains a separate page table for each process, and updates it to reflect the current occupancy of page frames by pages. There is one entry in a process's page table for each of its pages: the entry contains

(a)   an indication of whether or not the page is currently held in memory; and

(b)   if the page is in memory, then the address of the page frame holding it; otherwise the location of the page in secondary storage.

If the referenced page is in memory the address of its page frame is sufficient information to complete the transformation from program address to memory address. However, it is possible for a process to refer to a page which is not currently held in memory. In this case (called a *page fault*) the address transformation cannot be completed until the referenced page has been transferred from secondary storage into memory and the page table updated accordingly. The process becomes blocked while this is going on, and another process runs in the meantime. When the page transfer is complete the process becomes ready again, and is eventually selected to run. At this point the entire address transformation process is repeated, and this time is successful. The address transformation algorithm executed by the CPU is shown below, and is illustrated in Fig. 5.13.

> **module** *transform-address(a)*
> {Address transformation algorithm for paging. *a* is the program address; *z* is the page size}
> *set page number p to integer part of a/z*
> *set location w within page to remainder of a/z*
> *access pth entry of process's page table*
> **if** *page is held in memory*
>   **then** *extract page frame address pf from table*
>   *set memory address to pf + w*
>   **else** *cause operating system to transfer page into memory and update*
>   *page table accordingly*
>   {the process is blocked until this is complete, after which the
>   algorithm is re-executed}   (5.12)

Since the speed of address transformation is crucial to the overall speed of the computer, it is customary to hold a portion of the page table for the currently running process in a set of special CPU registers as well as in memory. We shall not describe this enhancement here, but refer the interested reader to the bibliography.

Note that paging allows a program to be larger than the computer's memory, since the program need not be wholly contained in memory in order to be executed. Paging therefore gives the illusion of a *virtual memory* which is larger than the actual memory available. It is this virtual memory which is "seen" by the programmer and by the programming language translator: both can be quite unaware of the underlying mechanisms that implement it.

Protection of memory from unauthorized access is automatically guaranteed by the use of a separate page table for each process. All memory addresses used by a process are interpreted relative to the process's own page table: thus there is no way in which a process can access page frames not allocated to it.

The major policy decisions taken by the operating system in a paging environment relate to which of a process's pages should be held in memory

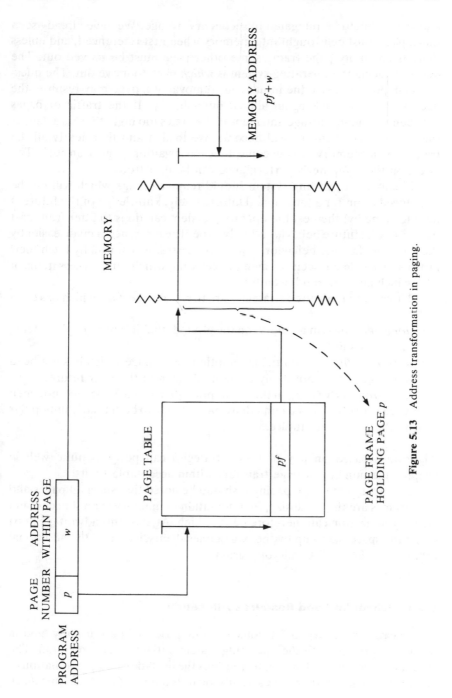

Figure 5.13 Address transformation in paging.

and which should be relegated to secondary storage. We have already seen that a page must be brought into memory when first referenced, and unless there is an empty page frame some other page must be moved out. The question facing the operating system is *which* page to move out. The question is important, since the injudicious removal of a page may result in the need to bring it back again almost immediately. If the traffic of pages between secondary storage and memory becomes too high, there is a danger that the I/O mechanisms will become overloaded and that nearly all the processes in memory will become blocked awaiting page transfers. The effect on the computer's performance can be disastrous.

Ideally the operating system should remove a page which will not be referenced again for a long time. Unfortunately, knowledge of the future is hard to come by: the best the operating system can do is to infer from past behavior what future behavior is likely to be. The inference is made easier by the fairly predictable behavior of most processes, which usually fetch their instructions from consecutive memory cells and which often access items of data which are stored adjacently.

Three commonly used strategies are to replace the page which has been

(1) *longest resident* in memory, on the grounds that it is probably not being used any more;
(2) *least recently used*, on the assumption that a page which has not been used recently is not likely to be used again in the near future;
(3) *least frequently used*, on the assumption that a page which has not been used very often in the immediate past is likely to be similarly unpopular in the immediate future.

Algorithms based on any of these strategies can perform quite well in keeping the number of page transfers within acceptable limits.

As a final remark on paging it should be noted that since all pages and page frames are the same size, fragmentation of memory cannot occur, and memory utilization can therefore be very high. Against this advantage must be set the space taken up by the page tables themselves, and the additional complexity of the CPU microprogram.

5.5.4 Scheduling and Resource Allocation

As indicated in Section 5.5.1, jobs awaiting processing are usually held in secondary storage until the operating system initiates their execution. The execution of a single job normally requires the initiation and coordination of several processes, either concurrently or in sequence (see Section 5.5.2).

The responsibility for initiating processes rests with an operating system module called the *scheduler*.

In deciding when to initiate a process the scheduler takes account of such factors as

(1)   the amount of resources (e.g. memory, processing time, I/O devices) which the process requires;
(2)   the amount of resources currently available;
(3)   the priority of the job with which the process is associated;
(4)   the length of time for which the associated job has been waiting.

The weight given to these factors varies from one operating system to another, depending on whether the major objective is high overall throughput or the provision of rapid service to a certain class of user (e.g. those currently accessing the system through terminals).

Information about the resource requirements of a process can be gleaned while the process is executing, or can be supplied by the user as part of the job control information of the associated job. (Job control information was mentioned in Section 5.5.1, and will be discussed more fully in Section 5.5.7). Information about the resources currently available is maintained by the scheduler and updated as resources are allocated and released.

Resource allocation may be either

(1)   *static*, meaning that all the resources required by a process are allocated when the process is initiated and reclaimed when the process is complete; or
(2)   *dynamic*, meaning that resources are allocated to a process when required and are released when the process has finished with them.

Under static allocation a process can be initiated only when all the resources required are available; under dynamic allocation a process may be initiated at any time, but it may subsequently become blocked if a resource is not available when needed. Dynamic allocation can lead to better resource utilization, but is more difficult to administer. In particular, measures must be taken to deal with *deadlock*—a situation in which two (or more) processes each hold a resource which is required by the other. If neither process can release the resource it holds then neither can proceed, and both will remain blocked indefinitely. (Deadlock is analogous to the traffic jam which can occur when two opposing streams of traffic, in trying to turn across each other's path, become completely immobilized because each occupies the road space required by the other.) Various measures can be taken to avoid or overcome deadlock: all of them have disadvantages of one form or another, and some of them can be quite complex and time-consuming.

5.5.5   I/O Handling

We saw in Section 5.5.1 that one of the functions of an operating system is to handle all I/O transactions on behalf of user processes. This burden is placed on the operating system for several reasons:

(1)   The I/O devices attached to a computer vary enormously in their operational characteristics—particularly in their speed, in the amount of data they transfer in a single operation, and in the way the data is represented on the input or output medium. It would be irksome for the user to have to be concerned with these details: it is far more convenient for him to call upon operating system modules to handle I/O operations for him.

(2)   For efficiency in processor allocation (recall Section 5.5.2), the operating system must know when I/O transfers are initiated and when they are completed: this is most easily arranged if the operating system handles all transfers itself.

(3)   Some I/O devices are *shareable* in the sense that they can handle successive I/O transfers which originate from different processes. A disk, for example, is shareable because different transfers can be directed to or from different areas of the disk without risk of confusion. Other devices are *unshareable*: the ways in which they operate imply that successive I/O transfers from different processes would lead to an inextricable mingling of data. A line printer, for example, is an unshareable device, since its use by several processes at once would cause the lines of output from the different processes to be interleaved on the same sheets of paper. Unshareable devices can be allocated to only one process at a time, and the operating system must ensure that a process uses only those devices which are allocated to it. This is most easily accomplished if the operating system handles all I/O transactions itself.

A process requests an I/O transfer by calling the appropriate operating system module with parameters which specify the nature of the transfer required. This module

(1)   checks the legitimacy of the request (e.g. that the I/O device is allocated to the requesting process);

(2)   initiates the transfer by executing instructions appropriate to the I/O device concerned;

(3)   blocks the requesting process;

(4)   calls the dispatcher to select some other process to run.

Completion of the transfer is signalled by means of an interrupt, which causes the CPU to execute a jump to a fixed location in memory (recall

Section 4.6). This location contains the first instruction of an *interrupt handler*, which is an operating system module for dealing with the interrupt. The interrupt handler

(1) identifies the source of the interrupt (i.e. which I/O device caused it), and hence the process which instigated the transfer;
(2) alters the status of the instigating process from blocked to ready, thus making the process eligible to be resumed;
(3) resumes the process which was running when the interrupt occurred. (Alternatively, the interrupt may be used as an opportunity to reallocate the CPU, in which case the interrupt handler calls the dispatcher to select another process to run.)

The details of the entire I/O operation are invisible to the requesting process, which need only call the appropriate I/O module.

One matter not addressed above is that of device allocation. As mentioned earlier, a process can use an unshareable device only if the device has been allocated to it. This implies that during periods of high demand several processes may be blocked waiting for access to heavily used devices, while during other periods the same devices may be idle. In order to spread the load on unshareable devices and reduce the possibility of bottlenecks it is possible to *spool* all I/O for heavily used unshareable devices. This means that all I/O transfers for such devices are redirected by the operating system through some intermediate shareable medium such as a disk. As an example, consider a process which wants to print output on a line printer. The process calls the operating system I/O module in the way described earlier, but this module sends the output to a disk instead of directly to the printer. All printer output from other processes is similarly sent to the disk, but as the disk is a shareable device no allocation problem arises. The output is eventually moved from the disk to the printer by an operating system process called a *spooler* to which the printer is permanently allocated. During periods of heavy printing activity a backlog of output may build up on the disk; this is cleared by the spooler as activity lessens.

5.5.6 The File System

In most computer systems there is a need to store information in easily accessible form for long periods of time. The kind of information stored naturally varies according to the purposes for which the system is used, but generally speaking it includes any programs or data which are to be used repeatedly. Examples are systems programs, data collected from scientific experiments or from surveys, programs written by users, and data bases for a wide range of applications. If the information is to be readily accessible it must be stored within the computer system itself—to input it each time is impracticable.

For technical and economic reasons the long-term storage of large amounts of information is effected on such secondary storage media as magnetic disks (see Section 4.6). It is the operating system's responsibility to manage this secondary storage in such a way that the information can be readily located and retrieved.

Information in secondary storage is usually held in the form of *files*, which can be of arbitrary size. Each file is a collection of information which is regarded as an entity by its users; it may for example be a program, the observations from an experiment, or a list of employees. The file is the logical unit which is stored and manipulated by the operating system.

The *file system* is that part of the operating system responsible for files. The specific functions of the file system vary according to the computer's application, but they typically include

(1)   creation and deletion of files;
(2)   provision of access to files;
(3)   management of secondary storage space;
(4)   protection of files from unauthorized access (though legitimate sharing, such as that between members of a project team, should be allowed);
(5)   protection of files against loss or corruption due to hardware or software failures.

Since the physical location of a file is of no concern to its users it is customary for each file to be given a name by its creator and for the file system to allow access to files through their names alone. The file system therefore maintains a *directory* of the names of files and their corresponding locations on the storage media. In an environment where several users are allowed to create and manipulate their own files the directory is usually broken into a two-level tree structure, as shown in Fig. 5.14. The root of the tree is the *master directory*, with an entry for each user; the leaves are *user directories*, with an entry for each of a user's files. This structure allows different users to call files by the same names without risk of confusion. The directories are usually held in secondary storage (as files themselves) and transferred into memory as required.

Each entry in the master directory contains the following information about a user:

(1)   the name by which the user is known to the system;
(2)   the location of the corresponding user directory.

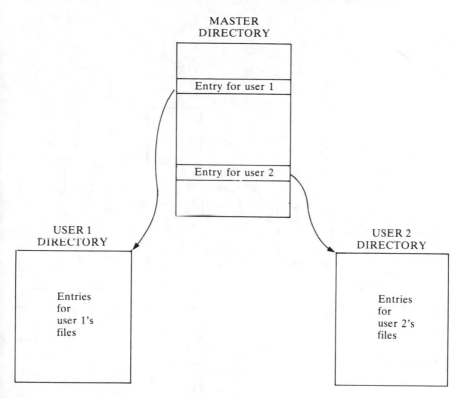

Figure 5.14   Two-level directory structure.

Each entry in a user directory contains the following information about one of the user's files:

(1)   the name of the file;
(2)   the location of the file in secondary storage;
(3)   the size of the file;
(4)   access control information supplied by the user, specifying who may use the file and what sort of access is to be permitted (for example access may be permitted for reading the file, but not for altering it);
(5)   various administrative information such as the date of creation of the file and the time of the last change to it.

In some systems the two-level directory structure is extended to several levels (Fig. 5.15). This allows a user to group together logically related files, and to access each group through a different directory. It also allows members of a project team to set up a joint directory, with their individual

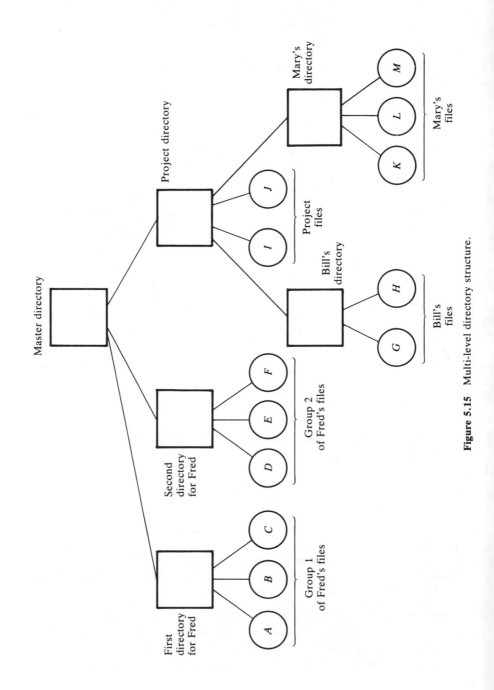

Figure 5.15 Multi-level directory structure.

directories at lower levels of the tree. Files in the joint directory (e.g. files *I* and *J* of Fig. 5.15) might be freely accessible to all members of the team, while those in individual directories (e.g. *G* and *K*) may have more selective access control.

Space in secondary storage is allocated in fixed sized units called *blocks* (the block size is typically equivalent to about 500 memory cells). Each file occupies an arbitrary number of blocks, which may be located anywhere on the secondary storage medium (they need not be contiguous). The file system must maintain information about which blocks are free and which are allocated to particular files. The algorithms and data structures used in allocation depend very much on the way in which the files are to be used; in particular they depend on whether the files are to be accessed *sequentially* from beginning to end, or *randomly* at any point. We shall not go into details here, but refer the interested reader to Section 6.1 and to the bibliography.

Since the contents of a file may represent many months' work or may consist of irreplaceable data it is important that the file system provide adequate mechanisms for backup and recovery in the event of hardware or software failure. This means that the system must maintain duplicate copies of all files so that they can be restored after any unfortunate occurrence. There are two principal ways of copying files:

(1) *Periodically*   The entire content of the storage medium is copied at periodic intervals. The copying may be done, for example, from one disk to another, or from disk to magnetic tape. The main disadvantages of this technique are the large volume of information which must be copied and the possibility of losing files which have been created or altered since the last copy was made.

(2) *Incrementally*   A file is copied only when it is created or modified. This technique reduces the amount of copying carried out, and also results in copies which are more up to date. Incremental copying is, however, more difficult to administer since out of date copies must be located and destroyed (or recognized and ignored during recovery after a failure). A variant of incremental copying is to copy not the whole file but only the changes to it. Recovery after failure can be quite complex, but the technique is useful when alterations are so frequent that copying the whole file is infeasible (e.g. airline reservation files).

5.5.7 Job Control

We conclude our discussion of operating systems by describing briefly how the user tells the operating system what he wants it to do. Broadly speaking, all user-requested operations concern the manipulation of programs and data which may be stored internally as files or presented externally through

I/O devices. The forms of manipulation vary widely: some of the more common ones are the input, output, and copying of data, and the compilation and execution of programs. Thus typical user requests may be

"Read the data which I type at my terminal and append it to my file called SURVEY82."

"Compile the program in my file ANALYZE, execute it with data from my file SURVEY82, and produce the output on the line printer."

"Give me a list of all my files, and tell me when I created them."

Instructions from the user to the operating system are expressed in a *job control language* (or *command language*). Most job control languages allow the following types of information to be conveyed.

(1) *Operational information*, specifying what operations the user wants performed (e.g. the copying of a file; the execution of a program).

(2) *I/O information*, specifying where the programs and/or data required for the operations are to come from, and where any output is to be sent (e.g. the program resides in a particular file; the output is to be typed on the user's terminal).

(3) *Resource information*, giving an estimate of the resources needed to perform the operation (e.g. the amount of memory; the length of processing time). Resource information is used by the scheduler in initiating processes (Section 5.5.4). In those cases where the user does not know or does not specify what resources are required the operating system makes its own default assumptions.

(4) *User identification*, specifying who the user is and establishing his bona fides (e.g. the user account number and password). This information is used to control access to the computer, and may also be used for accounting and billing.

Interpretation of job control instructions is performed by part of the operating system called (unsurprisingly) the *job control interpreter* (or *command interpreter*). The job control interpreter analyzes each instruction (or sequence of instructions) and carries it out. In some cases, such as the compilation of a user program, the instruction may be such that the interpreter cannot carry it out by itself. It therefore constructs a file specifying what is to be done. The file indicates what process(es) must be initiated, and may contain I/O and resource information extracted from the instruction or supplied by default. The scheduler periodically examines a list of such files when deciding whether to initiate another process (see Section 5.5.4).

Most job control languages have a very simple syntax, designed for easy interpretation. Unfortunately not all of them are designed for easy use: there is a tendency to expect the user to be acquainted with minute details of system operation, to memorize arcane symbols and obscure abbreviations, and to adhere to a rigid format. One hopes that such inadequacies will be eliminated in new job control languages in order to allow fluent and easy communication between user and operating system. Indeed, there is no reason why the principles applied to the design of high level programming languages cannot also be applied to job control languages.

EXERCISES

1 Extend the syntax of Fig. 5.1 by adding a production which defines a telephone directory as a sequence of entries. Write the additional production in two ways:

(a) using iteration (i.e. curly brackets);
(b) using recursion.

2 Define a BNF syntax for postal addresses (mailing addresses) in the country in which you live. The syntax should allow an address to include a person's name, house number, street, city, county (or state), and postcode (zip code).

Does your syntax allow addresses to be syntactically correct but semantically inconsistent?

3 The following BNF syntax describes expressions which are more general than those of Fig. 5.2:

expression → *term* | *term* + *term*
term → *factor* | *factor* × *factor*
factor → name | number | (*expression*)

Show that $a + b \times c$ and $(a + b) \times c$ are both valid expressions. Extend the syntax to include subtraction and division. Write down a few expressions that your extended syntax allows.

4 Extend the syntax of telephone directory entries (Fig. 5.1) to include format specification as suggested in Section 5.3.

5 Write down the sequence of tokens produced by the lexical analyzer of Section 5.4.1 from each of the following program statements (defined according to the syntax of Fig. 5.2).

(a) **set** *NET* **to** *GROSS − TAX*
(b) **while** $X \neq 0$ **do**
    set *X* **to** *X − Y*
(c) **if** $Y \neq 0$
    then if $X = 0$
        then set *X* **to** *Y + Z*

6 Draw the parse tree for each of the statements in Exercise 5.5.

7 Show that each of the following is *not* a valid statement in the language defined by Fig. 5.2.

(a) **set** *COST* **to** *PRICE × QUANTITY*

(b)   **if** $X = 0$
      then *set* X *to* $X + 1$
(c)   **while** $X \neq Y$ **do**
      set X *to* $X - Y$

Suggest alterations to the syntax of Fig. 5.2 which would make each of these examples a valid statement.

8   Sketch a module *parse-conditional* (similar to *parse-assignment* of Section 5.4.2) which parses the syntactic category *conditional* of Fig. 5.2.

9   Write down the code that might be generated (in the machine language of Section 4.5) for each of the program statements in Exercise 5.5.

10   Sketch a module *generate-condition* to generate code for a *condition* in the language of Fig. 5.2.
      Using *generate-condition*, sketch modules *generate-conditional* and *generate-loop*.

11   Write down as many advantages of multiprogramming as you can think of. Are these advantages always applicable?

12   What is the shortest time in which the three jobs of Fig. 5.8 can be completed if the computer on which they are running has two CPUs rather than one? Assume the jobs perform their I/O transfers (a) on different devices, (b) on the same device.

13   Sketch appropriate enhancements of the microprogrammed computer of Chapter 4 to provide address transformation by means of

(a)   base and limit registers;
(b)   paging.

Indicate how the microprogrammed interpreter of Section 4.5 would need to be altered in each case.

14   A particular program being executed on a paged computer uses the following sequence of program addresses:

51 1076 52 3974 2342 53 1511 3975 54 2782 3976 3123

Suppose that the page size is 1000, and that the program is allocated 2 page frames. Calculate how many page faults will occur during execution of the program if the page replacement algorithm is

(a)   longest resident;
(b)   least recently used;
(c)   least frequently used in the last six memory accesses.

Repeat your calculations for a page size of 500 and a memory allocation of 4 page frames (i.e. the same total allocation as before).
      Which page size gives the fewer page faults for each algorithm? Would you expect this to be generally true?

15   What factors do you think affect the choice of page size in a computer with paged memory?

16   Suggest possible measures for dealing with deadlock. Do your suggested measures have any drawbacks?

BIBLIOGRAPHY

Books about syntax definition and analysis:

A. V. Aho and J. D. Ullman, *The Theory of Parsing, Translation and Compiling*, Prentice-Hall, N.J., 1972.

R. L. Backhouse, *The Syntax of Programming Languages: Theory and Practice*, Prentice-Hall International, London, 1979.

The following give detailed accounts of how compilers work.

A. V. Aho and J. D. Ullman, *Principles of Compiler Design*, Addison-Wesley, Reading, Mass., 1977.

R. Bornat, *Understanding and Writing Compilers*, Macmillan, London, 1978.

D. Gries, *Compiler Construction for Digital Computers*, Wiley, New York, 1971

The following is a short account of assemblers and loaders.

D. W. Barron, *Assemblers and Loaders*, 3rd edn, MacDonald-Elsevier, London and New York, 1979.

The design of operating systems is discussed in

P. Brinch-Hansen, *Operating System Principles*, Prentice-Hall, N.J., 1973.

A. N. Habermann, *Introduction to Operating System Design*, Science Research Associates, Chicago, 1976.

A. M. Lister, *Fundamentals of Operating Systems*, 2nd edn, Macmillan, London, 1979.

D. C. Tsichritzis and P. A. Bernstein, *Operating Systems*, Academic Press, New York, 1974.

Finally, two books which span the entire field of system software:

P. Freeman, *Software Systems Principles*, Science Research Associates, Chicago, 1975.

J. Welsh and R. M. McKeag, *Structured System Programming*, Prentice-Hall International, London, 1980.

6 ALGORITHMS IN ACTION: SOME COMPUTER APPLICATIONS

It is less than 40 years since the first computer was built, yet in that time computers have penetrated almost every area of western life. Most people know that computers play a significant role in their lives, but few are aware of just how pervasive that role is. Computers are involved in almost all spheres of everyday life: from the supermarket checkout to the control of traffic signals, from the conduct of a bank account to the routing of telephone calls, from the preparation of the weather forecast to the production of the daily newspaper. Some examples of computer use in various fields are

Commerce: inventory control; invoicing; personnel management; financial control; document production

Industry: the control of machinery; safety monitoring; quality control

Science: analysis of experimental data; space flight navigation; solution of large sets of equations

Engineering: calculations of stress, heat loss, energy consumption, and cost

Social Sciences: analysis of survey data; predictive modelling of economies, populations, and social patterns

Medicine: diagnosis of illness; control of life-support systems; maintenance of medical histories

Education: computer aided learning and assessment

Arts: analysis of literary texts; production of animated films; production of graphic and architectural designs; composition of music

Recreation: video games; opponent in traditional games (e.g. chess, bridge)

The list is almost endless, and any attempt to exhaust it would be both tedious and futile. Rather than undertake such an exercise we shall look in some detail at two particular application areas: *data processing* and *artificial intelligence*. The first has been chosen because it currently occupies more computer time than any other application area; the second has been chosen for its inherent interest. In the spirit of the rest of the book our emphasis will be on the kinds of algorithms employed.

6.1 DATA PROCESSING

In a sense nearly all computer applications can be called "data processing", since most algorithms manipulate data in one form or another. However, the term *data processing* is usually understood in the narrower sense of comprising those applications in which the data is too voluminous for it all to be held in the computer's memory at once. The data involved in these applications must be held in secondary storage, and only relatively small portions of it can be placed in memory at any given time. The algorithms involved in data processing are therefore constrained by being able to operate only on small fragments of the data at a time. It is sometimes possible through the use of virtual memory (Section 5.5.3) for algorithms to ignore these constraints, but such algorithms are likely to be less efficient than algorithms which are carefully designed to optimize their use of the I/O mechanisms which transfer data to and from secondary storage. The challenge of data processing is to devise algorithms for performing the desired tasks in the minimum time. As an example, consider the problem of sorting 100 000 items of information when the memory is large enough to hold only 5000 of them at a time. The sorting algorithms of Chapter 2 (e.g. algorithm 2.20) are inadequate since they rely on being able to access all the data at any time: different algorithms, to be discussed later, are required.

Data processing is significant in being the major activity in which computers are currently involved, accounting for a considerable proportion of all computer time used. The chief application areas are in commerce (e.g. inventory control, payroll, accounts) and in government (the administration of such diverse fields as taxation, motor vehicle registration, and social security). All these applications are characterized by the need to maintain and manipulate large quantities of information.

The major activities in data processing are as follows.

(1) *Data input*
In human terms this is the most time-consuming part of data processing, since most input media (e.g. punched cards) require the data to be entered through some form of typewriter-like keyboard. The typing speed of a skilled operator is about 5 characters a second (painfully slow by computer processing standards), and so it is worthwhile looking at alternative methods of input.

Prospects for reducing the importance of the keyboard rest mainly with *magnetic character recognition, optical character recognition* and *speech recognition.* Magnetic character recognition is somewhat limited in scope, relying on input media (such as bank checks) which are pre-printed in magnetic ink. Optical character recognition is potentially more flexible, but current optical readers can handle only machine printed (not handwritten) material, and many are very limited in the print fonts they can accommodate. Speech recognition is an exciting prospect for data input in certain specialized applications, but is unlikely to be commercially viable before the late 1980s. Present day speech recognizers are limited in their vocabulary (typically a few hundred words), and have to be tuned to the voice of the person who is talking. They are also constrained by the great difficulty of understanding natural language (see Section 6.2.3). In the future, speech recognition is likely to be used mainly in simple dialogue, while numerical data continues to be input via a keyboard.

(2)   *Data validation*
Nowhere is the old adage "Garbage in, garbage out" more relevant than in data processing. The value that can be placed on output is limited by the accuracy of the input, and so considerable precautions must be taken to ensure that input data is correct. Commonly used forms of validation are

(a)   Redundancy checking: this involves inputting extra information whose sole purpose is to help detect errors. An example is to input the sum of a sequence of data items: if the sum is computed before and after input of the data then input errors can be detected.

(b)   Range checking: checking that data values fall within a predetermined sensible range (e.g. that the age of an employee lies between 15 and 65).

(c)   Consistency checking: checking that related data values are consistent with each other (e.g. that someone with marital status *widow* has sex *female*).

(3)   *Data manipulation*
This aspect of data processing includes all activities which operate on the data, either to make direct use of it or to reorganize it in some more usable form (e.g. by sorting it). The specific operations depend on the nature of the application: some typical ones are discussed later in this section.

(4)   *Data output*
The purpose of all data processing applications is to produce some useful output, such as pay slips, bank statements, or management statistics. The usefulness of the output depends crucially on

(a) how closely it meets user requirements in terms of relevance, sufficiency, and conciseness
(b) its format, which must be carefully designed for readability and assimi-
lation.

Since the utility of an entire data processing system ultimately depends on
the quality of its output, it is not surprising that considerable effort usually
goes into designing the output formats and modules.

6.1.1 Records and Files

Information in large quantities can be handled only if it is structured in some
way (cf. Section 2.11). The basic structural unit in data processing is the
record, which is a collection of information about a particular entity, such as
a particular person, stock item, or bank account. A record is composed of a
number of *fields*, which each hold a single item of information about the
entity the record describes. Some examples of different types of record, and
their component fields, are shown in Fig. 6.1. Note that records of the same
type (i.e. those which describe entities of the same type) have the same
component fields, though the information in the fields naturally varies from
one record to another.

Related records of the same type are held as *files* in secondary storage
(see also Section 5.5.6). In typical data processing applications a file might
contain thousands, or even hundreds of thousands, of records. Again,
Fig. 6.1 shows some examples.

Elementary operations, or *transactions*, on records are

(1) *reading*: that is, transferring the record from secondary storage to main
memory so that the information in its fields can be accessed;
(2) *writing*: that is, transferring the record from memory into secondary
storage;
(3) *adding* a record to a file;
(4) *deleting* a record from a file.

The reading and writing operations can be combined in

(5) *updating* a record: that is, altering the information in one or more of its
fields.

The transfer of records between secondary storage and memory is the
responsibility of the computer's operating system.

The organization of records within a file depends very much on the way
in which the file is accessed: in particular on whether its records are accessed
sequentially or *at random*. A *random access* file is, as the name suggests, a file

Application	File	Record	Typical fields
payroll	personnel	employee	name, address, grade
inventory control	automobile components	stock item	item number, cost, quantity in stock
banking	ledger	customer account	account number, customer name, current balance
airline reservations	today's flights	flight	flight number, date, seat availability

Figure 6.1 Typical files, records, and fields for various data processing applications.

which is organized for applications in which successive transactions occur at random, rather than in any particular order. An example is the file of flight records in an airline reservation system (Fig. 6.1). The pattern of access to the file is unpredictable, reflecting the pattern of enquiries and reservations by prospective passengers. Since response to passenger queries must be immediate there is no possibility of "saving up" transactions to be carried out later in some predefined order: each transaction must be carried out as soon as it is requested. Another example of a random access file is a bank ledger which is updated as soon as any deposit or withdrawal is made. Since transactions on accounts occur in unpredictable order, random access to the ledger file must be provided. These examples are particular cases of *real-time* applications: that is, applications in which each transaction must be completed within a short period of time, usually limited by human patience. Real-time transactions usually occur in unpredictable order, and by definition they cannot be delayed. It is therefore infeasible to defer them for ordered execution at some later time. It follows that the files used in real-time applications must usually be organized to permit random access.

A random access file must be organized in such a way that an arbitrary record can be quickly located. Note that a simple search from the beginning of the file is inadequate, as many thousands of records might have to be inspected before the required record is found. The time taken to transfer all these records into memory for inspection would be quite unacceptable in most applications. Details of more appropriate access mechanisms are referenced in the bibliography.

In a *sequential file* the records are arranged in an order determined by the content of a specified field, called the *key* field. For example, the records in a personnel file may be arranged alphabetically, the key field being the employee name; alternatively they may be ordered numerically, the key field being the employee number. The crucial point about sequential access is that the file is used in such a way that successive transactions operate on records in the same order as that in which the records occur in the file. This implies that the transactions can all be carried out by processing the records sequentially (i.e. during a single *pass* through the file).

An example of a sequential file is the personnel file of Fig. 6.1 which is used for producing the payroll. The transactions which are required to determine each employee's pay can readily be performed in the same order as that in which the employee records occur in the file. Another example is a commercial debtors file, which is normally ordered by customer account number, and which is updated each evening to reflect the day's business. If the update transactions are also ordered by account number then the whole process can be carried out in a single pass through the file. (We shall describe the process in detail in Section 6.1.4.)

The access mechanisms which the operating system must provide for a sequential file are relatively simple. Since the file is always accessed sequentially from beginning to end the operating system need provide only a means for locating the first record, for moving from one record to the next, and for recognizing that the last record has been reached. Again, the details are referenced in the bibliography.

We have seen that a crucial property of a sequential file is that the records are *ordered* according to the values in their key fields. The order must be established when the file is constructed, and must be maintained during subsequent operations on the file. Data processing therefore requires sorting algorithms for use in the construction of sequential files. Furthermore, the algorithms which perform subsequent operations on sequential files must not destroy the order. We shall discuss a few such algorithms in the following sections.

6.1.2. Sequential File Merge

A fairly frequent operation in data processing is the merging of two or more sequential files into a single sequential file containing all their constituent records. The files to be merged must of course be ordered by the same key field, and the ordering is preserved in the resultant merged file. Merging often occurs in connection with sorting, where, as we shall see in the next section, merge operations form the basis of certain sorting algorithms.

The merge operation is shown schematically in Fig. 6.2: all the records in a set of input files are merged to form a single output file. An outline description of the process is given by algorithm 6.1.

module *merge(INFILE1, INFILE2, ..., INFILEn, OUTFILE)*
{Draft algorithm for merging sequential files *INFILE1*, *INFILE2*, ...,
   INFILEn to form a single file *OUTFILE*}
read the first record of each input file
while *at least one file is not exhausted* **do**
   select the record with the lowest key
   append this record to OUTFILE
   read the next record from the corresponding input file   (6.1)

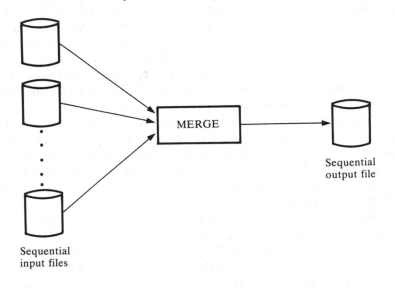

Figure 6.2   Sequential file merge.

   A problem which arises in implementing algorithm 6.1 is that the first
time some input file becomes exhausted the algorithm will attempt to read
the next record from that file. Since there is no next record in that file, an
execution error will occur. The problem can be circumvented by adding a
sentinel record to the end of each input file; this record contains no significant data, but its key field is set to a higher value than a key can legitimately
attain (possibly 999 if the key field is a 3-digit number, or ZZZZ if it is a
4-letter alphabetic sequence). The presence of a sentinel as the last record in
each input file ensures that the last record in a file is never selected as the one
with the lowest key. Hence no attempt is made to read any further records
from an exhausted file. (See Exercise 6.1 for verification of this.) The use of
a sentinel record is illustrated in algorithm 6.2, which is a modification of
algorithm 6.1. Note that the sentinel record is appended to the output file in
order to maintain the same format as the input files.

module *merge(INFILE1, INFILE2, ..., INFILEn, OUTFILE)*
{Algorithm for merging sequential files *INFILE1, INFILE2, ...,*
INFILEn to form a single file *OUTFILE.* Each file is terminated by a
sentinel record with a high key value}
read the first record of each input file
while *at least one record is not a sentinel* **do**
  select the record with lowest key
  append this record to OUTFILE
  read the next record from the corresponding input file
write sentinel record to OUTFILE   (6.2)

Algorithm 6.3 is a refinement of algorithm 6.2 for the case in which the
number of input files is two (the so-called two-way merge).

module *two-way-merge(INFILE1, INFILE2, OUTFILE)*
{Algorithm for merging 2 input files *INFILE1* and *INFILE2* to produce
output file *OUTFILE. INFILE1* and *INFILE2* are terminated by a
sentinel record}
read first record of INFILE1, and call it RECORD1
read first record of INFILE2, and call it RECORD2
while *either RECORD1 or RECORD2 is not a sentinel* **do**
  if *key in RECORD1 < key in RECORD2*
    then *append RECORD1 to OUTFILE*
      replace RECORD1 with next record of INFILE1
    else *append RECORD2 to OUTFILE*
      replace RECORD2 with next record of INFILE2
append sentinel record to OUTFILE   (6.3)

6.1.3. Sorting

As indicated earlier, sorting is an essential activity in data processing,
particularly in the construction and maintenance of sequential files. The
sorting algorithms used in data processing are constrained by being unable to
access all the data simultaneously: only a relatively small number of records
can be held in memory at once. The algorithms of Chapter 2 are therefore
inappropriate, since they rely on being able to access any data item at any
time.

The sorting algorithms used in data processing are generally based on a
strategy of building up ordered sequences of records by repeatedly merging
smaller such sequences. Each merge produces an ordered output sequence
which is longer than its inputs, and this in turn acts as an input to a further
merge. The ultimate goal is to build up an ordered sequence which consists
of all the records in the file being sorted.

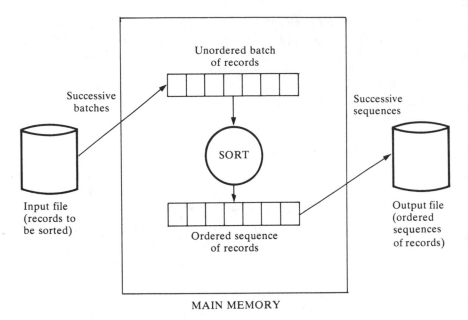

Figure 6.3   First (sorting) phase of the polyphase sort.

A particular algorithm which follows this strategy is the so-called *poly-phase sort*. As its name implies, the polyphase sort consists of a number of phases, which we describe in the following paragraphs. Our description will necessarily be brief, and will ignore some of the more technical issues concerned with the transfer of data between files and main memory.

The first phase (illustrated in Fig. 6.3) performs as much sorting as is possible with the amount of memory available. The records to be sorted are transferred into memory in successive batches, each of which is as large as the available memory can accommodate. While in memory each batch is sorted (using an algorithm such as those in Chapter 2), and the resulting ordered sequence of records is placed in an output file. At the end of this phase the output file contains a number of ordered sequences of records, the length of every sequence being equal to the number of records sorted in each batch.

Subsequent phases are alternately *distribution* and *merge* phases. The input to each distribution phase is the output file from the preceding phase (the initial sort, or a merge); this file contains ordered sequences of records. The sequences are then distributed evenly over several output files, so that if the number of output files is p the number of sequences on each file is $1/p$

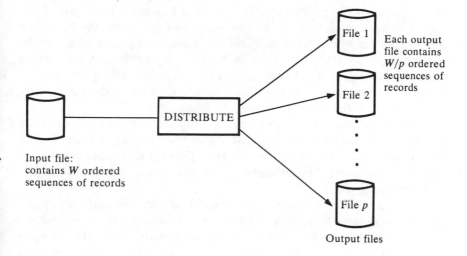

Figure 6.4   Distribution phase of the polyphase sort.

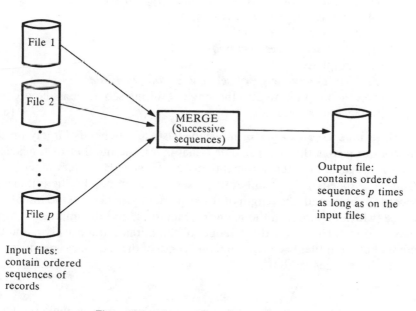

Figure 6.5   Merge phase of the polyphase sort.

times that on the input file (see Fig. 6.4). The number p of output files is usually chosen to be as large as possible, consistent with any limitation imposed by the operating system on the number of files which may be simultaneously in use. (If the files are held on magnetic tape their number will be limited by the number of tape drives available.) When the distribution phase is complete the output files containing the ordered sequences are used as input to the subsequent merge phase.

The merge phase is a p-way merge, in which successive sequences from each file are merged to form ordered sequences which are p times as long (the first sequence from every file is merged, then the second sequence from every file, and so on). The resulting sequences are written to an output file, as shown in Fig. 6.5.

The cycle of distribution and merging is then repeated, with the output file from each merge being used as the input to the next distribution, and vice versa. Each merge produces ordered sequences which are p times as long as before, and the cycle terminates when all the records are contained in a single ordered sequence. The entire sorting process can therefore be described by algorithm 6.4.

module *sort*
{Outline algorithm for polyphase sort}
{sort phase}
sort successive batches of records into ordered sequences
while *number of sequences* > 1 **do**
    {distribution phase}
    distribute sequences evenly over p files
    {merge phase}
    perform p-way merge of sequences from each file
    {when the loop terminates the single resulting sequence is the ordered
    sequence of all records}   (6.4)

The time taken to perform a polyphase sort depends largely on the number of passes through the data—that is, on the number of times each record is read and written. (Remember that I/O speeds are very much lower than CPU speeds.) The number of passes is determined by the number of records to be sorted, the length of the sequences produced in the initial sort phase (which depends on the memory available), and the number of input files used in each merge. If the length of the initial sequences is s, and the number of input files used is p, then the length of the sequences produced by successive merges is

$$s \times p, \ s \times p^2, \ s \times p^3, \ \ldots$$

Sorting terminates when the merge phase produces only a single sequence which contains all the N records to be sorted—that is, it terminates after k merges, where

$$s \times p^k = N$$

The number of distribute – merge cycles required is therefore

$$k = \log_p(N/s)$$

Each cycle involves two passes through the data (one during distribution and one during merging), and there is a single pass required in the initial sorting phase. Hence,

$$\text{total number of passes} = 2 \log_p(N/s) + 1$$

For a given value of N this number can be reduced by increasing s or p; that is, by using as much memory as possible during the initial sort and as many files as possible for distribution and merging. Since each pass through the data involves handling all N records, the asymptotic behavior of the poly-phase sort is $N \log_p (N/s)$, which for given values of p and s is proportional to $N \log_2 N$. (Recall section 3.2.1 for a definition of asymptotic behavior.) This asymptotic behavior is the same as that of the best sequential algorithms for sorting data which is entirely contained in memory, but the constants of proportionality are of course much higher.

6.1.4 Sequential File Update

One of the most common operations on a sequential file is that of updating it—that is, of altering some, but not necessarily all, of its records. Examples are the update of a bank ledger at the close of business, the update of an inventory file to reflect the day's deliveries and dispatches, and the update of a personnel file to reflect hirings, firings, and promotions.

The process of updating a sequential file is shown schematically in Fig. 6.6. The file to be updated is usually referred to as the *master file*: the update process transforms an *old* master file into a *new* master file. The update transactions are held in a *transaction file*, each record of which contains details of a single transaction. Each transaction may be one of the following types:

(1) *Insertion* The transaction record contains sufficient information to create a new master record. Examples of insertion are the opening of a bank account and the hiring of a new employee.

(2) *Update* The transaction record contains

    (a) the key (e.g. account number, employee number) of the master record to be updated

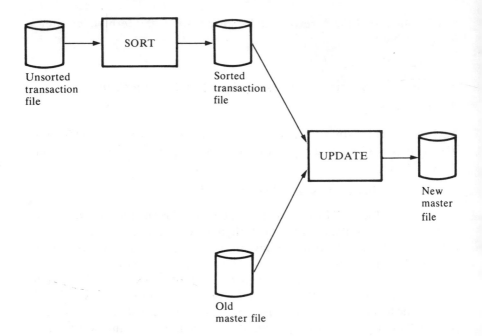

Figure 6.6   Sequential file update.

(b)   a specification of which fields in the master record are to be altered

(c)   for each such field, the details of the alteration required.

Examples of update transactions are the credit and debit of a bank account, and the promotion of an employee.

(3)   *Deletion*   The transaction record contains the key of the master record to be deleted. Examples of deletion are the closing of a bank account and the resignation of an employee.

The transactions to be applied to the master file are those which have accrued since the file was last updated. The transactions usually accrue in an arbitrary order (e.g. deposits and withdrawals in a bank), and must therefore be sorted into the same order as the master file before the update process can be carried out. Note that successive transactions may have the same key, implying several operations on the same master record (e.g. several credits and debits on the same bank account). Successive master records, however, have distinct keys.

An algorithm for updating the master file can be developed by stepwise refinement as follows. First we note that records with the same key, whether in the old master file or the transaction file, all refer to the same entity (e.g. an employee, a bank account, or a stock item). The update process can be viewed as combining all known information about each entity into a single record for that entity. The known information is derived from the old master file or the transaction file, or both, and the record containing the combined information usually becomes part of the new master file. However, if the combined information indicates that the entity no longer exists (e.g. a bank account has been closed) then there is no need to include the corresponding record in the new master file. An outline algorithm for the process is therefore

> **module** *update*
> {Draft algorithm for updating a master file}
> **repeat** *for each entity*
>   *combine into a single record all information about this entity*
>   **if** *the record is not null*
>   **then** *append it to the new master file*   (6.5)

Since each entity is identified by its key we can rewrite this outline as

> **module** *update*
> {First refinement of algorithm to update a master file}
> **while** *more keys* **do**
>   *select next key*
>   *combine into a single record all information*
>   *from records with this key*
>   **if** *the new record is not null*
>   **then** *append it to the new master file*   (6.6)

For convenience in further discussion we shall refer to particular files, records, and so on by the following names.

OLDFILE	old master file
TRANSFILE	transaction file
NEWFILE	new master file
OLDREC	next record in old master file
TRANSREC	next record in transaction file
NEWREC	the record which combines all information derived from records whose key is *CKEY*
CKEY	the current key (i.e. the one selected in line 4 of algorithm 6.6)

Using these names we can rewrite the outline algorithm 6.6 as follows:

module *update(OLDFILE, TRANSFILE, NEWFILE)*
{Updates *OLDFILE* with transactions in *TRANSFILE* to produce *NEWFILE*}
while *more keys* **do**
   determine next value of CKEY
   combine into NEWREC all information from records
     whose key is CKEY
   if *NEWREC is not null*
     then *append NEWREC to NEWFILE*   (6.7)

The value of *CKEY* is determined from the keys in *OLDREC* and *TRANS-REC*: to preserve order it must be the smaller of the two. There are two cases to consider:

(1)   The key in *TRANSREC* is smaller than the key in *OLDREC*. This is the case in which there is a transaction record for a particular entity but no old master record for it (the transaction is presumably an insertion). *CKEY* is determined to be the key in *TRANSREC*, and *NEWREC* is initially set to null. *NEWREC* is then built up from information in one or more transactions (the first of which must be an insertion).

(2)   The key in *TRANSREC* is greater than or equal to the key in *OLDREC*. This is the case in which there is an old master record for a particular entity, but not necessarily any transaction records (though if the keys are equal there is at least one transaction record). *CKEY* is determined to be the key in *OLDREC*, and *NEWREC* is initially set to *OLDREC*. Then *NEWREC* is updated by zero or more transactions. Once *OLDREC* has been used to initialize *NEWREC* there is no further use for it, and it can therefore be replaced by the next record from *OLDFILE*.

The above remarks lead to the refinement of algorithm 6.7 as shown in algorithm 6.8.

module *update(OLDFILE, TRANSFILE, NEWFILE)*
{Updates *OLDFILE* with transactions in *TRANSFILE* to produce *NEWFILE*}
while *more keys* **do**
   {select next key}
   if *key in TRANSREC < key in OLDREC*
     then *set CKEY to key in TRANSREC*
        initialize NEWREC to null
     else *set CKEY to key in OLDREC*
        initialize NEWREC to OLDREC
        replace OLDREC by next record in OLDFILE

update NEWREC with all transactions
  whose key is CKEY
{output resulting record to new master file}
if *NEWREC is not null*
  then *append NEWREC to NEWFILE*   (6.8)

The process of updating *NEWREC* with all transactions whose key is *CKEY* can be described by the following loop.

while *key in TRANSREC=CKEY* **do**
  {process current transaction}
  if *TRANSREC is an insertion and NEWREC is null*
    then *update NEWREC from TRANSREC*
    else if *TRANSREC is a deletion and NEWREC not null*
      then *set NEWREC to null*
      else if *TRANSREC is an update and NEWREC not null*
        then *update NEWREC from TRANSREC*
        else *report invalid transaction type*
  {move to next transaction}
  replace TRANSREC by next record in TRANSFILE   (6.9)

Note that the different transaction types are valid only if *NEWREC* satisfies certain conditions: for example, deletion of a null record is not a valid transaction.

The final step in refining the algorithm is elaboration of the condition *more keys* which governs the main loop. On each iteration the next key may be derived from either *OLDFILE* or *TRANSFILE*, and either of these files may become exhausted first. To avoid problems with exhausted files it is convenient to adopt the same strategem as in merging (Section 6.1.2)—that is, add a sentinel record with a high key to the end of all files. The condition *more keys* can now be expressed as

  either OLDREC or TRANSREC is not a sentinel

For this condition to be meaningful initially, the first record from each of *TRANSFILE* and *OLDFILE* must be read before the loop is entered. The complete algorithm for sequential file update is shown in algorithm 6.10.

module *update (OLDFILE, TRANSFILE, NEWFILE)*
{Algorithm for sequential file update. Updates *OLDFILE* with
 transactions in *TRANSFILE* to produce *NEWFILE*}
read OLDREC from OLDFILE
read TRANSREC from TRANSFILE
while *either OLDREC or TRANSREC is not a sentinel* **do**
  {select next key}

```
    if key in TRANSREC < key in OLDREC
      then set CKEY to key in TRANSREC
           initialize NEWREC to null
      else  set CKEY to key in OLDREC
            initialize NEWREC to OLDREC
            replace OLDREC by next record in OLDFILE
    {perform all transactions on current key}
    while key in TRANSREC = CKEY do
      {process current transaction}
      if TRANSREC is an insertion and NEWREC is null
        then update NEWREC from TRANSREC
        else if TRANSREC is a deletion and NEWREC not null
          then set NEWREC to null
          else if TRANSREC is an update and NEWREC not null
            then update NEWREC from TRANSREC
            else  report invalid transaction type
      {move to next transaction}
      replace TRANSREC by next record in TRANSFILE
    {append resulting record to new master file}
    if NEWREC is not null
      then append NEWREC to NEWFILE
    {terminate new master file}
    append sentinel to NEWFILE                              (6.10)
```

6.2 ARTIFICIAL INTELLIGENCE

Artificial intelligence is the computer application which perhaps more than any other has sparked the imagination, fears, and scepticism of observers. The reasons for this are not hard to find: it is an application which can be readily dramatized for the layman ("Electronic Brain Beats Chess Champion"), it evokes the images beloved of science fiction ("Robot Runs Amok"), and it raises issues which are deeply emotive ("Can Machines Think?"). It is also an application whose promise has so far greatly exceeded its achievement.

The term "artificial intelligence" is rather a broad one, being used in such diverse activities as robotics, game playing, and natural language understanding. The common feature of these activities is the exhibition by machines of behavior which would normally be considered intelligent if displayed by human beings. Artificial intelligence is the name given to the whole field of endeavor associated with producing such behavior in machines.

Most artificial intelligence applications are still in the research stage: the few areas which have reached practical fruition include industrial robotics, the analysis of complex molecular structures, and specialized forms of medical diagnosis. The major reason for the paucity of practical results is that many problems in artificial intelligence have turned out to be more difficult than originally envisaged. The rather naïve optimism which pervaded some early work has been replaced by a more sober appreciation of the problems involved. The potential, however, is enormous, not only for relief of physical and mental drudgery, but also for insight into man's own intellectual processes. It is easy to understand the challenge and excitement felt by those working in the field.

6.2.1 Can Machines Think?

The question posed above can be properly addressed only by considering what one means by "thinking", or more broadly, what one means by "intelligence". This is an issue which has occupied philosophers for centuries, and is not easy to resolve. It is clear, however, that intelligence has many aspects, such as the capacity to plan, to learn, to solve problems, and to use language. Behavior demonstrating any of these abilities is regarded by most people as "intelligent", and it is the aim of workers in artificial intelligence to make computers exhibit such behavior.

Behavior as a criterion of intelligence is the basis of a test proposed by Turing over 30 years ago as a means of determining whether a machine is intelligent or not. The essence of the *Turing test* is an attempt to distinguish between a machine and a human being by holding arbitrary conversations with each. It is assumed that for the sake of fairness the machine and the human being are isolated from the person carrying out the test, and that the medium of communication is neutral (e.g. messages typed on a keyboard). If the machine's responses to arbitrary statements and questions are such that it cannot reliably be distinguished from the human, then the conclusion from the Turing test is that the machine is indeed intelligent. Of course this is only one attempt at defining intelligence, and many criticisms have been levelled at it. These criticisms are often based on the fact that the test ignores what is occurring inside the machine, focussing rather on a single aspect of the machine's behavior.

Some experience with the Turing test has been provided by a program called ELIZA, which was written by Joseph Weizenbaum in the mid-1960s. ELIZA is a program which emulates the responses of a psychiatrist during consultation by a patient. The following session, taken from Weizenbaum's original paper, is an illustration. (The patient's remarks are shown in italics, while ELIZA's responses are in upper case.)

Men are all alike
IN WHAT WAY?
They're always bugging us about something or other
CAN YOU THINK OF A SPECIFIC EXAMPLE?
Well, my boyfriend made me come here
YOUR BOYFRIEND MADE YOU COME HERE
He says I'm depressed most of the time
I'M SORRY TO HEAR YOU ARE DEPRESSED
It's true, I am unhappy
DO YOU THINK COMING HERE WILL HELP YOU NOT TO BE UNHAPPY?
I need some help, that much seems certain
WHAT WOULD IT MEAN TO YOU IF YOU GOT SOME HELP?
Perhaps I could learn to get along with my mother
TELL ME MORE ABOUT YOUR FAMILY
My mother takes care of me
WHO ELSE IN YOUR FAMILY TAKES CARE OF YOU?
My father
YOUR FATHER?
You are like my father in some ways
WHAT RESEMBLANCE DO YOU SEE?
You are not very aggressive, but I think you don't want me to notice that
WHAT MAKES YOU THINK I AM NOT VERY AGGRESSIVE?
You don't argue with me
WHY DO YOU THINK I DON'T ARGUE WITH YOU?
You are afraid of me
DOES IT PLEASE YOU TO BELIEVE I AM AFRAID OF YOU?
My father is afraid of everybody
WHAT ELSE COMES TO MIND WHEN YOU THINK OF YOUR FATHER?
Bullies
DOES THAT HAVE ANYTHING TO DO WITH THE FACT THAT YOUR BOYFRIEND MADE YOU COME HERE?

It seems from this example that ELIZA's behavior is difficult to distinguish from that of human practitioners of a certain school of psychiatry, and that the program satisfies the Turing test within a limited domain of conversation. However, examination of the program shows that ELIZA's responses are no more than a sophisticated echo of the input from the patient.

The basis of the program is a *script* which contains a number of *templates* (or "skeleton sentences") such as

T1: WHAT MAKES YOU THINK XXX
T2: TELL ME MORE ABOUT XXX
T3: DOES IT PLEASE YOU TO BELIEVE XXX

where in each case XXX represents part of the sentence which is to be completed (or "fleshed out") by material derived from the preceding input. The way this material is derived is as follows. First the input sentence is inspected for the presence of a *keyword*: ELIZA's script contains a number of keywords (such as I, YOU, MOTHER, HATE) which are chosen for their probability of occurrence in a patient's remarks. Associated with each keyword is a set of *rules* for transforming a sentence containing the keyword into material which can be used in a response. For example, the keyword YOU might have an associated rule

R: YYY YOU ARE ZZZ $\Rightarrow$ I AM ZZZ

where YYY and ZZZ represent any sequences of words. The meaning of this rule is that any sentence containing the words YOU ARE can be transformed by stripping off its leading portion and replacing YOU ARE by I AM. (The rest of the sentence, represented by ZZZ, is unchanged, except for inversion of personal pronouns such as ME/YOU, MY/YOUR, and so on.)

The result of the transformation is then plugged into one of the templates, which is selected according to the keyword which was recognized and the rule which was applied. Thus the input sentence

You are afraid of me

might be transformed by rule R into

I AM AFRAID OF YOU

and then plugged into template T3 to produce the response

DOES IT PLEASE YOU TO BELIEVE I AM AFRAID OF YOU?

Alternatively, template T1 could equally well be used, producing the response

WHAT MAKES YOU THINK I AM AFRAID OF YOU?

The heart (if that is the correct word) of ELIZA is the script, which contains the templates, the keywords, and the transformation rules. However, several elaborations are necessary for ELIZA to have a "human" appearance. Firstly, ELIZA can remember earlier parts of a conversation and use them when no keyword can be detected in what the patient has just said (see, for example, the last line of the example conversation). Secondly, if the patient relapses into a sequence of monosyllables, then ELIZA counters with responses such as

YOU DON'T SEEM VERY TALKATIVE TODAY

Thirdly, the selection of a transformation rule for a particular keyword, and a template into which to plug the result, are both performed in such a way as to minimize the danger of repetition.

ELIZA satisfies the Turing test in a limited domain. Its behavior in that domain seems intelligent, but few people would regard the program itself as intelligent. Perhaps the principal objection to regarding ELIZA as intelligent is that it does not *understand* the conversations it takes part in. Although it recognizes MOTHER as a significant word it has no concept of what motherhood is—in fact its responses can be likened to those of a parrot.

Experience with ELIZA and similar programs suggests that intelligence is related to *understanding*; that is, to the ability to interpret information in the light of a body of knowledge which is already possessed. This knowledge represents a person's (or a machine's) view of the world – it is essentially a model of the world as the person perceives it. The model contains information about all objects which are known to exist, the attributes of those objects, and the relationships between them. Most people have a huge and intricate model of the world: it contains a large number of concrete and abstract objects, with wide and varied attributes, and with relationships between them which are often very subtle. Some part of this model may be inherited, but most of it seems to be acquired through experience. Indeed the process of learning can be seen in terms of additions and modifications to a person's model of the world.

To endow machines with similarly huge and intricate models of the world appears very difficult, and is certainly well beyond our current capabilities. One reason for this, which may be short-lived, is that the capacity of the largest computer memories is far less than that of the human brain. A more significant reason is that no generally convenient method of representing knowledge in a computer has yet been discovered. The major problem is not in storing knowledge, but in recognizing when particular items are relevant, and in retrieving them as required. A simple list of facts is inadequate: the *relationships between facts* are of crucial importance. Attempts to represent such relationships by complex data structures always seem to founder on the same two difficulties. The first is to know what relationships are relevant. The second is the time taken to locate and retrieve all information relevant to the problem at hand. This time rapidly becomes infeasible as the body of knowledge increases.

One obvious approach to resolving these difficulties is to study the human brain in an attempt to discover and emulate how knowledge is represented there. However, the brain is an extremely intricate mechanism, and no definitive results have yet been obtained. From the little we do know, it appears that the storage mechanisms of the brain are quite different from those of a computer: the memory elements in the brain may not be simply passive repositories of information but may also possess some active processing capability. If further research confirms this then the architecture of conventional computers may have to be rethought.

In the meantime, researchers in artificial intelligence have concentrated on problem domains which require relatively small amounts of knowledge. After the failure of more ambitious projects they have limited their endeavors to worlds which are very small and which can therefore be modelled by *ad hoc* techniques. Such worlds contain very few objects, with a small number of well-defined attributes, and a similarly small number of explicit relationships. A typical example is the world of the industrial robot, working, let us say, on an automobile assembly line. The only objects in this world are automobile components; the only attributes of these objects are size and shape; and the relationships between them are those of position. If the robot were confronted with a piano, or even with a different model of automobile, then it could make no sense of them, since its world does not encompass such objects. The industrial robot inhabits a narrow world indeed, but it represents the best practical achievement of current techniques.

The convenient representation of knowledge in machines is probably the key to any major breakthrough in artificial intelligence. In the next few sections we shall look at several areas of artificial intelligence research, each of which restricts itself to a narrow domain of knowledge. Although the results in some cases are impressive, the reader will see that further progress depends largely on the development of techniques for building massive bodies of knowledge into computer systems. We shall return to this point at the end of the chapter.

6.2.2. Game Playing

Game playing is a field in which considerable research effort has been expended, since it is in many ways a microcosm of artificial intelligence concerns. Game playing demonstrates several aspects of intelligence, particularly the ability to plan (at both the immediate tactical level and the long-term strategic level) and the ability to learn. Many programs have been written to play specific games, with degrees of accomplishment which vary with the complexity of the game concerned. Programs which play simple games like tic-tac-toe (noughts and crosses) are good enough never to be beaten by a human player; those which play more complex games like chess are presently at national competition standard. In the following paragraphs we shall see how game-playing programs can be constructed, and examine the source of their limitations.

We start with a very simple game, namely Nim. In this game two players take turns to remove matchsticks from a pile. There are initially five matchsticks on the pile, and each player may remove either one or two of them on his move. The player who removes the last matchstick is the loser. A strategy for playing Nim can be derived by constructing a *game tree* (Fig. 6.7) which shows the consequences of all possible moves. Each node in the tree represents a possible move. The leaves of the tree represent the possible conclusions of the game, and have been labelled with the identity of the winner. The tree clearly contains enough information to determine the best move in any situation. In fact the tree shows that the first player can always win. (How?—see Exercise 6.5.)

The game tree in Fig. 6.7 is *complete*: that is, it shows the entire course of the game for every possible move. Construction of a complete game tree is feasible only for very simple games: in most games the number of possible moves is so large that a complete tree cannot be constructed in any reasonable time or with any reasonable storage space. For example, the complete game tree for the relatively simple game of tic-tac-toe has about $300\,000$ nodes; the game tree for checkers (draughts) has about 10^{40} nodes, and the game tree for chess is even larger. In fact games for which a complete tree can be feasibly constructed are not very interesting, since the best course of play can be computed at the start (cf. Section 3.2.4).

The notion of a game tree is, however, still useful even in games where the complete tree cannot feasibly be constructed. The idea in such games is to build a game tree which extends as many moves ahead of the current position as is possible, given the constraints of time and space. An *evaluation function* is then used to evaluate those positions at the leaves of the tree—that is, those positions at the furthest extent of the program's ability to look ahead. The evaluation function is specific to the game being played: in chess, for example, it would take into account control over certain squares and the threat to various pieces.

Having evaluated the different positions the program selects a move which will lead to the position of maximum advantage. The selection is complicated by the need to consider potential moves by the opponent—he too is assumed to be playing for his own maximum advantage. As an example, Fig. 6.8 shows a game tree for three moves ahead of the current position (two moves by A, and one by B). The leaves of the tree represent the positions which can be reached after three moves, and are annotated with the result of some hypothetical evaluation function (the higher the value, the better for A). For convenience, the branches corresponding to certain moves

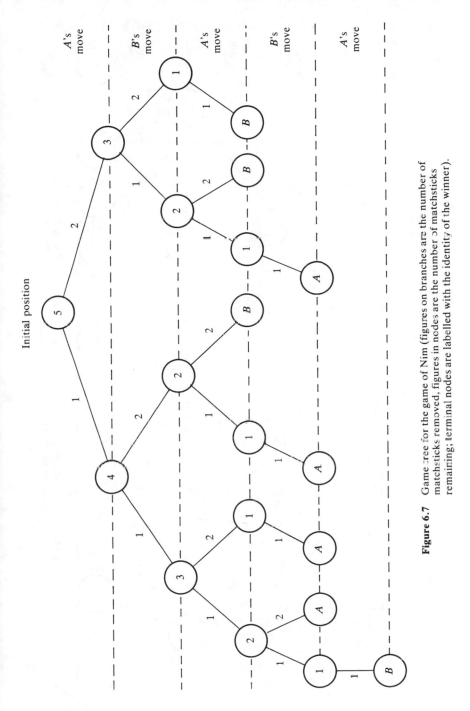

Figure 6.7 Game tree for the game of Nim (figures on branches are the number of matchsticks removed, figures in nodes are the number of matchsticks remaining; terminal nodes are labelled with the identity of the winner).

Figure 6.8   A game tree with 3-move lookahead (leaves are labelled with the result of an evaluation function).

have been labelled 1, 1', 2, 2', and so on. Clearly, the best position A could be in after three moves is the one with value 90, and it may therefore seem that A's first move should be 1'. However, the second move is B's, and since he too can look ahead he is unlikely to choose move 2' (which gives maximum advantage to A). Instead, he is likely to choose move 2, since in that case the best position that A can reach has value only 15. Thus if A starts with move 1' he will end up in a position with value 15 rather than the 90 he was aiming for. Further examination of Fig. 6.8 shows that A's first move should be 1, as this guarantees that despite B's best efforts A can reach a position with value at least 20.

A's strategy can be summarized as follows:

(1)   Generate the game tree for as many moves ahead as possible.
(2)   Evaluate the positions at the leaves of the tree.
(3)   Back up these values to positions higher up the tree, using the *maximum* values from the branches where the next move is A's and the *minimum* value from the branches where the next move is B's.
(4)   Choose the move leading to the position with maximum value at the first level of the tree.

The process described in step 3 is called *minimaxing*, since values are backed up the tree by alternately taking the minimum and maximum of the values lower down. Figure 6.9 shows the result of minimaxing on the tree of Fig. 6.8: it confirms that A's first move should be 1. Like many algorithms which manipulate trees, the minimaxing algorithm is essentially recursive: algorithm 6.11 is an outline.

> **module** *minimax(tree,move)*
> {Module for applying the minimax procedure to the given *tree*;
>   Parameter *move* indicates who moves next: us or opponent}
> **if** *tree is a leaf*   {this terminates the recursion}
>   **then** *result is the value of the evaluation function*
>   *for the leaf*
>   **else if** *move = us*
>   **then** *for each branch of the tree*
>   *minimax (subtree, opponent)*
>   *result is maximum of values obtained*
>   **else** *for each branch of the tree*
>   *minimax (subtree, us)*
>   *result is minimum of values obtained*   (6.11)

The effectiveness of minimaxing is limited by the depth of the game tree, which is itself limited by the time needed to construct and analyze it. (The time increases exponentially with the depth of the tree.) One way of

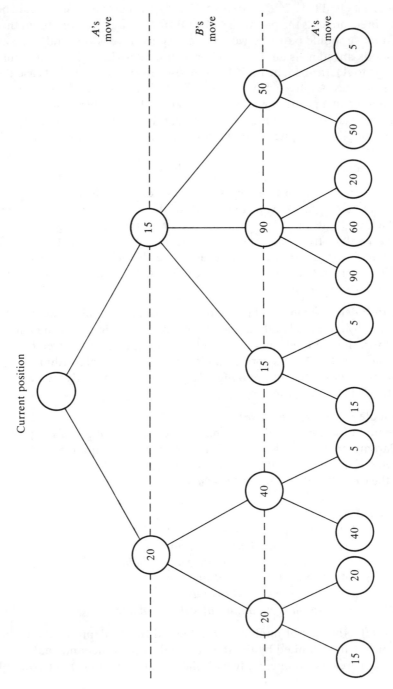

Figure 6.9   Result of minimaxing on the game tree of Fig. 6.8.

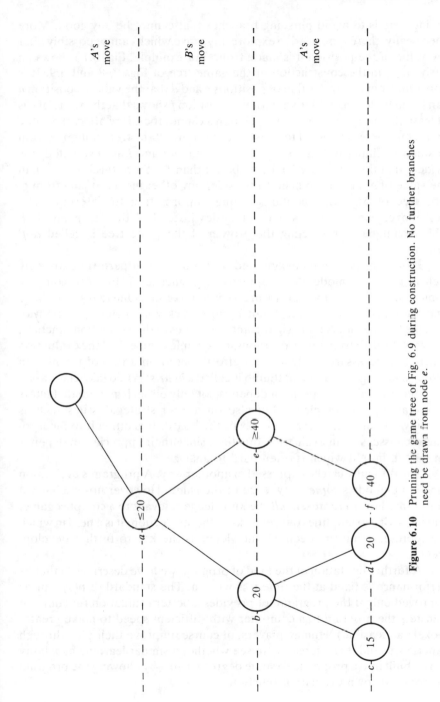

Figure 6.10 Pruning the game tree of Fig. 6.9 during construction. No further branches need be drawn from node e.

saving time is to avoid pursuing branches that cannot be any good. More specifically, there is no need to explore any move which cannot possibly alter the value of the position it is made from. For example, Fig. 6.10 shows an early stage in the construction of the game tree of Figs. 6.8 and 6.9. It is apparent from the evaluation of positions c and d that the value of position a can be no better than 20. Evaluation of position f shows that the value of e is at least 40: any other move from position e cannot therefore affect the value of a. Thus there is no need to construct any more of the tree stemming from position e. Similarly (Fig. 6.11) when positions i and j are evaluated it is evident that the value of g can be no better than 15. Since this is worse than the value of a there is no need to consider any other moves arising from g. The tree of Fig. 6.11 contains enough information to determine A's best move, but it contains only 11 nodes instead of the 19 in Fig. 6.9. This technique of restricting the growth of the game tree is called α–β *pruning*.

Programs using minimaxing and α–β pruning can perform extremely well in games of moderate complexity (e.g. checkers). In more complex games, such as chess, their performance is not so good. One reason for this is that the trees for such games branch more thickly, reducing the extent of feasible lookahead. A more significant reason lies in the evaluation function: it is very difficult to evaluate positions in a complex game, and the evaluation function is necessarily only a "best effort" based on a rule of thumb. (In artificial intelligence a rule of thumb is called a *heuristic*.) To take chess as an example, the value of a position depends not only on such immediate factors as threats to various pieces, but also on deeper strategic issues such as growing domination of certain areas of the board. It is difficult to incorporate such issues in an evaluation function, since their appreciation depends on human insight which is often hard to analyze.

The difficulty can be expressed in another way. A program's evaluation function embodies *some* knowledge of the game. However no-one has yet discovered how to represent *all* the knowledge relevant to a complex game. Game playing exemplifies our remarks of the last section: it is a field in which the representation of adequate knowledge is the key to further development.

A further limitation of the kind of program we have described is that its performance is fixed at the time it is written. The standard of play can be improved only if the programmer provides a better evaluation function (or transfers the program to a computer with sufficient speed to make greater lookahead feasible). Human players, of course, improve their play through experience, and it is interesting to see whether a similar learning capability can be built into a program. To some degree it can—by allowing the program to modify its own evaluation function.

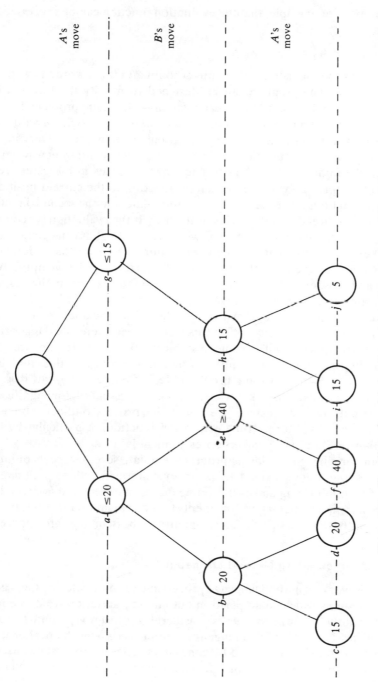

Figure 6.11   The effect of applying α–β pruning to the game tree of Fig. 6.9.

Suppose, for example, that the evaluation function can be expressed in the form

$$E = w_1 f_1 + w_2 f_2 + \cdots + w_n f_n$$

where the f's are the factors taken into account and the w's are the weights given to them. The program can be designed to modify the function by altering the weight accorded to each factor—the main problem lies in deciding when and how to do so. Fortunately there is a straightforward way to measure the effectiveness of the evaluation function. After every move the value of the current position can be computed in two different ways: first by using the minimax procedure to back up the values in the game tree; second by simply applying the evaluation function to the current position. Both computations make use of the evaluation function: the second directly, and the first indirectly via the leaves of the tree. If the evaluation function is perfect then the two values obtained will agree throughout the game. It is more likely, of course, that the values will differ: the greater the difference, the worse is the function's effectiveness. The differences between the two values can be systematically reduced by adjusting the weights in the evaluation function after every few moves.

The learning process outlined above is heuristic, and does not necessarily result in an optimum evaluation function (indeed there is a danger that the evaluation function will become unstable if adjustments in some weights over-compensate for adjustments in others). Learning of this kind has proved quite effective in some programs (e.g. for checkers), but it is no substitute for the deeper knowledge which is essential for significant improvements in performance. Certainly the process outlined above is limited by the initial form of the evaluation function, in particular by the factors which the programmer chooses to include.

Summarizing, game playing programs emulate several aspects of intelligence. *Knowledge* is embodied in an evaluation function; *planning* is effected by minimaxing and α–β pruning on a game tree; and *learning* is a process of limited systematic adjustments to the evaluation function. It is in the first of these areas that the most significant shortcomings are apparent.

6.2.3   Understanding Natural Langauge

Most early work on natural language processing was motivated by the desire to build systems which could perform automatic translation from one language to another. During the 1950s considerable effort was put into translation systems, in the belief that langauge translation is a mechanical process which can readily be performed by computers. These early systems used a dictionary to map individual words from one language to the other and then rearranged the output, adding suitable word endings as necessary, to conform to the grammatical rules of the language concerned. Unfortunately the resulting translations were not very good, and by the early 1960s it became evident that some other approach was required.

The major deficiency of early translation systems was that in concentrating on *grammar* (syntax) they ignored the importance of *meaning* (semantics) in language translation. Grammar alone is an inadequate basis for viable translation, as the two sentences

> *Cinderella attended the ball*

and

> *Cinderella kicked the ball*

readily demonstrate. Both sentences have the same grammatical structure, but *ball* is used in a different sense in each (and should therefore be translated differently on each occurrence). A person reading the above sentences distinguishes between the two uses of *ball* by relating the context in which the word appears to the knowledge he has of the world. He knows, for example, that a social function is not kickable whereas a spherical object is, and he interprets the second sentence accordingly. As another example, consider the two sentences

> *The house was built by the workmen*

and

> *The house was built by the river*

Grammatical rules give no help in translating the word *by*: one has to know that building is not an appropriate act for rivers and hence deduce that *by* in the second sentence is a preposition of location rather than of agency.

Realization of the importance of meaning has moved the focus of natural language processing from translation to *understanding*. Further impetus has come from attempts to use natural language in man–machine communication and from studies of language as a "window" into the brain. Only a small amount of progress has been achieved, the major obstacle being to find an appropriate representation of the kind of general world knowledge that a person uses in interpreting a sentence. Two of the many areas where knowledge of the world is crucial are

(1)   Resolution of word sense ambiguity, as in the examples involving *ball* and *by* above.
(2)   Resolution of pronoun references, as in the sentence

> *The soldiers shot the prisoners and I saw several fall*

Here the pronoun *several* refers to the prisoners, but in

The soldiers shot the prisoners and I saw several reload

it clearly refers to the soldiers. Correct interpretation relies on quite detailed knowledge about the act of shooting and its various consequences.

One way of attacking the problem of language understanding is to limit the *domain of discourse* (i.e. the things which are talked about) so that some insight can be gained from representing knowledge about a manageably small world. Perhaps the most celebrated system exploiting this approach is Terry Winograd's SHRDLU, developed in the early 1970s. SHRDLU simulates a robot with a single arm which can manipulate simple objects on a table top. SHRDLU's world is bounded by the edges of the table: the objects in this world are cubes and pyramids of various colors and sizes, together with a box for putting them in (Fig. 6.12). The current state of the world and the position of the simulated arm are displayed on a video screen. SHRDLU can respond to commands, answer questions, and accept new information about its world. Extracts from a dialogue with SHRDLU (taken from Winograd's account) are given below: explanatory comments have been added where appropriate.

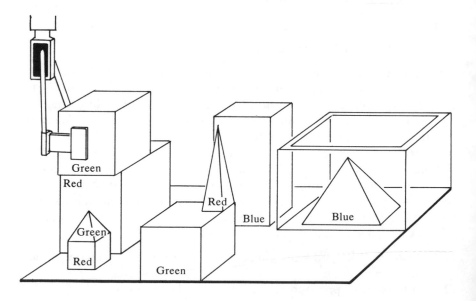

Figure 6.12   SHRDLU's blocks world.

Pick up a big red block
OK

> In order to pick up the red block the system had to find a space for the green one and move it away. The new state of the world is displayed on the screen.

Grasp the pyramid
I DON'T UNDERSTAND WHICH PYRAMID YOU MEAN

> There are 3 pyramids, and SHRDLU knows that *the* indicates a specific object the speaker has in mind.

Find a block which is taller than the one you are holding and put it into the box
BY "IT" I ASSUME YOU MEAN THE BLOCK WHICH IS TALLER THAN THE ONE I AM IIOLDING
OK

> The program points out the ambiguity of *it*, and uses a heuristic to choose one interpretation. It also deduces what *the one* refers to.

What does the box contain?
THE BLUE PYRAMID AND THE BLUE BLOCK
What is the pyramid supported by?
THE BOX

> On this occasion the system assumes that *the pyramid* is the one just mentioned.

Can the table pick up blocks?
NO

> The system knows that "picking up" must be performed by an animate object, and that the table is not animate.

Can a pyramid be supported by a block?
YES

> The system finds an example, so it knows it must be possible.

I own all blocks which are not red, but I don't own anything which supports a pyramid.
I UNDERSTAND

> The information is added to SHRDLU's knowledge of the world.

Do I own the box?
NO

> The box supports whatever it contains, including a pyramid.

Will you please stack up both of the red blocks and either a green cube or a pyramid.
OK

Is there a large block behind a pyramid?
YES, THREE OF THEM: A LARGE RED ONE, A LARGE GREEN
ONE AND THE BLUE ONE
Put a small one onto the green cube which supports a pyramid.
OK
Put the littlest pyramid on top of it
OK

> The meaning of *littlest* is deduced from the root form *little* and knowledge
> of common endings.

Had you touched any pyramid before you put the green one on the little cube?
YES, THE GREEN ONE

> The system maintains a record of its actions.

When did you pick it up?
WHEN I WAS STACKING UP THE RED CUBE, A LARGE RED
BLOCK AND A LARGE GREEN CUBE

> Time is described by naming the main goal being worked on.

Why?
TO GET RID OF IT
Why did you do that?
TO CLEAR OFF THE RED CUBE

> *That* refers to the action mentioned in the system's last answer.

Why did you clear off that cube?

> Here, *that* means the one just referred to.

TO PUT IT ON A LARGE GREEN CUBE
Why did you do that?
TO STACK UP THE RED CUBE, A LARGE RED BLOCK AND A
LARGE GREEN CUBE
Why did you do that?
BECAUSE YOU ASKED ME TO
A "steeple" is a stack which contains two green cubes and a pyramid
I UNDERSTAND

> The definition is added to the system's knowledge.

Are there any steeples now?
NO
Build one
OK
Thank you
YOU'RE WELCOME!

One of the most significant differences between **SHRDLU** and its predecessors is SHRDLU's representation of knowledge and meaning, summarized below.

(1) Only simple kinds of knowledge, such as the elementary attributes of objects, are represented by lists of "facts". Other knowledge is represented by pieces of program (modules). For example, the knowledge that *a steeple is a stack which contains two green cubes and a pyramid* is represented by modules which can determine whether any object is a steeple or not. Similarly, the knowledge that *I own all blocks which are not red, but I don't own anything which supports a pyramid* is represented by modules which can determine what objects I own. This so-called *procedural* representation of knowledge (*procedure* is another term for *module*) is very flexible.

(2) The representation of meaning is also procedural, rather than being a list of definitions. As a (simplified) example, the meaning of the phrase *red cube* might be represented by a module REDCUBE which is called whenever the phrase appears. The module searches the world for a red cube: that is, it looks for a block with attributes *red* and *equidimensional*. If the phrase *red cube* appears in a command (e.g. *Pick up a red cube*) then REDCUBE is called during execution of the command. If the phrase appears in a question (e.g. *Is there a red cube in the box?*) then REDCUBE is called in formulating the answer. If the phrase occurs in a statement (e.g. *Any red cube is mine*) then REDCUBE is incorporated in the procedural representation of the knowledge the statement imparts. As another example, the meaning of *one* (as in *Build one*) is represented by a module which looks back through the preceding dialogue and applies various heuristics to discover what *one* refers to.

(3) Grammatical rules are represented by modules which parse the corresponding grammatical structures. For example, the rule which can be expressed by the BNF production

$$verb\text{-}group \rightarrow transitive\text{-}verb\ noun\text{-}group\,|\,intransitive\text{-}verb$$

is represented by a module which parses verb groups. This idea is similar to that used in top-down parsing in compilers (Section 5.4.2). However, unlike the syntactic modules in compilers, those in SHRDLU do not operate in isolation: they frequently call semantic modules to decide whether a plausible parse makes sense.

SHRDLU was a significant advance on its predecessors, and is still one of the most impressive working systems. Its success can be attributed partly to the flexibility of its procedural representation of knowledge, but mainly to the following features.

(1)   SHRDLU's world is very small, comprising only a few objects. The attributes of these objects are relatively simple (e.g. color, shape, size), as are the relationships between objects (e.g. on top of, behind, inside). Thus the quantity and variety of knowledge which must be represented in the system is much smaller than that in any "real" world.

(2)   As indicated earlier, the modules concerned with syntax, semantics and knowledge do not operate in self-contained groups. In fact the modules in the three categories frequently call each other in order to interpret a given input sentence. For example, consider the input sentence *Put the blue pyramid on the block in the box*, in which it is not clear whether *the block* supports the pyramid or whether *the block* is in the box. The parsing modules may first suggest *the blue pyramid on the block* as a potential noun group. At this point semantic analysis commences, and it becomes apparent that the first word *the* means that a particular pyramid is being referred to. The knowledge modules are then called to see whether such a pyramid exists: if not, the parse is rejected, and the syntactic modules proceed to parse *the blue pyramid* as a noun group by itself and *on the block in the box* as a phrase indicating where the pyramid is to be put. Thus SHRDLU uses its knowledge about the blocks world to resolve ambiguities and to reason generally about the meanings of sentences.

Although SHRDLU is impressive it is doubtful whether the ideas it incorporates can be applied to larger domains of discourse. As the domain is widened, and correspondingly more knowledge modules are added to the program, execution time becomes infeasible. Some method is needed for storing vast amounts of knowledge in such a way that any relevant portion can be rapidly accessed and used. No-one has yet found such a method, and much current research is concerned with alternative representations of knowledge and meaning. As indicated in Section 6.2.1 artificial intelligence comes up against this problem time and again.

6.2.4   Visual Perception

Visual perception is an area of artificial intelligence concerned with enabling computers to interpret and analyze visual patterns or scenes. It is a field which has received considerable attention, as it promises several immediately valuable applications. Examples are

(1)   Computer analysis of satellite photographs for meteorological, environmental or military purposes (the last, not surprisingly, being the major source of research funds);

(2)   direct input of printed or handwritten text into computers;

(3)   enhancement of the capabilities of industrial robots—robots which can "see" as well as touch.

Another reason for strong interest is that visual perception is a field which can shed light on other areas of artificial intelligence. As we shall see, it is similar to language understanding in being a rich field for the study of knowledge-based reasoning.

A simple example is sufficient to show that knowledge plays an important role in visual perception: the symbol

$$\mathsf{H}$$

is perceived in different ways on its two occurrences in

$$\mathsf{T\,H\!E\ \ C\,H\!T}$$

The knowledge used in this case is quite simple, namely that *the* and *cat* are valid English words whereas *tae* and *cht* are not. In more complex cases, such as the interpretation of visual scenes, the type of knowledge required may be far more extensive. In fact human beings generally see what they *expect* to see: they base their perception on visual clues, on context, and on knowledge of what objects are likely to be present. Thus the same image may be interpreted as the Eiffel Tower in mist or an oil derrick in a sandstorm, depending on whether the context suggests Paris or Saudi Arabia.

As in other areas of artificial intelligence, workers in machine perception have tended to reduce their problems to manageable proportions by limiting the extent of knowledge required by their systems. They have done this (as in natural language understanding) by constraining their systems to operate in very small "worlds"; typical examples are the interpretation of handwritten text, the analysis of strip cartoons, and the interpretation of two-dimensional images of simple three-dimensional scenes. In the last case the objects permitted in the scenes have usually been restricted to having plane surfaces bounded by straight lines. In the real world, of course, objects can have curved surfaces with irregular boundaries, but the analysis of arbitrary real world scenes is well beyond the current state of the art. In the following paragraphs we shall use the analysis of simple scenes to illustrate some of the techniques used in machine perception. Like most perception systems we shall consider scenes containing only objects with planar straight-edged surfaces.

The various processes involved can be summarized as follows:

(1)   An image of the scene, provided by a TV camera or a photograph, is transformed into some digital representation. The most common digital representation is an *intensity matrix*: that is, a fine grid of squares each of which contains a number representing the average intensity of light in the corresponding part of the image.

(2) The intensity matrix is examined for the purpose of detecting high-lights, such as the corners and edges of objects. Because of the quality of the image or the nature of the lighting some corners and edges may not in fact be detected.

(3) Various heuristics are employed to extrapolate the information gained in (2) into a representation of the scene which is equivalent to a complete line drawing. This process can be regarded as "filling in" the features omitted in (2).

(4) Different portions of the representation produced in (3) are matched against the system's templates of permissible objects. The result is the identification of each part of the scene with an object the system knows about. At this point the scene has been fully interpreted.

We shall describe each of these processes in more detail in a moment, but we should first point out that despite the enumeration above they need not be carried out independently or in strict sequence. There can in fact be considerable interaction between the various phases of interpretation, with information gained in one phase being used to guide analysis in others. For example, a possible hypothesis about the scene shown in Fig. 6.13(a) is that it depicts a cube; this hypothesis might stimulate further analysis of the intensity matrix in an attempt to detect the missing edges and corners (Fig. 6.13(b)). Alternatively the hypothesis could stimulate analysis of the area "in front of" the supposed cube in order to find an object which could feasibly be hiding part of it (Fig. 6.13(c)). The interaction between the different phases of interpretation is similar to that occurring between the syntactic, semantic, and knowledge-based phases of natural language understanding (Section 6.2.3).

In the first phase of scene analysis an intensity matrix can be produced in a number of ways by a variety of optical equipment. One way, carried out

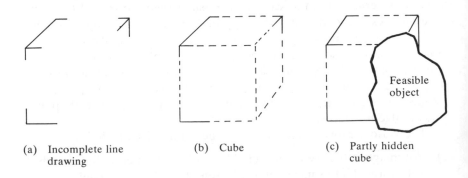

(a) Incomplete line drawing

(b) Cube

(c) Partly hidden cube

Feasible object

Figure 6.13 Possible interpretations of an incomplete line drawing.

Columns	4	5	6	7	8
Rows					
P	1	3	16	11	13
Q	2	2	15	15	14
R	9	1	2	16	14
S	7	8	2	3	16

(a) Part of an intensity matrix.

Columns	4		5		6		7		8
Rows									
P	1	(2)	3	(13)	16	(5)	11	(2)	13
	(1)		(1)		(1)		(4)		(1)
Q	2	(0)	2	(13)	15	(0)	15	(1)	14
	(7)		(1)		(13)		(1)		(0)
R	9	(8)	1	(1)	2	(14)	16	(2)	14
	(2)		(7)		(0)		(13)		(2)
S	7	(1)	8	(6)	2	(1)	3	(13)	16

(b) Intensity gradients for the matrix of Fig. 6.14 (a).

Columns	4		5		6		7		8
Rows									
P	1	(2)	3	(13)	16	(5)	11	(2)	13
	(1)		(1)		(1)		(4)		(1)
Q	2	(0)	2	(13)	15	(0)	15	(1)	14
	(7)		(1)		(13)		(1)		(0)
R	9	(8)	1	(1)	2	(14)	16	(2)	14
	(2)		(7)		(0)		(13)		(2)
S	7	(1)	8	(6)	2	(1)	3	(13)	6

(c) Probable edges in the scene represented by the matrix of Fig. 6.14 (a).

Figure 6.14 Processing an intensity matrix.

by a piece of equipment called a *digitizer*, is to scan a photograph of the scene with a small spot of light and to record the intensity of the reflected beam at every point. The precise details need not concern us, since the process is quite routine and does not fall within the artificial intelligence domain. A portion of a typical intensity matrix is shown in Fig. 6.14(a). The figures represent the intensity of light in the corresponding areas of the image: each area is usually a square of side about 1 millimetre. (The smaller the square the greater the resolution but the longer the processing time.)

In the next phase the intensity matrix is scanned with the aim of detecting edges and corners of objects. Edges show up as sudden changes in intensity, and can be detected by computing the *intensity gradient* (i.e. the difference in intensity between adjacent squares) at each point in the matrix. The intensity gradients for the matrix of Fig. 6.14(a) are shown as circled figures in Fig. 6.14(b). Possible edges are defined by joining adjacent points which have similarly high intensity gradients (Fig. 6.14(c)). Corners, of course, are simply those points where two or more edges meet. Note that some edges may remain undetected, since the process can be hampered by the quality of the image, the degree of resolution, and the nature of the lighting. Conversely, spurious edges may be detected where none exist: these can arise from the presence of shadows or of surface markings on objects.

The result of this phase is a two-dimensional representation, or *picture*, of the scene. Lines in the picture correspond to supposed edges in the scene, while the junctions of lines correspond to supposed corners. As noted above, the picture may be neither complete nor accurate.

In the third phase of analysis the picture is refined by various heuristics which attempt to fill in the gaps, remove spurious lines, and define closed regions. Thus collinear line segments may be joined together (Fig. 6.15(a)) and "hanging" lines extended to form a junction (Fig. 6.15(b)). There may

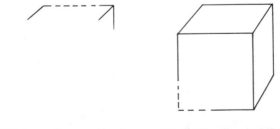

(a) Joining collinear segments   (b) Joining 'hanging' lines

Figure 6.15   Examples of processing incomplete line drawings.

of course be considerable uncertainty about how various parts of the picture should be filled in, and in some areas there may be a large number of possibilities. However, the number of possibilities can be reduced by a systematic characterization of lines and junctions as follows.

Each line in the picture can represent either

(1)   a *convex* edge between two visible surfaces: we shall label such lines with '+';

(2)   a *concave* edge between two visible surfaces: we shall label such lines with '−'; or

(3)   an edge at which one of the surfaces hides (or *occludes*) the other: such lines are labelled with an arrow. The direction of the arrow is such that the occluding surface is on its right.

These labellings (due to David Huffman and Max Clowes) are illustrated in Fig. 6.16. Junctions in a picture can be characterized by the labelling of the lines which form them: for example the junctions *A* and *B* of Fig. 6.16 are both of the type characterized by Fig. 6.17(a), while junctions *C* and *D* are both of the type characterized by Fig. 6.17(b). Since a line can have 4 possible labellings (+, −, → , and ←) it might be thought that the number of possible junction types is 4^2 for junctions formed by two lines, 4^3 for junctions formed by three lines, and so on. However, geometrical considerations imply that only very few of these junction types are physically possible. (For example Figs. 6.17(c) and 6.17(d) show two junctions types which are physically impossible.) Thus any interpretation of the picture, and any proposed "filling in", can be rejected unless it satisfies the constraints

(1)   each line has the same labelling all along its length; and

(2)   each junction is physically possible.

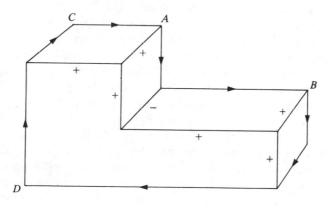

Figure 6.16   Huffman–Clowes line labelling.

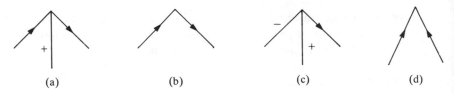

     (a)   (b)   (c)   (d)

Figure 6.17   Example junction types. Types (a) and (b) are physically possible; types (c) and (d) are physically impossible.

These constraints can be regarded as "semantic" knowledge of the 3-dimensional scene which guides "syntactic" interpretation of the 2-dimensional picture. It is analogous to the semantic information used to guide parsing in natural language understanding (Section 6.2.3). The relatively simple form of this knowledge is a direct result of the restriction to a narrow domain in which only objects with planar faces can appear.

The result of this third phase of analysis is a representation of the scene which is equivalent to a complete line drawing. The lines, junctions and closed regions correspond to supposed edges, corners and surfaces in the scene.

In the fourth and final phase an attempt is made to match various parts of the picture against object templates stored in the system. For example, part of the picture may match a pyramid template, and an adjacent part may match a cube template. The corresponding portions of the scene can therefore be identified as a cube supporting a pyramid. Note that the templates must be stored in such a form that objects can be recognized whatever their size or orientation. Recognition is easier if the position of the camera is known: this may be given in advance, or it may have to be deduced after positive identification of one or two objects. The recognition of all objects in the scene must of course be consistent with a single camera position.

The object templates embody the system's knowledge of its world: an object with no template cannot be recognized. A visual perception system can therefore be seen to have three levels of knowledge, summarized in Fig. 6.18. The corresponding three levels of knowledge in a natural language understanding system are shown by way of analogy.

The techniques described above have achieved some success in the application areas mentioned earlier. However, the type of perception system we have described takes no account of color, motion, or non-planar surfaces. Although there are specialist systems which can handle each of these phenomena in a limited fashion, no system comes remotely close to the power and flexibility needed to analyze the real world scenes which humans deal with every waking minute. As the reader might suspect, it is the

Level of knowledge	Visual perception	Natural language understanding
syntactic	line finding modules	parsing modules
semantic	geometric constraints	word meanings
world	object templates	object attributes

Figure 6.18   Analogous types of knowledge in systems for visual perception and natural language understanding.

appropriate representation of large bodies of knowledge which is the major obstacle to further progress.

6.2.5   The Representation of Knowledge

We have noted in earlier sections that an adequate representation of knowledge is the key to further progress in many areas of artificial intelligence. It therefore seems appropriate to conclude our survey of artificial intelligence with a brief examination of current trends in this field.

One promising approach to knowledge representation is to recognize that knowledge is valuable only if it is *used* for something—to answer questions, to plan actions, or to infer further knowledge. It therefore seems reasonable to represent knowledge in a form which indicates the ways in which the knowledge can be used. More precisely, each item of knowledge can be represented by a "rule" which specifies *when* to use it and *how* to use it. Such a rule takes the form "When a condition of type C applies then A is the appropriate action to take," or, more concisely,

$$C \Rightarrow A$$

A rule of this kind is called a *production* (not to be confused with the productions used in syntax definition, though there is a common ancestry). A system which represents knowledge as a set of productions

$$C_1 \Rightarrow A_1$$
$$C_2 \Rightarrow A_2$$
$$\vdots$$
$$C_n \Rightarrow A_n$$

is called a *production system*. The set of productions can be regarded as defining actions which are triggered when the corresponding conditions are satisfied.

A production system has one other essential component. This is the *working memory*, which contains short-term information about the current state of the world. The information in the working memory is updated by the actions $A_1,...,A_n$ of the production system; conversely, the information it contains is matched against the conditions $C_1,...,C_n$ to determine which action to take. Thus the production system operates in the following cycle:

repeat
   select some C_i which matches the information
   in working memory
   carry out the corresponding action A_i
forever   (6.12)

To give an example, a production system might represent the knowledge *All men are mortal* by the production

(MAN X) $\Rightarrow$ assert(MORTAL X)

meaning "if any object X is a man then assert that X is mortal". (*Assert* is an action which adds a piece of information to the working memory.) Suppose that at some stage the working memory contains the information

(MAN SOCRATES)

This item of information matches the condition in the production above, and so the corresponding action can be carried out. The effect is to add

(MORTAL SOCRATES)

to the working memory.

The action specified in a production may modify the content of the working memory (as in the example above), or it may provide interaction with the outside world. For example, a production system modelling a "blocks world" like that of Winograd's SHRDLU (Section 6.2.3) might contain the production

(WANT-TO-MOVE X) and (CLEAR-TOP X)
   $\Rightarrow$ pick-up X; assert(PICKED-UP X)

This production expresses knowledge about when to pick up an object (when we want to move it and its top is clear) and about the effect on the state of the world.

Other ways of interacting with the outside world are by asking for information and by answering questions. Consider, for example, how our earlier production system might respond to the question *Is Socrates mortal*? We assume that the system contains productions which can interpret the question, and which place the information

(ASKED (MORTAL SOCRATES))

in the working memory. An appropriate response can then be provided by the productions

(ASKED (MORTAL X)) and (MORTAL X)
    ⇒ reply("YES"); delete(ASKED (MORTAL X))
(ASKED (MORTAL X)) and (MISSING (MORTAL X))
    ⇒ reply("DON'T KNOW"); delete(ASKED (MORTAL X))

The reply "YES" is given if the information (MORTAL SOCRATES) is in the working memory; if this information is missing from the working memory then the reply is "DON'T KNOW". In either case the fact that the question has been asked is deleted from the working memory, indicating that the question has been dealt with.

This method of answering questions assumes that the system has already placed in the working memory all the information it is capable of deducing. For example, if (MAN SOCRATES) is in the working memory then (MORTAL SOCRATES) is assumed to be there too. The drawback to this approach is that the working memory may be cluttered with information which is never used. For example, if we inform the system above that Tom, Dick and Harry are all men, then it will generate and store the information (MORTAL TOM), (MORTAL DICK), and (MORTAL HARRY), irrespective of whether this information is ever needed. Moreover, any realistic system would need to know more about men than the fact of their mortality, and so a whole set of productions would add to the working memory the information that Tom, Dick and Harry are all animate, that they are all mammals, that they are all bipeds, that they each have a head, and so on. The working memory would rapidly become cluttered with information which might never be needed. Such cluttering is undesirable because the size of the working memory may be limited. More importantly, the time to access relevant information is likely to be infeasible if too much information is being stored.

A way out of this difficulty is to modify the system so that information can be inferred *when required* rather than being generated indiscriminately and stored indefinitely. In our example this can be done by replacing the production

(MAN X) ⇒ (MORTAL X)

by the productions

(WANT-TO-KNOW (MORTAL X)) and (MORTAL X)
    ⇒ assert(RESULT TRUE)
(WANT-TO-KNOW (MORTAL X)) and (MISSING (MORTAL X))
    ⇒ assert(WANT-TO-KNOW (MAN X))

The second of these productions is an *inference rule*: that is, a way of inferring one piece of information (the mortality of X) from another (the manhood of X). In order for this particular inference to be carried through it is clearly necessary to specify how the manhood of X can be determined. The following productions might be provided for this purpose.

> (WANT-TO-KNOW (MAN X)) and (MAN X)
>   ⇒ assert(RESULT TRUE)
> (WANT-TO-KNOW (MAN X)) and (MISSING (MAN X))
>   ⇒ assert(RESULT UNKNOWN)

Here we have assumed that manhood is a "basic" property which cannot itself be inferred from other properties; if this is not the case then we would write an inference rule similar to that for mortality. A chain of such inference rules must of course lead back to some basic property.

Returning to the origin of our discussion, the question *Is Socrates mortal?* can now be handled by the inference rules above and by the productions

> (ASKED (MORTAL X))
>   ⇒ assert(WANT-TO-KNOW (MORTAL X));
>   delete(ASKED (MORTAL X))
> (RESULT TRUE) ⇒ reply("YES"); delete(RESULT TRUE)
> (RESULT UNKNOWN) ⇒ reply("DON'T KNOW");
>   delete(RESULT UNKNOWN)

Summarizing, to avoid an information explosion in the working memory it is possible to build inference rules into the production system. The inference rules can themselves be expressed as productions.

In general the inference rules may be more complex than the example we have given. For instance, there is a need for rules such as "to infer that X is mortal, establish that X is a man or that X is a woman," and "to infer that X is an ostrich, establish that X is a bird and that X has its head in the sand." These more complex rules can also be expressed as productions, but there is a danger that the increased number of productions can lead to an explosion of its own. The more productions there are the longer it takes the system to find one it can execute. Thus attempts to incorporate a large amount of information in the productions can lead to infeasible execution time.

Up to this point we have concentrated on the use of knowledge in making inferences and answering questions. Knowledge is also used in *planning*: that is, in attempting to achieve a goal by formulating and achieving subgoals. This aspect of knowledge can also be represented in production systems. To give an example, the following production might occur in a system for a simple robot like SHRDLU:

(WANT-TO-MOVE X) and (SUPPORTS X Y)
$\Rightarrow$ assert(WANT-TO-MOVE Y)

This production formulates a subgoal and adds it to the working memory; some other productions are responsible for achieving the subgoal. This technique can be generalized for arbitrarily complex plans.

Production systems can also model *learning*. We have already seen how information can be added to the working memory; however, this cannot be regarded as learning since the information is deduced by the system itself and is therefore nothing new. By "learning" we mean the acquisition of more permanent and fundamental knowledge, such as that expressed in the statement *All men are mortal.* This knowledge is represented not in the working memory, but in the productions themselves. In a production system the ability to learn is therefore the same as the ability to extend the set of productions. It is in fact possible to devise productions to do this (see, for example, Exercise 6.12), but the details are beyond our scope. The result is a production system which can add to its own productions, and which can therefore be said to have the capacity to learn.

Since production systems can model inference, planning and learning, they are clearly an attractive means of representing knowledge. There is a further feature which adds to their attraction. This arises from the modularity of the productions—each production is a self-contained entity which interacts with other productions only through the working memory. This means that productions can be invoked in parallel, provided that the information in the working memory matches their respective conditions. This facility is of little consequence if only a single processor is available, since in that case only a single production can be invoked at a time. (The choice can be made according to arbitrary selection criteria.) However, if a large number of processors is available the situation becomes more interesting. A processor can now be allocated to each production, and a production can be invoked as soon as its enabling condition is satisfied. This increases the processing speed of the system, but the cost is an increased number of processors.

It is interesting to speculate on whether or not there is any analogy between production systems and the human brain. Each production can be regarded as an autonomous agent, waiting to perform its particular action as soon as the appropriate conditions arise. Similarly, a group of neurons (brain cells) can be regarded as a minute agent which is "fired up" to perform its particular function as soon as the appropriate stimuli are received. There may also be an analogy between production systems and certain psychological models of the brain, with the working memory being identified with the psychologists' "short-term memory" and the set of productions with the "long-term" memory which contains a person's skills, knowledge and recollections. However, these ideas are only speculative, and the necessary evidence is lacking.

Production systems have been sucessfully used in small domains of knowledge. The major successes are in *expert systems*, which perform analytic and diagnostic tasks in narrow fields of speciality. (Examples are the analysis of organic compounds, the identification of bacteria, and the prescription of antibiotics.) These systems are "taught" by human experts, and usually proceed to perform better than their tutors.

In summary, production systems appear to provide an attractive framework for representing knowledge. The main drawback has been hinted at earlier—namely, the explosion of information as the domain of knowledge widens. The explosion is reflected in the amount of information in the working memory, or in the number of productions, or both. The result is infeasible execution time as the system tries to determine which productions it can execute. Note that parallel execution of the productions is no help, since the problem is to know *which* productions are executable. What seems to be needed is some convenient mechanism for associating items in the working memory with the productions they affect. This would allow a production to be executed as soon as relevant information appeared in the working memory. Unfortunately, no such mechanism has yet been devised.

Generalizing, the convenient representation of knowledge seems to require storage mechanisms quite different from those found in present-day computers. What is needed are mechanisms which cause information to "jump out" when relevant, rather than having to be searched for. Such mechanisms are apparently present in the human brain, but no-one has yet discovered how they work, much less implemented them on a computer. One realizes how much remains to be done if one compares the abilities of the most sophisticated current systems with those of a new-born child. The comparison provokes a healthy humility.

EXERCISES

1   Consider two (very short) sequential files whose records are ordered by an alphabetic key field. The values of the key fields for each file are
    File 1: Bill, Dick, Jane, Mary
    File 2: Fred, Sue, Tim
    Trace the execution of algorithm 6.1 in merging these files. At what point does an execution error occur?
        Suggest a suitable sentinel for the two files, and show by tracing execution of algorithm 6.2 that use of the sentinels avoids the execution error above.

2   A particular file contains 128000 records, each of which requires 10 memory cells to hold it. The file is sorted using a polyphase sort with 8 output files and a memory allocation of 20000 cells. How many distribute–merge cycles are required to sort the file?
How many output files would be needed to reduce the number of cycles to one? Alternatively, how much memory would be needed?

3   A bank ledger is to be updated by a sequence of transactions. The ledger file and the transaction file, which for simplicity can be regarded as ordered by customer name, are shown below (figures denote the current balance, or the amount to be credited or debited).

ledger file	transaction file
Brown, 76	Green, debit 14
Green, 41	Green, credit 12
Jones, 84	Johnson, open account
Smith, 15	Johnson, credit 28
Turner, 23	Jones, debit 84
	Jones, close account
	Smith, open account
	Smith, credit 24

Trace the execution of algorithm 6.10 which performs the update, and write down the resulting ledger file.

4   Suppose that ELIZA contains the transformation rule
YYY MY MOTHER ZZZ ⇒ YOUR FAMILY ZZZ
Show how this rule, together with one of the templates given in Section 6.2.1, can produce the response

   TELL ME MORE ABOUT YOUR FAMILY

to the input

   Perhaps I could learn to get along with my mother

What response would the same rule and template produce for the input

   I think my mother hates me

Would any of the other example templates produce a better response?

5   Deduce from the game tree of Fig. 6.7 a winning strategy for the first player in the game of Nim.

6   Devise an evaluation function for the game of noughts and crosses (tic-tac-toe). Try out the function on a few sample games, using a lookahead of two moves (one by each player). (*Hint*: use symmetry to reduce the size of the game tree.)

7   Why would it be inappropriate for a game-playing program to adjust its evaluation function
(a) after each move?
(b) after each game?
When *should* it adjust the evaluation function?

8   Think of two sentences in which word sense ambiguity can be resolved only by semantic knowledge.

9   What difficulty would be encountered by a program trying to understand a story prefaced by "I had this weird dream in which ..."? How do you think people overcome this difficulty? Can the same means be used in a program?

10   Apply the Huffman–Clowes line labelling technique to the "devil's pitchfork" illustrated in Fig. 6.19. What conclusion can be drawn? Can a program draw the same conclusion?

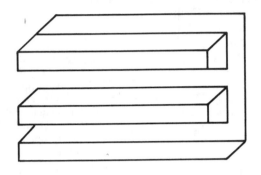

Figure 6.19

11   Devise a production system which is capable of distinguishing between a lion, an elephant, an ostrich, an emu, and a sparrow. Assume that the system can ask questions which require a YES or NO answer—e.g. ask ("LONGLEGGED?")—and that the answers are stored in the working memory.

12   A certain production system can learn (i.e. add to its own productions) by a production of the form

(*X* says "all *P* are *Q*") ⇒ add production ((*P*   *X*) ⇒ assert (*Q*   *X*))

Thus, for example, if the working memory contains the information

(Newton says "all apples fall downward")

then the production

(APPLE *X*) ⇒ assert (FALL-DOWNWARD *X*)

is added to the system.

To allow for known liars the system also contains the production

(LIAR *X*) and (*X* says "all *P* are *Q*")

⇒ add production ((*P*   *X*) ⇒ assert (not *Q*   *X*))

What happens when the system learns of Epiminedes the Cretan's observation that "all Cretans are liars"? (Epiminedes is reputed to have died laughing at his own foolishness.) Is there any way that the system can resolve such inconsistencies?

BIBLIOGRAPHY

A few introductory books on data processing are

V. T. Dock and E. Essick, *Principles of Business Data Processing*, Science Research Associates, Chicago, 1974.

D. R. Judd, *Use of Files*, 2nd edn, MacDonald-Elsevier, London and New York, 1975.

J. Martin, *Computer Data Base Organization*, 2nd edn, Prentice-Hall, N.J., 1977.

A detailed analysis of many algorithms applicable to data processing is in

D. E. Knuth, *The Art of Computer Programming, Vol. 3 Sorting and Searching*, Addison-Wesley, Reading, Massachusetts, 1973.

Three overviews of artificial intelligence are

A. Bundy (ed.), *Artificial Intelligence: an Introductory Course*, Edinburgh University Press, 1978.

E. B. Hunt, *Artificial Intelligence*, Academic Press, New York, 1975.

P. McCorduck, *Machines Who Think*, Freeman, San Fransisco, 1979.

Some thought provoking material about machines and intelligence can be found in

F.A. Feigenbaum and J. Feldman (eds.), *Computers and Thought*, McGraw-Hill, New York, 1961.

A. Newell and H. A. Simon, *Human Problem Solving*, Prentice-Hall, N.J., 1972.

A. Turing, Computing machinery and intelligence, published in 1950 and reprinted in *Computers and Thought* (see above).

An account of a game-playing program which learns is

A. L. Samuel, Some studies in machine learning using the game of checkers, reprinted in *Computers and Thought* (see above).

Understanding natural language is treated in

E. Charniak and Y. Wilks (eds.), *Computational Semantics*, Fundamental Studies in Computer Science No. 4, North-Holland, Amsterdam, 1976.

R. C. Schank and K. M. Colby, *Computer Models of Thought and Language*, Freeman, San Franciso, 1973.

T. Winograd, *Understanding Natural Language*, Edinburgh University Press, 1972.

J. Weizenbaum, ELIZA—a computer program for the study of natural language communication between man and machine, *Commun. Assoc. Comp. Mach.*, **9** (1), 36–45, 1966.

A. Zampoli (ed.), *Linguistic Structures Processing*, Fundamental Studies in Computer Science No. 5, North-Holland, Amsterdam, 1976.

The following two books discuss visual perception.

R. L. Gregory, *The Intelligent Eye*, McGraw-Hill, New York, 1970.

P. H. Winston (ed.), *The Psychology of Computer Vision*, McGraw-Hill, New York, 1972.

Finally, the following is an account of expert systems, which are based on production systems.

D. Michie, Expert systems, *Computer Journal*, **23**(4), 369–76, 1980.

7 SOCIAL ISSUES

At the start of the last chapter we saw that computers are used in a wide variety of applications spanning almost the whole range of human activity. In this chapter we shall look at some of the social implications of such widespread and rapidly growing computer use.

Perhaps the most interesting and important effect of the computer revolution will be its impact on people's lives and on the structure of society. It is possible, for example, that the entire monetary system will need to be redesigned. At present, the use of credit cards entails a lot of paperwork sent from shops to credit companies, collated there, and the totals billed to the customer at the end of each month. It may eventually be economically viable to replace the paperwork and collating by direct links from shops to the credit company's computer. The system could then easily be extended for cash-paying customers, by having the computer make a direct withdrawal from a customer's bank account. Thus the computer revolution may result in what has been referred to as the *cashless society*, since money in the form of cash may become obsolete.

The business office is another sphere in which the computer revolution could have a major influence. There is already a rapid trend away from ordinary typewriters, in favor of *word-processing systems*. These are effectively typewriters linked to a computer which can store the entire document being typed. The computer allows the typist to correct errors and perform revisions of the document, needing only to type the changes, rather than re-typing the entire text. Current word-processing systems can also remember standard form letters, so that a large number of similar documents can be produced with a minimum of typing. This feature is especially useful in applications such as a law office, in which a whole contract can be typed by providing the text of a few special clauses, and telling the computer which standard clauses to add.

It is not hard to visualize extensions of word-processing systems which would automatically file any documents produced. Furthermore, it is not only typists and filing clerks whose workload could be reduced or eliminated by automation. Many tasks performed by managers are repetitive—for example, gathering information and projecting trends. There is much scope for automatic management information systems to aid the decision making role of managers. The automated office could be quite different from the business office as we know it.

The home is another potential area of change due to automation. Applications of computers in house appliances and home entertainment are virtually unlimited. The home telephone, too, could be quite transformed by the addition of a computer. The telephone could take messages from friends, or give out information to selected callers when the owner is away. It could place shopping orders, periodically try calling a number until a successful connection was made, or pay a bill via an instruction to the bank's computer.

Automatic robots which clean, polish and dust are also not impossible, although these seem remote for the time being. However, industrial robots with relatively simple and well-defined tasks are being deployed in ever greater numbers, and may eventually totally automate mass-production lines.

The computer revolution may also result in a more even distribution of political power. Individuals could, on a daily basis, gain relevant information and input their personal choices on a wide range of issues via a network of interconnected home computers. Such networks might entirely replace large centralized governments as we know them.

It seems possible to speculate endlessly on the impact of the computer revolution. In this chapter we shall discuss only a few of the issues which such speculations highlight: the effect on employment; the possible erosion of privacy; vulnerability to computer crime; and the chance of total human redundancy.

7.1   EMPLOYMENT

Since the early 1950s there have been dire predictions that the computer revolution would bring dramatically shorter working hours and massive unemployment within a few decades. These predictions have not been fulfilled to date, at least not to the extent predicted. Certainly automation has caused a steady increase in productivity, but this has been largely matched by *increased consumption*, rather than increased leisure time. The complex forces which mold western society have thus far solved the problem of automation by increasing the demand for material wealth. For example, in some socio-economic classes demand for material wealth has so increased that married couples have found it *economically* desirable (as well as desirable for other, non-economic factors) for both husband and wife to undertake paid employment in order to achieve the standard of living which they seek.

Even though the overall level of employment has not dramatically changed because of automation, *job dislocation* has occurred as a result of shifting patterns in areas of employment. The general trend has been away from primary industries (e.g. agriculture and mining) towards sales, service industries and government. Again, the changes have occurred more slowly than expected in early predictions, allowing time for job retraining and gradual attrition of redundant workers by retirement, death and resignation.

Of course, many people expect more from employment than simply having a job and receiving a pay packet. Factors involved in employment include gaining satisfaction from a stimulating career, increasing self-esteem from success, satisfying a desire to contribute to society, exercising authority over others, exercising control over events, and bending to social pressure and conditioning. Automation can affect not only the amount and distribution of employment, but also these non-material factors.

In general, the nature of computers leads one to expect that dull and repetitive tasks will be automated, as will some jobs in environments unpleasant to humans. Examples include reductions in clerical jobs caused by word-processing and other data processing equipment, replacement of menial operator jobs by automatic control equipment, and the loss of some specialized employment categories such as typesetters in the printing industry and welders in the automobile manufacturing industry. On the other hand, some new jobs will be created, particularly those requiring a level of intelligence and creativity beyond that of current computers. The new requirements for computer programmers and technicians are obvious examples. Thus one might hope that job satisfaction will increase in the majority of cases.

Of course, anomalies are to be expected. For example, in fully automated industrial plants it may be necessary to retain highly skilled operators in case of a severe emergency which the control computer cannot handle. The job performed by such operators may be extremely boring and highly demoralizing for most of the time. Some union battles to retain jobs have resulted in similar situations. A classic historical example was the retention of a fireman—whose task it was to shovel coal in a steam engine—in every diesel train on American railroads.

The destruction of old jobs and the creation of new ones may have an impact on the level of skill and education required of the workforce. People who find it difficult to acquire new skills and adapt to new tasks may be more severely affected than those who find it a pleasant challenge to learn a new skill. Studies show that the workforce has indeed become more educated over the past few decades, in terms of level of formal education achieved. However, it is not clear whether this has resulted from a greater need for skills acquired in education or whether the screening process for job applicants has become tighter as a result of other social and economic factors. The level of education required after computerization seems to depend heavily on the individual application, and no clear trend is at present discernible.

One thing is certain: we must not be complacent about the effects of automation on society. Is it desirable, or even possible, for demand to continue to keep pace with increased productivity? If so, then massive unemployment and social dislocation may be avoidable. It is also possible that as increased production causes the depletion of raw materials, more labor-intensive collection and recycling of raw materials may become necessary. Again, we may find that once an initial dramatic increase in productivity through computerization is attained, further increases can be achieved only by considerable effort and sophistication. Thus the effect of diminishing returns may be that, after a certain point, highly skilled technological jobs may be created faster than repetitive tasks are eliminated.

On the other hand, feelings of environmental responsibility and other complex social factors may curtail the demand for ever-increasing material wealth. In that case, increased productivity will result in less time being spent by the workforce in the production of the required goods. It would then be necessary for society either to find more activities with which to satisfy the workforce, or else to learn to cope with increased leisure time.

Finding additional activities for the workforce is a challenging endeavor. A range of activities is required which can be satisfying to different people with varying physical and intellectual gifts, and at the same time not so routine or repetitive that machines could more efficiently and economically perform them. One example of such a range is the set of tasks which some people regard as "improving the quality of life". Increased public works such as improving and beautifying public buildings, parks and the waterfront come to mind as tasks which are hard to automate but which may provide job satisfaction. Picking up litter is another job which is difficult to computerize. Improved health care and better staff/student ratios in educational institutions are also labor-hungry activities. Visiting the aged, the sick or the physically or intellectually handicapped are further occupations to which computers are unsuited, as are artistic and musical activities and jobs associated with the old concept of craftsmanship. It is ironic that the ultimate in automation and mass production may, by freeing people's time, allow a return to individuality, art and craftsmanship.

Rather than finding new activities to satisfy the workforce, society may decide to come to grips with increased leisure time. The increased leisure time can arise in one of two ways: either from a general reduction in working hours, or by having a group of people who are permanently or periodically unemployed. In both cases, the success of any proposed solution depends upon people feeling happy with their new role in society and having a satisfying method of filling their leisure time. Increased entertainment facilities, both communal and in the home, are possibilities. More opportunity for travel, enlarged libraries, and greater access to educational facilities can both occupy some people, and provide more jobs for others. Even personal home improvements, gardening, and more time with the kids can be satisfying activities to fill the otherwise empty hours created by the computer revolution.

7.2 PRIVACY

Computers are having a significant impact on society as they are increasingly used to gather, store, and efficiently access vast volumes of information. A potential conflict arises between cases where such practices seem reasonable and desirable, and others where a citizen's individual right to privacy is threatened.

Organizations which gather large volumes of personal data include government departments, law enforcement agencies, credit bureaux, banks, insurance companies and other corporations, educational institutions, libraries (long term records of book loans to individuals), magazine and mail order companies (mailing lists), newspapers, and some research organizations.

Data collection aids the smooth functioning of government, business and research. Personal data is used for tax assessment, job selection, credit rating assignment, and many other purposes. Aggregate data is useful for planning and formulating social policies. The general availability of data supports freedom of speech and freedom of the press.

Conversely, the gathering of data can erode personal privacy. Data can be used for blackmail, especially large scale political blackmail by governments or police with too much power. Harassment of individuals by law enforcement agencies and monopolistic corporations (including utility companies) can also occur. Errors in data collection can lead to many unfair practices, such as denial of employment or denial of credit. Outdated or incomplete data can cause similar problems. Unfettered publication of personal data can lead to personal trauma. Retention of information for long periods can result in excessive punishment of a person for a misdemeanor long since atoned for.

As with other conflicting demands in our society, a balance is necessary between unrestricted use of data on the one hand, and total secrecy on the other. Before the advent of computers, such a balance was maintained largely by the difficulty inherent in storing and efficiently accessing large masses of information. Cumbersome filing techniques resulted in practical limitations on the dissemination of stored information, and made it almost impossible to amalgamate many pieces of information about a single person from diverse sources. However, the speed and mass information handling capability of modern computers have tipped the balance in favor of the information gatherers to the detriment of personal privacy. It is now feasible for an organization such as a government to amalgamate many collections of information and to have efficient access to all the data. The potential for abuse is enormous. For example, political profiles (or "dossiers") of government opponents could be created by combining detailed information about

(1) financial transactions, obtained from bank and taxation records, including any charities, religious groups and political parties to which donations were made;

(2) the placement of telephone calls, gleaned from telephone company billing computers;

(3) reading habits, as recorded by computerized library lending systems;

(4) medical and psychological history, taken from hospital and health insurance records;

(5) attendance at rallies and demonstrations, recorded clandestinely by secret service organizations;

(6) criminal history, including speeding and parking misdemeanors, obtained from police files;

(7) other personal details regularly recorded on census forms.

Society will need to either adapt to the new situation of reduced privacy, or pass legislation limiting collection, storage and access of personal information. Limitations which have been suggested include the following:

(1) People should be informed about what type of information is being kept.
(2) People should have a right to access any stored information about themselves.
(3) People should have a right to request corrections to that information, and have a right of appeal to the courts if the data collectors refuse to accept the change.

(4) People should have a right to request the removal of information related to their distant past, to avoid excessive punishments as mentioned earlier. They should also have the right to request removal of information which is impossible to substantiate.

(5) People should have a right to specify restrictions on the use of any information they divulge. For example, they may restrict access to the information to certain persons only, and then only for specific purposes (as is supposed to be the case with taxation returns). Alternatively, they may specify that the information be used only in aggregate data (as is the case with census information or information gathered for research projects).

(6) Each access to information about an individual should be recorded, and the records made available to that individual for inspection.

(7) Transfers of information to other collections of data should be recorded, so that any changes can be propagated to all copies of the information.

(8) All information should be signed by the person who stored it.

(9) Adequate safeguards should be maintained to ensure that information is secure from unauthorized access. Security of computer systems is further discussed in Section 7.3.

If such rules are to be made effective, they will have to be backed by law. Moreover, individuals must have reasonable recourse to the courts in case disputes arise, and to law enforcement agencies to force compliance with court rulings.

Exceptions to the rules must also be written into legislation to handle the rare cases in which access by individuals to data about themselves is undesirable. Such a case can occur during investigation of a person by a law enforcement agency. The person's rights may still be protected by requiring the law enforcement agency to show reasonable grounds for suspicion before a court order permitting the secret collection of personal data for a limited period is obtained. This is analogous to the laws found in some countries which permit law enforcement agencies to perform wire tapping or searches of personal property in exceptional cases.

Lack of an adequate balance between data collection and personal privacy can have undesirable social consequences. Quite apart from violating the United Nations Declaration of Human Rights, inadequately limited data collection can lead to a situation of "voluntary" conformity in society. Observation of similar situations in the past has shown that individuals tend to conduct their affairs in order to maximize the favorable information which is collected about them. For example, people will tend to shy away from associations with people, organizations, and even books and magazines which are known to be regarded with suspicion by data collection agencies. Who would subscribe to a sex magazine if it was known that this piece of information would be duly recorded, and subsequently retrieved by a prospective employer?

A perceived imbalance can also lead to sabotage of the data collection system. Individuals can contrive to have all sorts of erroneous data entered into the system, using aliases, misspellings and blatantly wrong information. A mild example is the use of slightly different spelling of one's name when subscribing to various magazines or when ordering items by mail, in order to trace the sale of mailing lists from one organization to another. Large scale entry of erroneous data would certainly help restore the balance towards privacy. However, it is not a socially desirable method of achieving that goal, since it would tend also to sabotage the legitimate uses of data collection.

7.3 SECURITY AND CRIME

In the previous section we mentioned that data collection organizations should maintain adequate safeguards against unauthorized access to personal information. More generally, it is essential for computer installations to provide tight security against all types of *computer crime*.

Computer crime can be defined as any crime committed by unauthorized tampering with a computer. It is distinct from *computer-related crime*, which is crime connected with a computer, but committed by conventional means. Examples of computer-related crime are the theft of computer equipment or blueprints, or of computer programs or data printed on paper or stored on magnetic tapes. Computer-related crimes can usually be countered by conventional security measures. However, computer crimes entail new and specialized criminal techniques, and can often be detected and prevented only by a good technical understanding of a computer system.

Before a computer crime can take place, the criminal must gain *access* to the computer. Often the criminal has been a trusted employee in the computer installation, such as an operator, programmer, bank teller or even manager, and thus access has been relatively easy. There have also been a number of cases reported of outsiders gaining computer access through the use of remote telephone-dial-up terminals. Outsiders have either broken security codes and passwords, discovered them by tapping the telephone of a legitimate computer user, or simply found them written on discarded documents in waste-paper bins! Increased security precautions in this area can include

(1) use of longer passwords;
(2) use of "scrambler" codes to transmit data over the telephone lines;
(3) frequent changes to passwords and codes to reduce the chance of cracking them and minimize the effects if they are broken;
(4) restrictions on access by employees to computer facilities which are not essential to their individual jobs;
(5) the shredding of sensitive documents and computer print-outs before they are discarded.

Computer crimes can be roughly categorized under three headings: direct theft, indirect theft, and sabotage. *Direct theft* involves accessing the computer to steal programs, data or computer time. Some protection can be obtained by storing sensitive data and programs in secret codes. Further protection can be achieved by using separate passwords for individual programs and collections of critical data. These passwords should be changed regularly, and distributed on a strictly "need-to-know" basis. It is also important to ensure that any temporary copies of a program or data which are made inside the computer be similarly protected, and erased as soon as they are no longer required.

Indirect theft is the area of computer crime which seems to have the greatest appeal to the press. It is typified by the unauthorized alteration of programs or data inside the computer for illegal purposes. Classical cases include

(1) The *resting money* method, in which a program that transfers money from one account to another is instructed to deposit the transferred amounts for short periods of time in the criminal's own account. This account then appears to have a significant average balance.
(2) *Rounding error* collection, where fractional parts of a cent, which arise naturally during calculations involving division (such as discounts), are subtracted from the accounts to which they should be credited, and instead are accumulated in the criminal's own account. It is surprising how rapidly these fractional cents can amount to a significant figure.
(3) Alteration of check writing programs to send additional checks to *fictitious creditors* (later collected and cashed by the criminal).
(4) Transfer of funds from *inactive accounts* (which the owners have forgotten, or never check) to the criminal's account.
(5) The *Pacific Telephone* swindle in which a high school student gained unauthorized access to the telephone company's computerized ordering system and placed fictitious orders for telephone equipment. At the time he was discovered, he employed ten people and a large warehouse in his telephone equipment reselling company.

Some of these indirect thefts are so subtle that they would require very fine auditing programs for their detection. One aid to prevention of some of the crimes is to divide a computer installation's activities into many categories, and have no employee assigned to more than one category. This precaution, coupled with restricted access between the categories of activity, can limit major abuses to the (comparatively rare) cases of conspiracy between a number of employees from different categories. A case in which such a strategy would have been useful is that of a university programmer who recently confided that at one time or another he had been involved with every component of the group of computer programs which administer student records. This lack of security could have permitted him, if he had been so inclined, to graduate himself without ever attending a single class!

The final type of computer crime is outright *sabotage*. A disgruntled employee, a commercial competitor, or a political saboteur may try to erase masses of data or valuable computer programs. Errors could be maliciously inserted into programs, or bogus jobs given to the computer in order to overload it and thereby reduce its effectiveness. A case is on record in which a programmer secretly added a special test to the payroll program to see if his name was still on the payroll. If not, the program tried to delete as much data as possible from the entire computer system. When the programmer was fired at a later date over a different issue, all havoc broke loose after the next payroll run. In addition to the other security measures mentioned earlier, it is clear that keeping regular "back-up" copies of all data and programs can be a very worthwhile insurance against many types of data loss, purposeful or accidental.

Unfortunately, security precautions in practice tend to be poor, and consequently computer installations are vulnerable to all types of computer crime. The sorry state of the art of computer security is perhaps best summarized by the following statement from the data processing manager of a large computer installation: "We don't need all these checks and security measures. We have not detected a single case of computer crime"!

7.4 HUMAN REDUNDANCY

The all-pervasiveness of the computer revolution, the impact of computers on our society, the takeover by computers of human jobs, all leave a nagging thought in our minds: are humans expendable? Will future society be a society of machines with humans as their servants? Will it consist of no humans at all? These questions are highly complex, as their answers depend not only upon machine capabilities, but also upon which of their capabilities man will allow machines to exercise. Machine capabilities have by no means been explored to their fullest. Nor is the possible extent of those abilities well understood.

Nevertheless, machines do have certain limitations. Section 3.1 showed that there are some tasks for which no algorithm exists. There are problems which cannot be solved by any routine method. Presumably, such problems require creative thinking and ingenuity for their solution. Thus the existence of machine limitations tends to suggest that humans are not expendable. If there are tasks which machines cannot perform, and indeed these tasks are quite fundamental and important, then surely jobs will remain for which the special abilities of mankind are required. Possible examples are jobs which involve visual perception or understanding natural language (see Chapter 6).

In the short term, therefore, the possibility of total machine takeover appears to be nil. There is still a wide gulf between the capabilities of modern computers and the capabilities of humans.

It is interesting to consider the characteristics which make humans so much more successful than computers for tasks requiring "intelligence". Unfortunately, our current knowledge of the human brain is either too detailed or too vague to answer this question. Neurophysiology studies the workings and interconnections of individual nerve cells in the brain, producing a mass of detailed facts. In contrast, psychology studies the behavior of the brain from largely external observations, yielding only vague conclusions. It is a challenge to computer science to understand the architecture of the brain from a computational viewpoint. What are the major computational structures in the brain? Which functions do they compute? How are they interconnected? What is the form of the computation inside the human brain?

Although we do not currently know the structure of the human brain it is reasonable to suppose that it nevertheless does have a very definite structure. One can imagine this structure written down in the form of a blueprint which shows exactly what the components of the brain are, and how they are interconnected. Such a line of thought leads to the conclusion that we ourselves are machines. Given a blueprint of the brain and enough time and resources, it should in principle be possible to build the brain artificially. If this is true then the human brain, as complicated as it appears, is only a machine and is therefore capable only of executing algorithms. That is to say, humans may be limited in the same way as computers to performing *routine* mental tasks, and real creative and original thinking (if such a thing even exists) may be beyond us. If one accepts this view then the total replacement of humans by machines is a real, if distant, possibility.

It is not necessarily an insult to human intelligence to say "man is a machine". Although the machines with which we are familiar are relatively unsophisticated, and cannot by any stretch of the imagination be called intelligent, nevertheless machines can in theory be very complex. It may well be the case that extremely complex machines can begin to exhibit intelligent behavior. If humans are fundamentally limited to carrying out nothing but algorithms, this may not be as severe a limitation as it first appears. Like machines, algorithms can be very complex, and complex algorithms can be very interesting. Some of the algorithms in Chapter 3 illustrate the point. They suggest that even relatively short algorithms can have some striking and unexpected properties. It is not beyond the realm of possibility that an enormously complex algorithm could appear to behave intelligently.

The total replacement of humans by machines—the end of human society—seems to be the very worst thing which could befall us. Perhaps some solace can be found in the following thought. As individual human beings, we are continually becoming redundant, and being replaced by our offspring. Our offspring are not identical to ourselves. Mankind is slowly evolving, changing its appearance and its capabilities. If we were to return to a human society millions of years from now, we would feel very out of place indeed. We might not even be recognized as intelligent beings. It is not a new experience for mankind to bequeath its achievements and even its existence to its offspring. Why not, then, bequeath them to electronic offspring? Indeed, we might feel prouder of our electronic children than our biological ones, since so much more conscious effort has gone into their design and construction! However, for the moment, and for some time to come, the discontinuity between machine and man will remain. Computers will perform routine and repetitive mental tasks. Humans, with their apparent abilities for the creative, the innovative and the original, will not be redundant.

EXERCISES

1   Prepare a list of activities currently carried out by humans which can/cannot be automated.

2   Discuss changes in employment patterns caused by automation which tend to increase/decrease skill levels required of humans.

3   How do the "suggested limitations" of Section 7.2 compare with the collection, storage and access of your scholastic records?

4   Discuss the suitability of the "suggested limitations" for controlling the use of personal information for research purposes.

5   Find a reported case of computer crime. Under which type of computer crime would you classify it? What security measures could have prevented this crime?

6   Describe one area of vulnerability of a particular computer system with which you are acquainted. What security measures would you suggest?

7   Suggest a definition of intelligence which seems reasonable to you. Discuss the extent to which your definition differentiates between humans and machines.

8   It is possible that the fundamental difference between humans and current computers lies in the ability of the former to recognize relationships between independently presented pieces of data. Assuming this to be true, discuss the possibility of a total machine takeover in either the near or distant future.

BIBLIOGRAPHY

A selection of works which discuss the impact of computers on society is

M. A. Arbib, *Brains, Machines and Mathematics*, McGraw-Hill, New York, 1964.

M. A. L. Farr, B. Chadwick, and K. K. Wong, *Security for Computer Systems*, National Computing Centre, Manchester, 1972.

C. C. Gotlieb and A. Borodin, *Social Issues in Computing*, Academic Press, New York, 1973.

L. J. Hoffman, Computers and privacy: a survey, *Computing Surveys*, 1(2), 85–103, 1969.

M. Laver, *Computers and Social Change*, Cambridge University Press, 1980.

D. B. Parker, *Crime by Computer*, Charles Scribner's Sons, 1976.

Z. W. Pylyshyn, *Perspectives on the Computer Revolution*, Prentice-Hall, N.J., 1970.

B. C. Rowe (ed.), *Privacy, Computers and You*, National Computing Centre, Manchester, 1972.

D. Van Tassel, *Computer Security Management*, Prentice-Hall, N.J., 1972.

N. Wiener, *The Human Use of Human Beings*, Houghton, Massachusetts, 1950.

INDEX